T0374661

Managerial Capitalism

Managerial Capitalism

Ownership, Management and the Coming New Mode of Production

Gérard Duménil and Dominique Lévy

First published 2018 by Pluto Press
345 Archway Road, London N6 5AA

www.plutobooks.com

Copyright © Gérard Duménil and Dominique Lévy 2018

The right of Gérard Duménil and Dominique Lévy to be identified as the
authors of this work has been asserted by them in accordance with the
Copyright, Designs and Patents Act 1988.

British Library Cataloguing in Publication Data
A catalogue record for this book is available from the British Library

ISBN   978 0 7453 3754 8   Hardback
ISBN   978 0 7453 3753 1   Paperback
ISBN   978 1 7868 0221 7   PDF eBook
ISBN   978 1 7868 0223 1   Kindle eBook
ISBN   978 1 7868 0222 4   EPUB eBook

This book is printed on paper suitable for recycling and made from fully
managed and sustained forest sources. Logging, pulping and manufacturing
processes are expected to conform to the environmental standards of the
country of origin.

Typeset by Stanford DTP Services, Northampton, England

Simultaneously printed in the United Kingdom and United States of America

Contents

PART III: PAST ATTEMPTS AT THE INFLECTION OF HISTORICAL DYNAMICS

PART IV: PROSPECTS FOR HUMAN EMANCIPATION WITHIN AND BEYOND MANAGERIALISMS

List of Figures

List of Tables

Introduction

Seizing the opportunity created by the two-hundredth anniversary of Marx's birth on May 5, 1818, this book defends a two-sided thesis. First, as analytical framework, Marx's theory of history remains unchallenged; second, despite the failure of the expectations regarding the ability of the proletarian class to supersede capitalist relations of production, the struggle of popular classes is the single force capable of impacting the course of history in the direction of social progress.

There is, however, a "but." Marx's analysis of history requires a thorough revision in one key respect: Rather than straightforwardly paving the way to the implementation of a classless society, current relations of production undergo a process of transition toward a new mode of production, "managerialism," whose upper class is the class of managers.

In the available literature, managerial traits are typically treated as an odd feature of contemporary capitalism, quite adequately denoted as "managerial capitalism" on such grounds, but the hybrid character of relations of production in the full Marxian sense of the phrase is overlooked. The consequences of this misreading of historical dynamics are severe. In our opinion, the revision of Marx's analytical framework—the single alternative to its outright abandonment—is the precondition to the interpretation of past and current economic, social, and political trends.

Major political consequences are implied. One cannot change the world with ideas but, as Marx did, we believe they can help. To contribute to this analytical revolution is the main ambition of the present endeavor.

1
An overview

This book combines a broad variety of distinct approaches in a rather unusual and dense fashion. A number of chapters make an extensive use of data sets regarding income distribution and technical change; others attend to theoretical frameworks, first of all Marx's theory of history; a third field is the examination of sequences of economic and political events since World War I. Wide use is also made of the work of historians in the analysis of secular social transformations and ideologies.

As suggested in the Introduction, the relationship between our thesis and Marx's analytical framework is an uncommon mix of fundamentalism and revisionism. On the one hand, the analysis is grounded in the principles of Marx's theory of productive forces and production relations, classes, and class struggle; on the other hand, the approach to class patterns is extended to the consideration of managers as forming a new class.

This first revision is prolonged by the thesis that capitalism is not the last mode of production in the chain of modes based on class antagonisms. In the same way that capitalism is the mode of production whose upper class is the class of capitalists, managerialism is a new mode of production whose upper class is the class of managers. While in capitalism the main channel of extraction of surplus-labor is surplus-value, the extraction of surplus-labor within managerialism follows from the hierarchy of wage inequality. Within contemporary societies, the transition between capitalism and managerialism is still underway; well advanced though not completed. The resulting hybrid social formation is known as managerial capitalism.

The first part of this book harks back to fundamental principles. A close examination reveals the dual nature of Marx's theory of historical dynamics. The most familiar facet is the "theory of class societies," attending to the stubborn reproduction of class dominations as successive links in the chain of modes of production: Along such lines, the contradictions of the last such phase, in capitalism, were expected to lead to the destruction of antagonistic patterns of any forms, and the establishment of what Marx and Engels called socialism or communism (in the terminology used in the middle of the nineteenth century). A second, less familiar, facet of Marx's and Engels' analysis is, however, the acknowledgement of the march forward of mankind in the conquest of rising degrees of what we call "sociality," that is, the increasing sophistication of social interactions. Production is realized within large firms, including broad national and international networks of affiliates; the division of labor among firms is dramatically increased; central authorities, specifically states, are at the head of vast networks regarding transportation, education, welfare, etc. In Marx's and Engels' view of history, the process of socialization was conducive to dignified forms of social organization in socialism, provided that the appropriate political inflection were imparted. The theory of sociality without the theory of class societies would amount to sheer ideology, and the demonstration that the historical progress of sociality is embedded within the sequence of classes and dominations along the chaotic course of capitalism was Marx's and Engels' key concern.

Managers play a central role in managerialism in the above two respects, class dominations and sociality: simultaneously as a social class and for being the main agents of socialization. Managers will be the upper class of managerialism as a new mode of production; new degrees will be reached in the historical process of socialization thanks to the organizational capacity of managers, thus overstepping the potential inherent in capitalist relations of production.

The study of the interaction between the historical dynamics of socialization and class societies—the object of this book—defines a broad field of analysis, but in our investigation not all aspects of social relations are considered, only aspects lying at the intersect of the two theories, that is, fundamentally, economic and state relationships. For example, the "production of material life," as Marx and Engels put it in *The German Ideology*, is conferred a central role, as are the functions of states in the management of class relationships or the conduct of the economy. Many other components of life in society—including important sources of dominations and alienation such as gender dominations—are not directly subject to class dynamics, only secondarily. They do not belong to the field here outlined.

A first expected outcome of this analytical revolution is the recovery of the capability to interpret the course of managerial capitalism.

Abstracting from intermediate groups, the class pattern is the three-polar structure of capitalists, managers, and popular classes (production workers and other categories of subaltern employees). The first steps of managerial capitalism were accomplished at the end of the nineteenth century. The ensuing twelve decades were punctuated by large crises, delineating three periods of a few decades, which we denote as social orders. A social order is a configuration of social powers defined by the hegemony of a class, the corresponding class dominations, and the potential alliances between classes. One can notably contrast the alliance between popular classes and managers after the Great Depression within the post-depression/postwar compromise or "social-democratic compromise" and the alliance at the top between managers and capitalist classes in neoliberalism after the crisis of the 1970s. These politics of managerial capitalism, as expressed within social orders, must be understood in relation to the historical trends of technology and distri- bution, and the secular rise of the class of managers, thus harking back to Marx's analyses of the dynamics of productive forces and relations of production, and historical tendencies. This renewed Marxian interpreta- tion of managerial capitalism is the object of the second part of the book.

The third part attends to the long-term aspect of Marx's analysis regarding the capability of popular classes to inflect the course of history. Looking backward, the stubborn and frustrating character of the historical dynamics of class societies is all too obvious. In the early stages of the development of capitalist relations of production, as during the revolutions of the seventeenth century in England and eighteenth century in France, the attempts at the establishment of advanced forms of democracy in line with the ideology of modernity were discouraged by the implacable course of the concentration of capital. The radical attempts at the inflection of the course of history in the direction of social progress—were they utopian or "scientific," in Marx's and Engels' parlance—failed. Utopian attempts at the alteration of the course of history were undermined either by the outright negation of authority, in total contradiction with the course of socialization, or by the author- itarian concentration of power in the hands of a small minority or a single leader. Notably, new paths toward advanced forms of managerial- ism were opened within the countries of self-proclaimed socialism. But these endeavors ended up in sudden switches toward the structures of managerial capitalism at the end of the twentieth century. Seen from the early twenty-first century, no alternative trajectories seem in sight. This is the dark side of the history of mankind.

There is a brighter side, discussed in the fourth part of this book, but the road toward class emancipation is long and winding:

1. For economic and political reasons, there will be no outright leap from managerialism, as a new mode of production, to a classless society. For a considerable period of time, the main class contradiction will oppose popular classes and managers, and the forms of interaction—more or less acute or compromising—between the two classes will define basic political circumstances.
2. All managerialisms are expressions of the domination of managers as upper class, but a broad variety of such economic and political configurations may exist along the spectrum of historical social progression–regression.
3. Periods of strong social regression, such as the decades of the industrial revolution or neoliberalism, temporarily obstruct the road of social progress. They are the main hurdles on the route toward class emancipation.
4. These periods are finally superseded as an effect of their internal economic and political contradictions and the struggle of popular classes, historical trajectories being "bent to the left" under the pressure of popular classes.
5. A key political factor governing such favorable resolutions is the weakening of the cohesiveness of the various fractions of upper classes and forms of interclass alliances between popular classes and fractions of upper classes, as during the post-depression/postwar compromise.

Despite the occurrence of episodes of devastation lasting several decades, layers of social conquests accumulate. Going back at least as far as feudalism, each step in the course of historical societies from one mode of production to the next opened new opportunities for popular classes. The ideology of modernity (the declaration of liberty and equality) concomitant with the emergence of capitalist relations of production, in the context of the old aristocratic values on the wane during the bourgeois revolutions, opened new perspectives. The same is presently true under the circumstances created by the rise of managerialism from within capitalism. The substitution of the new ideology of meritocracy for the old values of the private ownership of the means of production (and their reproduction by inheritance) open new territories to be conquered by popular classes. Under such circumstances, the advance of managerialism itself, given the enhancement of social interaction and the progress of education, would be subject to continuing internal contradictions, and the monopoly of decision-making would become harder to preserve. A new stage would be reached in the march toward class emancipation, in what one might decide to call "socialism" despite the current abuse of the term.

PART I

Modes of Production and Classes

This first part is devoted to historical dynamics. The main notions are productive forces, relations of production, class patterns, and class struggle.

Chapter 2 uses data on income distribution in the United States during the recent decades and since World War I as a starting point in the double aim of the illustration of: (i) the permanence of class divides; and (ii) the rising importance of wages within the income of upper classes underlying our thesis regarding managerialism.

Chapters 3 and 4 hark back to Marx's analytical framework, emphasizing the unquestionable explanatory power of basic principles but also the limitations inherent in Marx's theory with respect to the emergence of the managerial class.

Chapter 5 introduces the basic notions of sociality and socialization. Elaborating on Marx's analysis of the labor process, these notions are extended to social relationships at a general level of analysis.

Chapter 6 attends to the relations of production typical of managerialism as a new mode of production and managerial capitalism as a hybrid social formation.

Chapters 7 and 8 supplement the above analysis in two quite distinct respects: (i) other interpretations of the class location of managers in contemporary societies; and (ii) lessons to be drawn from the emergence of capitalist relations of production from feudalism, regarding the deciphering of hybrid social formations. Chapter 8 is the first of a set of four (with Chapters 14, 15, and 16) addressing historical developments in a more "narrative" fashion and widely relying on the work of historians. The style of these chapters is correspondingly quite distinct from others in the book.

2
Patterns of income distribution

Assessed in light of the broad historical perspective in the overview given in Chapter 1, the empirical analysis of income hierarchies does not seem to measure up to the ambitious endeavor aiming at the identification of class patterns and their historical transformation. The present chapter is, however, much more than a technical introduction. It is the first component of a twofold inquiry into the nature of social relations: here with the empirical analysis, while the following chapters attend to the theory.

Two laws of income distribution

The empirical analysis is based on the work of a team of economists and physicists, called econophysicists, regarding income distribution in various countries (in particular the research conducted around Victor M. Yakovenko). The section explains the basic methodological principles and presents the main results. A more detailed account of the method is provided in the appendix to this chapter.

The object of investigation is less the now-familiar assessment of the degrees and trends of income inequality than the unveiling of the class pattern prevailing in the United States:[1] An upper social category is singled out. The implications of income inequalities with respect to social structures are so blatant that, independently of theoretical foundations, the reference to class patterns came spontaneously to the fore in the presentation of results by the authors.

In the United States, the Internal Revenue Service (IRS) publishes statistics of households' yearly taxable incomes (therefore, pretax incomes), in which households are classified by income levels.[2] In the pyramid of incomes, a fractile sets out a group of households whose income is located within a bracket defined in percentage terms. For example, the 90–100 fractile is formed of the 10 percent of all households receiving the highest incomes. Depending on the period, 15 to 30 fractiles of unequal size are distinguished with the specification of the average income of one household in each fractile. Fractiles and average income are the only variables considered in the studies, but what the presentation demonstrates is remarkable.

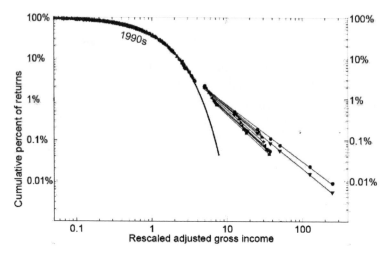

Figure 2.1   Two laws of income distribution for two classes, 1990s

Each dot accounts for one fractile in one year. The variable on the horizontal axis is the average income in each fractile (as a ratio to the average income of the lower class composed of the bulk of households, set to 1 on the axis). The variable on the vertical axis is the percentage of all households belonging to the fractile and to all fractiles with a larger income. Thus, 100 percent of households belong to a fractile with an average income larger than or equal to the average income of the lowest fractile. The percentage diminishes for fractiles with larger average income, up to an income equal to about 250 times the average income. (Only 0.01 percent, that is, 1 out of 10,000, of households belong to the upper fractile.)

Source: A. Silva and V. Yakovenko. "Temporal evolution of the 'thermal' and 'superthermal' income classes in the USA during 1983–2001." *Europhys. Lett.*, 69 (2): 304–10, 2005, Figure 2.

The results are presented in Figure 2.1, and the method is briefly described below and in the appendix to the chapter:

1. The main finding is the distinction between two separate groups, to which the authors refer as classes. (The blank in the line mirrors the deliberate absence of a trendline between the two groups.) The boundary coincides with the inflection in the profiles of the

sequences of observations for an income equal to 3 or 5 times the average income in the lower category. The ordinate of the separation on the vertical axis is between 1 and 3 percent of households. Thus, approximately 97–99 percent of the total number of households belong to the lower group and, correspondingly, 1–3 percent to the upper. It is worth emphasizing that 1 percent means 1,200,000 households. (The slogan "We are the 99 percent" refers to this upper group in a negative fashion.) Thus, 3 percent amounts to 3,600,000 households, that is, a minority but not a small community.

2. As already mentioned, the criterion used in the separation is the distinct profiles of the two distributions within each class. The contour for the lower category, to the left, is concave to the origin, compared to the upper category, to the right, for which straight lines are observed. The concavity manifests a lower degree of inequality. The authors contend that the income distribution of the bulk of households is governed by a strikingly stable "exponential law" over the period considered by the authors (1983–2001, of which only the 1990s are shown in Figure 2.1). The reference to the exponential distribution is equivalent to the statement that, if equal fractiles were considered, the difference between the average incomes of any two subsequent fractiles would be the same.

3. The profile for the upper fractiles is linear and, thus, given the log-arithmic scales on the two axes, governed by a "power law": If equal fractiles were considered, from one fractile to the next, the income would be multiplied by a constant coefficient. Thus, a more acute inequality is revealed within the upper category than within the lower.

In the study of income inequality, a difference must be made between: (i) the degree of inequality within each class; and (ii) the degree of inequality between the two classes. The finding of a stable law of distribution for the lower class is equivalent to the observation that the degree of inequality within the group remained stable. (All dots representing the fractiles during the successive years are located on the same curve.) The law for the upper class was significantly altered. Thus, the segments accounting for individual years differ more visibly. The degree of inequality within the upper class actually increased.

Similar results are presented for other countries.[3]

Inequalities as such should not hide the main finding, namely the underlying class structures. The observations in Figure 2.1 are strikingly evocative of the dual social pattern typical of a capitalist economy, pitting capitalists with high incomes and comparatively large degrees of inequality at the top, against salaried workers with lower incomes and less dramatic degrees of inequality at the bottom. The respective percentages of households belonging to the two groups (1–3 and 97–99 percent) apparently match or, at least, do not contradict this "standard" interpretation.

Marxist scholars obviously hailed the above spectacular illustration of a pattern of income inequalities so adequately matching their views of social structures. Besides the blatant gap between incomes at the top and the bottom of income hierarchies, the observations show that distinct social dynamics govern the distributions of the income of the bulk of the population and a small minority at the top. We obviously share this enthusiasm but, in our opinion, the narration of these findings is only the first episode in a longer and even more fascinating story to which the remainder of the book is devoted: A closer empirical analysis reveals that the dual pattern fails to identify the most telling aspect.

Wages and capital income

The consideration of the composition of income, distinguishing between wages and capital income, sheds considerable light on the findings in the previous section.

The variable used in the forthcoming analysis is the ratio of wages to the sum of the wages and capital income received by households (based on Thomas Piketty's and Emmanuel Saez's data). Wages include pensions, bonuses, stock-option exercises, etc. Capital income is the sum of dividends, interest, and rents. Abstraction is made of capital gains, since these gains are at the origin of excessive fluctuations in the series that blur underlying trends and do not fundamentally modify the overall configuration. (Entrepreneurial income, which amounted to an almost constant fraction of the income of households since World War II, is also set aside.)

Since the upper class in the previous section varied between 1 and 3 percent of all households, we limit the investigation to the top 1 percent, which consistently belonged to the upper group. The comparison is made with the fractile 90–95, which remained a component of the lower group (near the top of the lower class).

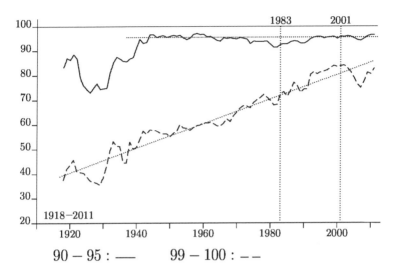

$$90 - 95 : \text{———} \qquad 99 - 100 : \text{– –}$$

Figure 2.2 The ratio of wages to the sum of wages and capital income within the fractiles 90–95 and 99–100 (percent)

In this analysis, we use the data collected by Piketty and Saez. (The presentations in the figure and interpretations are ours.)

Source: T. Piketty and E. Saez. "Income inequality in the United States, 1913–1998." *The Quarterly Journal of Economics*, CXVIII (1): 1–39, 2003, Table A7. Tables and figures (http://eml.berkeley.edu/saez/TabFig2015prel.xls).

Figure 2.2 shows the composition of income for each of the two fractiles, specifically the share of wages in the sum of wages and capital income (denoted as "income" for brevity, leaving aside entrepreneurial income):

1. The first observation is that, during the years 1983–2001 considered in the previous section (marked by the vertical dotted lines in Figure 2.2), the share of wages in the income of the top layer of the upper category had reached 78 percent (average 1983–2001) and, correspondingly, capital income only amounted to 22 percent of the total. One-fifth (22 percent) of income as capital income is far from negligible, but the bulk of the income of the group was clearly made up of wages. Going down in the pyramid of incomes, the percentage of capital income diminished rapidly. Still considering the average

for the period 1983–2001, the percentage of wages was reduced to 6 percent for the fractile 90–95.

2. The historical profiles of the two percentages since World War I are particularly telling. During the 1920s, only 40 percent of the income of the top 1 percent was made up of wages, while 60 percent was capital income. This latter percentage declined steadily to the end of the period, bottoming out at less than 20 percent on average since 2000. This is in sharp contrast to the historical transformation of the composition of income for the fractile 90–95. Regarding this group, a major reduction in the share of capital income occurred after the Great Depression and during World War II, testifying to the elimination of a large fraction of the households benefiting from small amounts of capital income (other than independent producers). After World War II, the percentage remained constant and equal to 96 percent.

Two important conclusions follow from this analysis: (i) The great mass of the income of the upper category is made up of wages, and capital incomes are only a secondary component; and (ii) The establishment of this pattern of income distribution is not recent and did not occur in one blow but was established gradually, since at least the Great Depression. A dramatic historical trend is thus revealed.

The importance of the distinction between wages and capital incomes suggests a return to the separation of households between two classes, as in the previous section, where the analysis was conducted with reference to total income: the sum of wages, capital income, and entrepreneurial income. The data regarding the share of wages in the income of upper fractiles dismiss the standard interpretation locating capitalists within the upper class, with large degrees of inequality, and wage earners within the lower class, with smaller degrees of inequality.

Limiting the analysis to wages, the same division into two classes with distinct degrees of inequality as in the previous section would again be revealed. The data is not directly available, but estimates can be realized on the basis of Piketty and Saez's data. The answer is unambiguously positive: The separation between the two categories of households is confirmed when only wages are considered. Thus, the split between the two groups in Figure 2.1 is not the mere effect of the concentration of capital income within upper-income fractiles but also manifests a strong bias of wage distribution in favor of upper classes.

Managers within income hierarchies

As already stated in the synthesis in Chapter 1, we made the important decision to call "managers" the wage earners belonging to the upper fractiles of income hierarchies. The relevance of the term can be questioned, as it tends to be used nowadays in a broad variety of contexts (within lower levels of hierarchies), but "the management" and the epithet "managerial" also convey social connotations pointing to the upper segments of social hierarchies, notably in the phrase "managerial capitalism." It should go without saying that we do not use the criteria underlying legal or administrative frameworks, for example the institutions in charge of the allocation of retirement benefits in France. Within such contexts, individuals are classified in various categories according to given administrative rules, generally the result of negotiations. "Managers" in this sense defines a much broader group. Such categorizations may have a sociological relevance that we will not discuss here. Along such lines, what we denote as managers could also be called "high managers."

Combining the demonstrations in the previous sections, we contend that the observations made point to a three-polar social structure typical of contemporary societies. The three categories are, respectively, the beneficiaries of high capital income, managers (as recipients of high wages), and the remainder of the population. Obviously, the reference to three poles does not exclude intermediate or hybrid positions, notably small entrepreneurs, or individuals belonging to the upper layers of social hierarchies who are simultaneously owners of significant capital and active in upper management.

The distinction between two social categories as suggested by Figure 2.1 must be understood as a first assessment of social structures straightforwardly derived from income hierarchies. The findings convincingly support the existence of distinct dynamics of income distribution at the top and within the bulk of the population. Unquestionably, the split between "those above" and "those below" is and will remain a fundamental feature of social structures until the territories of emancipation are reached, but the separation between wages and capital income emphasizes the importance of the separation between the two basic sources of income, as well as the dramatic historical transformation of the mix between the two sources of income within the upper category.

The upper segment of the population is steadily becoming a group of wage earners.

A set of additional comments can be made concerning numbers. In the United States, a distinction exists between production workers and other wage earners. Production workers amount to about 80 percent of the overall population of wage earners. The criterion clearly does not match the separation in the previous sections, where segments of 97–99 percent of households have been considered. A further difficulty is that the unit of analysis in the available statistics of income distribution is one household (one tax unit) and not one individual. The social positions of the members of a same family may obviously differ. Thus, the boundary within the upper fractions of the lower group and the upper group does not rigorously reflect differences in individual social status. The analytical miracle is that the separation appears so neatly within income data despite ambiguous features. One of the merits of the study of econophysicists is to provide an objective criterion supporting a separation whose otherwise arbitrary character could feed endless controversies. Given the income mix at the top of income hierarchies, a ballpark figure regarding the number of managers in the above definition could be 2 or 3 percent of wage earners, that is, between 3 million and 4.5 million people in 2015.

Time is now ripe for the reference to class patterns in the full sense of the term. Not only terminology is involved. The notion conveys of whole body of implications, the object of the "leap upward" the realm of theoretical analysis in the following chapter.

APPENDIX TO CHAPTER 2: THE METHODOLOGY USED IN THE CONSTRUCTION OF FIGURE 2.1

The purpose of the present appendix is pedagogical. The list of fractiles is arbitrary, and the average incomes (the only data used) are forged, though likely values have been picked up.

1. The fractiles are presented along the top of Table 2.1.
2. Line (1) shows the yearly average income of one household in a fractile (in thousands of dollars). As suggested by the horizontal line in the table, no other data are inputted. All other figures are calculated.
3. The two figures in Line (5) are the average income of the three lower fractiles to the left, jointly identified as the "lower class," and the average

income of the two upper fractiles to the right, the "upper class" (in thousands of dollars).

4. Line (2) shows the "rescaled income," that is, the income of the fractile in Line (1) divided by the average income of the lower class (equal to 47). This value is used as the unit of measurement for the yearly average incomes of all fractiles.

5. The figures in Line (3) are the percentages of total households belonging to the fractile.

6. The figures in Line (4) are the percentages of households belonging to the fractile and to all fractiles with a larger average income, that is, the sum of all percentages in Line (3) beginning with the fractile considered and ending with the rightmost fractile. For example, 30 in the column 70–95 means that 30 percent of households belong to a fractile whose income is equal or larger to the income of this fractile (with 30=25+4+0.9+0.1). This percentage (30 percent) is also called the "cumulative probability," that is, the probability to receive an income greater than or equal to a given income.

Table 2.1   Data used in Figure 2.3

Fractiles	0–70	70–95	95–99	99–99.9	99.9–100
(1)	33	117	235	376	705
(2)	0.53	1.88	3.7	6.03	11.3
(3)	70%	25%	4%	0.9%	0.1%
(4)	100%	30%	5%	1%	0.1%
Class	Lower class (0–99)			Upper class (99–100)	
(5)	47			409	

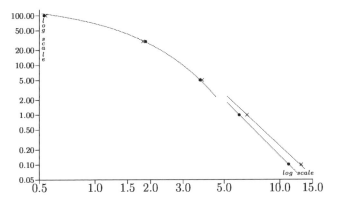

Figure 2.3   Cumulative probability with forged data

Figure 2.3 is based on the data in Table 2.1. The variable on the horizontal axis is the rescaled income in Line (2) of the table. The variable on the vertical axis is the cumulative probability in Line (4). (Logarithmic scales are used on both axes.) Each of the five fractiles, whose rescaled incomes are given in Line (2) of Table 2.1, is denoted by a dot. The × symbols denote the same fractiles for the next year (whose data are not provided), at a slight distance from the dots. The cumulative probabilities are not altered. (They are inherent features of the definition of fractiles.) Thus, the ordinates of the dots and the × symbols are unchanged. The ordinate of the lowest-income fractile is 100, since 100 percent of all households belong to a fractile whose average income is larger than or equal to the average income of the group. This cumulative probability is gradually lower when fractiles with larger incomes are reached (as in Line (4) of Table 2.1).

The two laws of distribution are represented by dotted lines. For the bulk of households within the three lowest fractiles (that is, 99 percent of all households), the analytical form of the law is exponential. The analytical expression for the upper class is a power law, thus, represented in the figure by a straight line (due to the use of logarithmic scales). A lower declining slope mirrors a larger degree of inequality, and conversely. Thus, the variation between the two years expresses a stable pattern of inequality within the lower class and an increasing degree within the upper class.

3

Marx's theory of history

Can Marx's analysis of history be described as "the" theory of history or, equivalently, the "science of history" in the Althusserian tradition of the 1970s?[1] It would actually be more adequate, in our opinion, to approach Marx as the author of "a" theory "on" the history of human societies—specifically the theory of class societies—as Marx's framework obviously does not have the monopoly on the interpretation of historical dynamics.

The present chapter recalls the main principles, makes explicit the notions and terminology used in the remainder of the book, and engages in some of the controversial aspects of Marx's theory. The theory of the state will be discussed in a stepwise fashion beginning in Chapter 5. (We will not enter into the analysis of states as rival international entities.)

A materialist interpretation of history

We recall that Marx's theory of class societies was known as historical materialism, materialism being understood as "processual materialism," that is, hinging around human practices instead of with reference to the matter of the sensitive object, as, notably, within Ludwig Feuerbach's materialism. This was the object of Marx's first "Thesis on Feuerbach":

> The chief defect of all hitherto existing materialism—that of Feuerbach included—is that the thing, reality, sensuousness, is conceived only in the form of the object of contemplation, but not as sensuous human activity, practice, not subjectively [*not in relation to an active subject*]. [...] Feuerbach wants sensuous objects, really distinct from the thought objects, but he does not conceive human activity itself as objective activity.[2]

In this sense, Marx's theory of history is, indeed, a historical materialism.

To existing idealist interpretations of the course of history, Marx opposed the reference to the framework of social relationships into which human beings enter in the conduct of production and the mechanisms governing the distribution of the ensuing product. This was done for the first time in Chapter I of *A Critique of the German Ideology*, entitled "Feuerbach."[3] There, Marx and Engels summarized the basic principles of historical materialism in a number of propositions beginning with the production of necessities: "The first historical act is thus the production of the means to satisfy these needs, the production of material life itself [...]."[4] From this first statement, the authors derived the fundamental concepts, such as modes of production or classes, in the sequence of what, a few pages earlier, had been described as "the most general results." Regarding historical dynamics, the key notions were there. (The abstract formulation of such general statements was defined as the maximum ambition for what would survive as the best of philosophy.[5])

The fragile balance maintained within Marx's later work between objective and subjective determinants must be cautiously preserved. The issue of degrees of consciousness comes, thus, to the fore. As Marx wrote in *The Eighteenth Brumaire*:

> Men make their own history, but they do not make it as they please; they do not make it under self-selected circumstances, but under circumstances existing already, given and transmitted from the past.[6]

The perspective in the book tightly matches Marx's statement, combining historical determinants, such as the trends of technical change or class patterns, with deliberate class strategies.

Modes of production: The channels of exploitation

The most compact and comprehensive text devoted by Marx to the theory of history can be found in the Preface to *A Contribution to the Critique of Political Economy*, published in 1859, in this respect supplementing *The Communist Manifesto* eleven years earlier.[7] The *Contribution* is still an early, though very sophisticated, text in Marx's writings.[8] In the Preface, Marx summarized the results of about ten or fifteen years of research whose main objects were history and political economy, notably the work of English classical economists (as had been the case of Hegel, already struck by the laws of political economy that he had discovered in Adam Smith[9]).

The basic concepts in Marx's *Capital* are commodity, value, money, capital, etc.; mechanisms such as the historical trends of technical change and crisis are discussed. Thus, the object of *Capital* is unquestionably a political economy, not merely a "criticism" of political economy. (It is simultaneously such a critique of the existing bourgeois political economy.) Marx's political economy must not be confused with his theory of history as in the present chapter.[10] The object of Marx's political economy is the analysis of capitalism, but capitalism as a mode of production in the historical sequence of these modes is a component of Marx's theory of history. There would be a political economy of feudalism, but it is not the object of *Capital*. As contended below, at the end of *Capital*, Marx defined class patterns in capitalism in the light of the concepts of the political economy of capitalism. Not all aspects of class patterns in capitalism can, however, be explained on this basis.

The difference between the analysis in the Preface to *A Contribution* and *The Communist Manifesto*, written with Engels a decade earlier, was the stronger insistence on the crises of capitalism and class struggle in the *Manifesto*, where capitalist classes were described as apprentice "sorcerers" unable to master the product of their own magic.

The key notions in Marx's theory of history are familiar, namely "relations of production," "material forces of production," and the "mode of production of material life." The social character of production was a pivotal notion, accounting for the analytical transition from production to relations of production. Marx described relations of production as the real foundations of social structures as opposed to a "legal and political superstructure" and "forms of consciousness" (also "legal, political, religious, artistic, or philosophic" forms): The economic foundations determine the superstructure and not the reverse.

Unfortunately, Marx was never truly explicit regarding definitions. For example, only "property relations" (the expression of relations of production in "legal terms") are mentioned, and the reference to the ownership of the means of production is not precisely set out. The same is true of productive forces or the mode of production, with the exception that this latter notion is meant in tight relation to the production of material life. Some light was shed on actual content when Marx finally spelled out the list of modes of production, "the Asiatic, ancient, feudal, and modern bourgeois modes of production,"[11] directly evocative of familiar social structures. This account remained obviously schematic. A richer presentation was given in the famous text "Forms which precede capitalist relations of production."[12]

Concepts are theoretical tools, the product of the human brain, whose explanatory power—the single use-value of concepts—is expressed in their joint mobilization in the aim of the analysis of a particular process.[13] A science is a system of concepts whose definitions have been conceived in anticipation of this combination. Thus, the content given to the distinct concepts within a same science must be carefully articulated. When applied to Marx's analysis, these attributes of knowledge are specifically relevant regarding the concepts of political economy, namely value, money, price, capital, surplus-value, profits, and the like. For example, prices are a form of value, and capital is value taken in a movement of self-enlargement. But Marx never elaborated his theory of history in this fashion. The problems of definition raised earlier are the straightforward expressions of this difficulty. The title of the great opus is "Capital," not "Capitalism." No clear definition was given of capitalism as a mode of production. Marx more frequently used "capitalist production," still without defining the notion.

A central theme within Marx's theory of history was the description of the historical dynamics underlying the succession of modes of production: "At a certain stage of development, the material productive forces of society come into conflict with the existing relations of production."[14] Conditions are created for the revolution of production relations: "Mankind thus inevitably sets itself only such tasks as it is able to solve."[15] On the one hand, conditions are created; on the other, the transformation is a task that mankind sets to itself. The reference is obviously implicit here to the power of class struggle.

Entering into the field of historical transformations, the theme of dynamics comes to the fore, namely the dynamics of productive forces and relations of production. Dealing with Marx's analysis, the mention of a dynamic process immediately suggests the reference to dialectics. A broad new field is thus opened, and the relation of Marx to Hegel's philosophy comes center stage. Dialectics play a key role in the present book. For obvious reasons, we will, however, not address the topic per se, only sketch a few principles.[16]

Dialectics first convey a definitional component always underlying Marx's analysis. (This definitional aspect is directly evocative of Hegel's distinction between the categories of the understanding and the concepts of reason.[17]) Behind the difference between productive forces and production relations looms their higher unity within an "unnamed" concept of "productive forces/relations of production," that is, one of the components of what we denote as historical dynamics (the other component being class struggle). It is, for example, not possible to identify productive forces with the existing technology, on the one hand, and relations of production with property rights, on the other (as Marx sometimes does in a desperate attempt to be understood). To become effective, the existing technology must be set in motion within organizational and social frameworks whose analysis belongs to the field of production relations. The symmetrical relationship is obvious: Property relations, for example, are impossible to conceive independently of given methods of production technically defined or particular spheres of activity.

A second aspect of dialectics, also quite relevant to the present analysis, is the view that social processes are governed by the development of their internal contradictions.[18] This is unquestionably an aspect of Marx's approach to the dynamics of history when referring to the "conflict existing between the social forces of production and the relations of production." One must, however, be careful not to confuse dialectics with straightforward strife, be it individual or social. As applied to productive forces and relations of production, there is a clear link between the two aspects, the dialectics inherent in knowledge and the dialectics of factual contradictions, but it is not always unambiguously so.

A mode of production is the institutional locus of the confiscation of a fraction of the labor realized by the bulk of workers (the product of this labor) by a minority of the population. The labor thus extracted is denoted as surplus-labor. Each mode of production is defined by the main channel of extraction of surplus-labor. Limiting the analysis to feudalism and capitalism, the channels are, respectively, the capability of the lord to impose forced labor on workers as serfs (notably in agriculture), the corvée, and a broad variety of taxes, regarding feudalism; and the surplus-value, regarding capitalism.

In this definition, the reference to a "main" channel of exploitation is important. Even in capitalism, and focusing on basic mechanisms, the purchase of the labor power of the worker at a given wage and the sale of commodities and services at given prices may be at the origin of variegated forms of exploitation to the extent that the mechanisms governing the formation of wages and prices, or the quality of goods and services, are biased in favor of upper classes; the actual practices within firms are the object of constant cheating on alleged "market mechanisms"; and the multiple fields of non-market mechanisms regarding culture, health, environment, and the like are subject to similar distortions.

There is always a collective aspect to exploitation, as surplus-labor may be extracted in one social locus and realized in another. Complex procedures of allocation of the benefits of surplus-labor were already observed in feudalism (notably through the relationships between vassals and lords). The mechanisms were thoroughly altered by the establishment of capitalist relations of production. Within capitalism, the theory of the social process of exploitation (the extraction and realization of surplus-value) is the theory of the valorization of capital or theory of surplus-value based on the labor theory of value. Value is an elementary concept of the theory of commodity, and the explanatory power of the theory is subject to the sufficient extension of exchanges and the ensuing transformation of products into commodities. Consequently, as long as markets and monetary mechanisms had not reached sufficient degrees of maturity, there was no room for a theory of value. Conversely, capitalism generalized commodity relations.

As briefly stated, the concepts of Marx's theory of history were never defined with the same care as the concepts of political economy in *Capital*. We believe this was probably impossible "by nature." Obviously, the construction abided by the basic principles of scientific knowledge, to which Marx was always faithful, a key feature being the constraint imposed on the definition of elementary concepts by their reciprocal relationships within the theoretical framework. Regarding Marx's theory of history, a similar tight link exists between the definitions of modes of production and the channels of extraction of surplus-labor. There can be no exception or even "flexibility" in this respect. To put the matter in a more familiar formulation, such relationships are definitional. On this basis, it is possible to "graft" on the analysis of a mode of production a number of further social attributes, to the extent that these attributes can be derived from the identification of the definitional criterion, namely the channel of extraction of surplus-labor.

What has been described above as the relationship between the channels of extraction of surplus-labor and relations of production is the linchpin of Marx's theory of history. The link is in any case the pillar of the construction in the remainder of this book, the aim being to restore the explanatory power of Marx's theory regarding contemporary societies.

Economics and economicism

Important criticisms have been directed against an alleged economics-based, narrow, or minimalist approach to modes "of production," and Marx's theory of history was correspondingly charged with economicism. It is not possible here to provide a faithful account of these debates, but major names were involved. A forefront example is Karl Polanyi, the author of the concept of "the economistic fallacy."[19] In *The Great Transformation*, Polanyi accused Marx of following David Ricardo in the analysis of class patterns based on economic relationships or interpreting political debates in relation to social tensions among various fractions of capitalist classes.[20] One could also cite Cornelius Castoriadis' criticism of Marx's economicism and many others. As we will contend, Edward P. Thompson's stand on the issue remained uncertain.

The more the analyst looks at the features of a period, the more he or she is fascinated by the discovery of the complex character and diversity of aspects transcending the analytical rigors of the reference to the main channel of exploitation in a mode of production. There is always a narcissistic aspect in this fascination. Besides outright rejection, there is a questionable tendency to "stretch" the notion of mode of production beyond its definitional boundaries to encompass the main features of an epoch, including what Marx would have classified among superstructures. These issues were at the origin of important controversies during the 1970s and remain a source of discomfort in the assessment of Marx's framework.

It should go without saying that the core theory of modes of production, as recalled in the previous section, does not purport to account for every aspect of an epoch in history. Important differences are apparent when patterns of events are compared between countries or regions and distinct periods. For example, serfdom was not truly the same institution within Western and Eastern Europe, and major differences were observed in the chronologies. There was in the past and there is still today more than one form of capitalism. The relevance of Marx's theory of history lies in the identification of the common features and, at a more sophisticated level of analysis, in the derivation of discrepancies as branches of the same original trunk.

The traits resilient to monocausal, allegedly economicist, interpretations are often broad features of the history of human societies, common to distinct modes of production. As we will contend in Chapter

4, devoted to Marx's analysis of managers, this is, for example, how Marx approached bureaucracies. Many other features were regarded as self-explanatory or not amenable to theoretical generalization.

Reference is sometimes made to Marx's notion of "social formation" or "economic formation," which may be regarded as a broadening of the notion of mode of production.[21] The phrase is used once in the Preface to the *Contribution to the Critique of Political Economy* as a synonym for mode of production, and at the beginning of Chapter 31 of Volume I of *Capital*.

A further difficulty is the overlap observed in the succession of modes of production. The transition from feudalism to capitalism was a long and complex process, segmented by major geographical idiosyncrasies and a wealth of variegated institutional combinations. This is so true that it is hard to imagine a society unambiguously defined by the reference to a single mode. A mode of production typically "dominates" in a given historical context. Earlier forms survive to various extents and, even more strikingly, the germs of new sets of social relations are manifested from the first steps of each new mode, thus anticipating the subsequent.

The acknowledgement of such patterns of hybridization is key to historical analysis and a new expression of the role to be conferred on dialectics in the two senses above: Both the dual nature of the process and its internal contradictions are involved. In the remainder of this book, we will use the phrase "social formation" to refer to the combination of social relations typical of two overlapping modes of production, in a way we judge to be rather well in line with Marx's use of the phrase "economic formation of society" in Chapter 31:

> But the Middle Ages had handed down two distinct forms of capital, which ripened in the most varied economic formations of society, and which, before the era of the capitalist mode of production, nevertheless functioned as capital—usurer's capital and merchant's capital.[22]

The hybridization of relations of production in social formations is a central theme in this book, as expressed in the notion of managerial capitalism and the comparison with the transformation of relations of production between feudalism and capitalism in Chapter 8, in which usurers' and merchants' capitals play an important role.

The charge of economicism against the reference to modes of production is directly linked to the controversies hinging around the distinction between super- and infrastructures during the 1970s. Modes of production were strictly defined by Marx in relation to infrastructures, quoting Marx:

> The totality of these relations of production constitutes the economic structure of society, the real foundation, on which arises a legal and political superstructure and to which correspond definite forms of social consciousness. The mode of production of material life conditions the general process of social, political and intellectual life. It is not the consciousness of men that determines their existence, but their social existence that determines their consciousness.[23]

We fully follow Marx in these respects.

The thoroughly obvious nature of the relationship was emphasized by Althusser in his study *Sur la Reproduction*, regarding the reciprocal action of superstructures on infrastructures:

> We have tried to shed a little light on this "reciprocal action", which is, fundamentally, not a reciprocal action at all, since the specific relation in which the superstructure stands to the base is that of reproducing the conditions of its functioning.[24]

There is probably no better illustration of the nature of the relationship than the ideology of the free market, that is, the ideological cornerstone of economic liberalism. Free-market ideology can only be understood with reference to capitalist relations of production, since capitalists claim a total freedom of action on "markets." Symmetrically, free-market ideology does not provide the theoretical foundations required by the analysis of capitalist relations of production, since capitalism is much more than a market economy. Free market is the "image" of the economy that upper classes attempt to impose in negation of the class features of capitalism. But obviously free-market ideology does have an impact on the preservation of capitalist relations of production; the ideology has been forged in this aim, as Althusser felt necessary to recall.

Many things can be written about the complexity of historical transformations between the fifteenth and eighteenth centuries, that is, during the period of emerging capitalist relations of production. We believe, however, that the dizzying wealth of information will never alter the fundamental explanatory power of the transition between a pattern of income of upper classes based on feudal coercion (independently of its arbitrary character or inscription within customary law) to a contractual channel rooted in the mechanisms of capitalist production. The shift within relations of production will play not a secondary but the central role in the overall interpretation. This is what Marx's theory of history is about.

Classes and income distribution

Class analysis is the obvious supplement to the theory of modes of production. The identification of class patterns has two main analytical purposes: (i) the elucidation of the mechanisms of domination and exploitation in a given mode of production, the object of the present analysis; and (ii) the disentangling of the complex of social struggles, to be discussed in the following section.

Regarding capitalism, the more detailed analysis of class patterns prolongs the emphasis on the channel of extraction of surplus-labor by the consideration of the division of surplus-value into two separate flows, namely profits and rents. Three criteria are, thus, combined in class analysis: (i) the position vis-à-vis the means of production; (ii) the main channel of appropriation of surplus-labor; (iii) the allocation of the benefits of surplus-labor between various segments of upper classes.

Chapter 52 of Volume III of *Capital* is entitled "Classes." Reference is made in the first paragraph to the "three great classes of modern society." The chapter coming at the end of *Capital*, the criterion used is the link between the list of classes and the basic concepts of political economy as introduced in the three volumes, specifically wages and the two fractions into which surplus-value is divided:

> The owners of the mere labour-power, the owners of capital and landowners, whose respective sources of income are wages, profits and ground-rent—in other words wage-labourers, capitalists and landowners—form the three great classes of modern society based on the capitalist mode of production.[25]

One fraction of the upper classes receives a share of surplus-value, the rent, on account of the ownership not of capital but of land or another appropriable natural resource. In Marx's framework, land is not a capital, though it may have a price. Thus, three classes are distinguished in capitalism instead of two if the single criterion of the benefit of surplus-value had been retained. Further decompositions can be performed at any stage. For example, various categories of capitalist may be distinguished, such as the money and functioning capitalists, each receiving fractions of the total surplus-value, respectively the interest (and dividends) and the profit of enterprise. But the rationale is the same.

Not all sources of income are involved. Marx explicitly raised the question: "What makes a class?", with the answer "At first sight, the identity of revenues and revenue sources." But the analysis went on as follows:

> From this point of view, however, doctors and government officials would also form two classes, as they belong to two distinct social groups, the revenue of each group's members flowing from its own source. The same would hold true for the infinite fragmentation of interests and positions into which the division of social labour splits not only workers but also capitalists and landowners—the latter, for instance, into wineyard-owners, field-owners, forest-owners, mine-owners, fishery-owners, etc.

(This is the pathetic last sentence in the manuscript.) Obviously, Marx wrote this paragraph with the aim of the refutation of the above "point of view": The "identity of revenue" per se, without further specification, is not the appropriate criterion.

Class struggle as an "objective" component of historical dynamics

Within circles of stricter or looser Marxist obedience, the definition of class patterns and class struggle remains as controversial as the reference to modes of production or, maybe, more. At one end of the spectrum, one can locate rigid or "paradigmatic" approaches, in which class conflicts are strictly referred to the revolutionary warfare of the proletariat against the capitalist or bourgeois class. At the other end, the anchorage of classes in relation to production is charged with economicism, and socio-cultural determinants favored; the reference to class struggle is diluted within a broader notion of social conflicts. In our opinion, none of these approaches is truly convincing.

Beginning with what has just been called rigid approaches, the mention of a fundamental class antagonism as in the analysis of modes of production suggests a very strict definition of class struggle. Along such lines, the basic antagonism in capitalism is between the capitalist and proletarian classes and, correspondingly, class struggle pits the two classes against each other. Revolution is center stage, as in the *Communist Manifesto* or in Lenin's *The State and Revolution*.[26] The victory of the proletarian class is premised on a strong and deliberate organization, and a high degree of class consciousness is assumed.

The emphasis on class consciousness appears all the more natural given that political consciousness is always strong within the ranks of upper classes. The solidarity among the more accommodated segments of the population is rapidly expressed when the struggle from below endangers privileges at the top or, more fundamentally, questions the existence of upper classes altogether. The scramble to the secure base, the state, is thus initiated.

In this context, the distinction is sometimes made between a class "in itself" and "for itself." There is actually a single paragraph in Marx's work pointing to a historical process in which the mass of workers "constitutes itself as a class for itself" as opposed to the class "against capital" that it was previously:[27] The class against capital was typically fighting for wages, up to the point where the confrontation became a "civil war," that is, a "political struggle." The historical relevance of this statement is unquestionable: Class conflicts become straightforwardly political when higher degrees of consciousness and organization are reached.

There is no questioning the fact that the above rigid approach to class struggle in capitalism as deliberate and radical class confrontation between the bourgeoisie and the proletariat is a pillar of Marx's theory of history. This approach must, however, be considered with caution, as too strict an appraisal may lead to exceedingly narrow perspectives depreciating the manifold struggles between popular classes and distinct segments of upper classes. Not only is the analysis of specific conflicts of the past at stake, but also the capability to interpret general historical dynamics in the past and within contemporary capitalism.

The truth of the more flexible approach lies in the observation that class struggle is also manifest within upper and lower classes—given the constant reshuffling of alliances among various factions. The struggles may be conducted from above and below, with victories and setbacks on the part of all components of social forces. Many distinct aspects are involved, in everyday life: within firms, regarding education, within media, within religious practices, within philosophy and economics, in military conscription, and the like. The sense of being exploited is often very strong and explicit among popular classes, even if expressed in rough or biased formulations while no clear class consciousness in the strict sense has been established.

The discussion of the boundaries that should be set to the notions of class and class struggle is tightly linked to the distinction between super-structures and infrastructures. An interesting example of the uncertainty surrounding these issues is Thompson's uneasy assessments regarding superstructures and classes.[28] On the one hand, Thompson wrote of the distinction between super- and infrastructures that "it is impossible to give any theoretical priority to one aspect over the other" or that the reference to infrastructures tends to endow "blind, non-human, material forces" with "volition—even consciousness—of their own."[29] Nonethe-less, the Preface to the *Making of the English Working Class* unambiguously stated: "The class experience is largely determined by the productive relations into which men are born—or enter involuntarily."[30]

In our opinion, the basic trait earmarking a conflict as a component of class struggle is whether the interplay of fight and repression is an "objective" component of historical dynamics in the definition given earlier, that is, the march forward of productive forces and relations of production and the sequence of class patterns. The unity of the basic principles of Marx's theory of history—productive forces/relations of production, class patterns, and class struggle—is, thus, preserved.

Limiting the analysis to the early stages of the implementation of capitalist relations of production, when the reference to the transition between feudalism and capitalism was still relevant, the following famous historical examples can be recalled. The two sets of develop-ments were not anecdotic but pivotal components in the rise of capitalist relations of production. The controversies surrounding the definition of these conflicts as class struggles are puzzling:

1. Mechanization and the factory system were major steps in the estab-lishment of capitalist relations of production. They had devastating consequences on the situation of workers. The fight of the Luddites in England, engaged in the destruction of machinery at the beginning of the nineteenth century, provides a clear example of such conflicts. (Similar struggles had already been waged since, at least, the early seventeenth century.) Marx wrote in the first volume of *Capital* that the participants in the movement had not yet learned to distinguish

between the machine and its employment: "It took both time and experience before workers learnt to distinguish between machinery and its employment by capital, and therefore to transfer their attacks from the material instruments of production to the form of society which utilizes those instruments."[31] In this assessment, it is clear that Marx was clinging to the core of his own view of history at a very general level of analysis. Thompson devoted a careful study to the Luddite struggle in his *Making of the English Working Class*. The emphasis was on the observation that the Luddites were not simply backward workers, ignorant of the historical course of history, but communities of people fighting for their survival and defending a way of life and a culture.

In our opinion, the movement testified to early forms of social strife that should unquestionably be considered as components of class struggle in a period in which workers were not yet conscious of overall underlying circumstances and stakes, thus fighting for their economic and cultural survival.[32] The point is that we, as analysts and with the benefit of hindsight, as Marx himself had done, can understand this struggle as an episode in the historical class confrontation between workers and capitalists during the Industrial Revolution as a new phase in the implementation of capitalist relations of production, not as the mere expression of a local or atemporal, or trans-relations of production rebellion, while the Luddites did not. And, along such lines, we can establish the link between this particular conflict and a broad set of other upheavals during the same years, independently of well-identified individual or collective connections. Being an actor in class struggle is not premised on a degree of consciousness and political consistency.

2. A second major aspect of the progress of capitalist relations of production was the elimination of all restrictions to trade. One can mention here the Flour wars during the Ancien Régime in France in the eighteenth century, in which popular classes fought for their survival against the consequences of the policies inspired by the "economists" (physiocrats in France and classical economists in England) in favor of the free expansion of the devastating capitalist relations of production on the rise, in which the capital of merchants played a central role.[33] There should be no denying the fact that workers in the countryside shared something like Thompson's "moral economy of the English crowd,"[34] but the fight was unquestionably a

component of class struggle. (We do not mean here that Thompson himself denied it.) It is now well understood that the Flour wars in France played an important role in the unfolding of the French revolution.[35]

To these examples, one could add the fight for the limitation of the labor day, to which Marx devoted much attention. And the list is certainly not limitative.

When social struggles interfere with the historical dynamics of productive forces and relations of production, and contribute to or delay the accomplishment of key steps in the historical process of emergence of new relations of production, the overall consistency of Marx's historical framework is recovered. These conflicts must unquestionably be interpreted as components of class struggle independently of the degrees of consciousness reached by their actors. This defines, in our opinion, the objective criterion.

Regarding the above social confrontations, the difficulty was that class consciousness had not yet explicitly emerged; nowadays, it has been lost, but this loss does not alter their nature. As we will contend in the second part of the book, the capacity to interpret contemporary developments in terms of class struggle has crumbled, including the most straightforward reading of social conflicts in terms of class power and alliances, such as the imposition of neoliberalism (see the discussion of Michel Foucault's framework in the appendix to Chapter 10). The setback of Marx's analytical framework had devastating theoretical and political consequences.

4

Managers in Marx's analysis

In the discussion of production relations and class patterns in the previous chapter, two distinct lines of investigation were successively followed regarding: (i) the position of individuals and classes vis-à-vis the means of production; and (ii) the extraction of surplus-labor, its main channels, and its allocation among various fractions of the upper classes. The link between the two aspects is straightforward: The position vis-à-vis the means of production is the key determinant governing the access to surplus-labor. When applied to capitalism, the relationship is quasi-definitional: Capitalism is the mode of production grounded in the private ownership of the means of production and, in turn, ownership conditions the extraction of surplus-labor.

Within capitalism, the main benefit to be derived from the ownership of capital is the making of profit. But, as Marx once wrote, capital does not yield profit as pear trees yield pears.[1] Besides the ownership of capital, the obtainment of profit requires constant cares in what is nowadays known as management. Thus, the present chapter attends to a second facet of social relations in capitalism, so far neglected: The capitalist owner is also the agent of the valorization and circulation of capital and, immediately behind the capitalist, looms the figure of the manager, supported in his or her tasks by subaltern employees. ("Valorization" defines the extraction and realization of surplus-value; "circulation" refers to the changing forms of capital, as money capital, commodity capital, and productive capital in the circuit of capital.)

A second theme in this chapter is that the reference to management in Marx's work was strictly targeted to the functioning of private firms. There is, however, a second component to the managerial class in the extended sense we give to the notion, namely the upper segments of what Marx called bureaucracies. No link was established by Marx between firms' managers and government administrative bodies. In addition, senior officials were not singled out within the mass of bureaucrats; only bureaucracy as a whole, civil and military, was considered. (The phrase "government officials" is also used by Marx.²) New fields of investigation are, thus, opened.

The capitalist as owner and manager

Seen from the mid-nineteenth century, the separation between active capitalists and passive partners had already a long history. There is, therefore, no surprise in the discovery that the distinction between the "functioning capitalist" (or active capitalist), in Marx's terminology, and the mere owner of capital was the object of important developments in Volume III of *Capital*. The alternative figure to the functioning capitalist was called the "money capitalist." His or her involvement was confined to a financial contribution. Two categories of income were consequently distinguished by Marx, namely the "profit of enterprise" accruing to the active capitalist as owner and manager, and "interest" (actually interest and dividends) as return on the financial contribution of the money capitalist (on the "interest-bearing capital"). The distinctions between legal ownership and active management, and the two categories of income, were explicitly spelled out:

> But it is no sinecure to be a representative of functioning capital, unlike the case with interest-bearing capital. On the basis of capitalist production, the capitalist directs both the production process and the circulation process. The exploitation of productive labour takes efforts, whether it does it himself or has it done in its name by others.³

The functioning capitalist could, to some extent, be involved in the production process itself. Marx clearly identified the historical process of concentration of the "intellectual" facet of labor in the person of the functioning capitalist as an aspect of the division of labor within the manufactories:

> It is a result of the division of labour in manufactories, that the labourer is brought face to face with the intellectual potencies of the material process of production, as the property of another, and as a ruling power. This separation begins in simple co-operation, where the capitalist represents to the single workman, the oneness and the will of the associated labour. It is developed in manufacture, which cuts down the labourer into a detail labourer. It is completed in modern

industry, which makes science a productive force distinct from labour and presses it into the service of capital.[4]

But the main component of the action of the functioning capitalist was the accomplishment of the so-called capitalist functions, such as the management of the workforce, the purchase of inputs, the selling of the product, and the like.

An important additional function of the capitalist class is the allocation of capitals between various industries (as in Marx's analysis of competition at the beginning of Volume III of *Capital*[5]). This can be performed within the same firm by the differentiation of products; depending on historical circumstances, distinct firms are, however, typically involved, and financial and credit mechanisms play a pivotal role. This "collective" function of financial institutions may be at the origin of hierarchies among capitalists, as between bankers and industrialists.

Unfortunately, Marx never disentangled the complex social relationships to which the above observations should have led, notably regarding the delegation of the upper productive and managerial tasks to salaried workers, to which we now turn.

Salaried workers as profit-rate maximizers

Marx went one step further, as the same developments in Volume III of *Capital* ushered in the person of the salaried manager as a central character in the conduct of firms' management: "[...] the work of supervision is readily available, quite independent of the ownership of capital."[6] Or, even more specifically:

> Joint-stock companies in general (developed with the credit system) have the tendency to separate this function of managerial work more and more from the possession of capital, whether one's own or borrowed. [...] and since on the other hand the mere manager, who does not possess capital under any title, neither by loan nor in any other way, takes care of all real functions that fall to the functioning capitalist as such, there remains only the functionary, and the capitalist vanishes from the production process as someone superfluous.[7]

Marx was clearly anticipating here what would become a central theme of interest among scholars during the first decades of the 20th century, namely the "separation between ownership and management" and the rise of financial institutions (in which salaried managers may play a pivotal role in the process of allocation of capital among industries). From the viewpoint of Marx's general framework, the above statements meant, however, a risky step forward: A complex of new social relations loomed behind the status of wage earner.

But this was only a first step. Besides the salaried managers, lower-ranking workers, for example clerks, also contributed to the accomplishment of capitalist functions. Confronting these difficulties, Marx remained faithful to a strict definition of productive labor as labor creating value from which the surplus-value is extracted. The rigors of the criterion surrounding the formal channel of income distribution as wage-labor were, thus, abandoned: Salaried workers involved in trade (selling goods) or clerks in offices (for example, keeping the books of firms) and, with some provisos, foremen in the workshop were not classified among productive workers, as was the case with salaried directors.

Abstracting from potentially productive intellectual tasks within the production process in the strict sense, it was clear to Marx that the labor of managers, like the labor of the capitalist, was targeted to the maximizing of the profit rates of firms. (For example, the work of a trade worker accelerates the rotation of capital and increases the profitability of the firm.) The wages paid to such categories of workers were classified by Marx among "costs," for example, commercial costs (costs of circulation, in Marx's parlance), to be subtracted from the correspondingly enhanced profits, but not the basis of the extraction of surplus-value.

Thus, independently of the individual or group in charge of the tasks, any form of labor within capitalist firms, distinct from the labor of productive workers, was considered as having a single purpose, namely the maximizing of the profit rate. Marx was cautious enough to maintain such rigorous theoretical distinctions.[8] What could have been called profit-rate maximizing labor was, thus, larger than management in the strict sense, since it included the work of employees belonging to the lower layers of the workforce.

The notion of the costs of maximization of the profit rate could rather easily be incorporated within the theory of capitalist production relations, as Marx did. Thorny issues remained, however, unresolved. Independently of the positions within hierarchies, the question of the potential exploitation of the social categories in charge of profit-rate maximizing tasks besides the capitalist, that is, managers and low-ranking unproductive workers, was not given convincing answers.[9] The introduction of a second channel of exploitation besides the extraction of surplus-value was certainly not welcome.

The most convincing insight Marx had regarding the historical rise of private management was the view that these developments could be interpreted as harbingers of the superseding of capitalist production relations, that is, in Marx's mind a transition toward forms of socialism:

> This [*the separation of ownership and management, as in joint-stock companies*] is the abolition of the capitalist mode of production within the capitalist mode of production itself, and hence a self-abolishing contradiction, which presents itself *prima facie* as a mere point of transition to a new form of production.[10]

Or, even more specifically:

> This result [*as above*] of capitalist production in its highest development is a necessary point of transition towards the transformation of capital back into the property of the producers, though no longer as the property of individual producers, but rather as their property as associated producers, as directly social property. It is furthermore a point of transition toward the transformation of all functions formerly bound up with capital ownership in the reproduction process into simple functions of the associated producers, into social functions.[11]

Bureaucracies

Marx's treatment of government officials raises much more difficult issues. (The appendix to the following chapter attends to Marx's most explicit exposition regarding states and bureaucracies in *The Eighteenth Brumaire*.)

The key point is that Marx never considered administrative bodies as classes. The bureaucracy was described as an "artificial caste" created "alongside the actual classes of society."[12] This assessment was the logical consequence of the principles introduced in the previous chapter of this book. The criteria used in the definition of classes could not be applied to the bureaucracy: The position of the bureaucracy within social structures is not defined in relation to the means of production; bureaucracies develop within all modes of production, and the formation of the income of the bureaucracy does not match the criterion of the successive historical channels of extraction of surplus-labor. Within the confines of Marx's framework, the income of the bureaucracy could only be understood as one among the outlets of the transfer by the channel of taxation of the surplus-labor extracted from productive workers. There is no questioning the fact that the upper layers of officials may garner comparatively high wages, but Marx's social theory attended to class patterns and should not be mistaken for an analysis of inequalities. Theoretical foundations were required.

The problem raised by the distinction between high officials and members of the upper classes is not only theoretical. In the course of history, a tight border between the upper layers of government officials and upper classes has always been difficult to maintain. In the French Ancien Régime, for example, reaching high positions within the administration was one of the ways of accessing to nobility, as in the "noblesse de robe." In the Russia of the tsars, individuals in charge of important functions within state institutions could gain access to hereditary or nonhereditary nobility. This access to nobility should not be understood as a sheer stimulation or a reward for good services. The exercise of power by individuals alien to the ruling class contradicted the ideology of the privileges of command underpinning social hierarchies.

Stretching explanatory powers

Although to various degrees and with distinct content, the limits of the explanatory power of Marx's theories of history and political economy regarding private management and the upper layers of government officials are rapidly met:

1. Marx observed the delegation of the tasks of the active capitalist to salaried managers. There was, however, no actual analysis of the changing relations of production supporting this historical trend in *Capital*. Marx did not disrupt the categories of his political economy with the aim of accounting for these developments. Marx had, however, a powerful insight regarding the relationship between the historical transformation of relations of production as preliminary steps toward "new forms of production," meaning socialist or presocialist social structures.

2. In a similar manner, Marx was also aware of the growth of bureaucracies, of which he emphasized the police and military repressive
functions. He remained, however, at the edge of a more thorough
analysis of state relationships. To our knowledge, Marx never established the link between the increasing number of and the powers of
private managers and government officials.

A more profound revision of Marx's framework appears necessary in
these two respects. Only then will it become possible to address "managerialism" as a new autonomous episode in the sequence of modes of
production and the hybrid figure of managerial capitalism in Chapter 6.

5
Sociality and class societies

The thesis in the present chapter is that the harmonious unity of Marx's theory of historical dynamics in Chapter 3 hid a dual pattern.

Capitalism was first of all described by Marx and Engels as a mode of production, that is, a given epoch in the history of human societies as class societies. There is, however, a second facet to the historical dynamic—also a component of Marx's and Engels' analysis—which should not be overlooked for its rather "common-sense" character: Human beings interact within sets of relationships in the realization of production and the conduct of general social processes, such as government or law, which are governed by mechanisms whose intelligibility oversteps the limits of class relations. This latter aspect of human societies belongs to what we denote as the "theory of sociality." This acknowledgement does not question the fact that historical dynamics must be understood as a single process: The advance of sociality has always been accomplished within the framework of class societies. There is no possible thorough "factual" disconnection. The contention is that historical dynamics are a two-sided process and must be understood as such. The deciphering of a multifaceted phenomenon requires the combination of the explanatory powers of distinct theories.

As recalled in Chapter 3, economics is a central component of the analysis of social relations. As Marx and Engels had noted in *The German Ideology*, the fundamental ground on which human beings interact is the production of material life. As implied in the notion of sociality, the scope of human interaction is, however, much broader, potentially encompassing all aspects of social relations. Social organization is implied, as in law, and potential forms of transclass dominations such as inequalities of gender or "races."

Historical dynamics are also involved in the analysis of sociality. Besides the demonstration of the necessary superseding of capitalist relations of production, Marx and Engels pointed to a tendency toward rising degrees of sociality or, equivalently, socialization, notably the socialization of production associated with the advancement of productive forces. In this respect, capitalism was understood by Marx and Engels as the great architect of gradually more sophisticated and "efficient" economic and, more generally, social relations. Thus, in a rather puzzling fashion, the new society of organization and emancipation from class dominations to follow capitalism would simultaneously be the outcome of, on the one hand, the process of self-destruction of capitalist relations of production and, on the other, the generation of "socialism" from within capitalism along the march of socialization. And, in Marx's and Engels' minds, the acknowledgement of this paradoxical combination was the criterion separating scientific from utopian socialisms: Utopian socialism is the product of human "constructions," while scientific socialism is the product of the historical dynamics of human societies (though it is obviously susceptible to analysis).

By "emancipation," Marx and Engels meant emancipation from class dominations. It was implicit that, once class dominations were eliminated, other aspects of domination or alienation would vanish—an obvious gross simplification. The entire field of the relationship between the theories of sociality and class societies is here implied.

"Sociality": Governing the workshop

One can very simply illustrate the distinction between the theories of sociality and class societies with reference to Marx's well-known analysis of the production process in the workshop. The capitalist, potentially a manager, is compared to the conductor of an orchestra. The action of a leader is a requirement in the conduct of a collective process but, whenever necessary, the director may also be the agent of the imposition of a specific form of discipline grounded in social relations, as in all class societies:

> The labour of supervision and management is naturally required wherever the direct process of production assumes the form of a combined social process, and not of the isolated labour of independent producers. However, it has a double nature.
>
> On the one hand, all labour in which many individuals co-operate necessarily requires a commanding will to co-ordinate and unify the process, and functions which apply not to partial operations but to the total activity of the workshop, much as that of an orchestra conductor.

This is a productive job, which must be performed in every combined mode of production. On the other hand [...], this supervision work necessarily arises in all modes of production based on the antithesis between the labourer, as the direct producer, and the owner of the means of production.[1]

The easiest way to gain insight into the "double nature" of economic mechanisms is to begin with the straightforward approach to production as collective process, abstracting from the determinations resulting from the conduct of production within a class society, and then move to the class attributes of production.

Considering production from the first viewpoint, that is, the viewpoint of sociality, individuals are located within distinct positions depending on their skills. A variety of tasks has to be performed; there is a division of labor within firms, as well as among firms connected by markets or interacting through given forms of central coordination or organization. Conversely, from the viewpoint of class societies, individuals are located within distinct positions vis-à-vis the means of production; the pivotal notion is the relation of production (which defines these distinct locations), and the emphasis is on the channels of extraction of surplus-labor.

To put the matter very simply, there are two ways of looking at the distinct positions of human beings vis-à-vis the means of production: either as distinct producers in a technically articulated production process or as, respectively, owners and producers. A "vertical" dimension may be technically involved in the production process, one task being in a sense above another task, though not intrinsically as the expression of a class hierarchy. Relations of production and classes point to the specific configurations in which these respective technical positions and the division of labor are "redistributed" and "molded" by social relations and express class dominations. The technical division of labor is altered by the class bias in the aim of the reproduction of social hierarchies.

The socialization of production: Capitalists and managers

The historical progress of sociality as process of socialization is also explicit in Marx's and Engels' work. In the chapter entitled "The historical tendency of capitalist accumulation" of Volume I of *Capital*, Marx mentioned the "socialization of labor" inherent in the historical dynamics of capitalist relations of production: Capitalism "socializes" labor.[2] The term "labor" appears rather restrictive in this context; a more adequate formulation would have been the "socialization of production." The theme of "socialized production" is, correspondingly, central in Chapter III of Engels' study *Socialism: Utopian and scientific*.[3] The view is that more sophisticated forms of organization are historically implemented within firms or the overall economy. Though no systematic treatment of socialization can be found in Marx's and Engels' work, we believe the notion was one of the pillars of their understanding of history.

Marx's and Engels' insight regarding the historical trend of socialization was fully vindicated by later historical tendencies during the following decades and centuries. Regarding theoretical foundations, not much has to be added to Marx's and Engels' analysis in this respect. Capitalist classes were key agents in the progress of the socialization of production. Capitalist merchants were at the origin of broad articulated production and trade networks in agriculture, and of various forms of "putting-out" systems in manufacture; then came the factory system and the large industry, with the collective production process described by Marx. Dramatic transformations of the institutions of capitalist ownership were required. Markets and transportations were also involved, both nationally and worldwide.

Along with capitalist owners, and gradually more so, managers were the key agents in the progress of organization. It is actually impossible to date the origins of management to a particular period in the history of mankind. When the collaboration of sufficiently large bodies of workers is required, the collective work must be governed from above, as stated by Marx. The construction of pyramids in Egypt was realized under the control of "managers"! Not only discipline had to be imposed on workers; the project also had to be conceived and its progress placed under tight overseeing. Without even mentioning the conduct of wars, millennia ago, ships had to be commanded. Everywhere, the social structures of management were the natural offspring of the complex of social relations on which class dominations were established within the countryside and cities.[4] The delegation of the tasks of overseeing and supervision is, thus, much older than mature capitalism.

Moving to the early forms of capitalist agriculture and industry, the management of large estates and many categories of businesses was delegated to estate stewards and managers. In his book *The Genesis of Modern Management*, Sidney Pollard drew a fascinating picture of the early forms of management during, or even prior to, the Industrial Revolution in England.[5] The two aspects, discipline and organization, as in Marx's quotation earlier in this chapter, were inextricably enmeshed. A lot of the activity of managers was devoted to disciplining workers, but many other tasks were also delegated to "managers, pursers, engineers, and so forth,"[6] both within firms or as outside consultants, notably the buying of raw materials or the implementation of equipment. A broad use was made of the delegation of tasks to independent "sub-contractors" employing their own workforce, notably children.[7] The importance of these mechanisms is also vividly described in John Foster's book *Class Struggle and the Industrial Revolution*.[8] Foster emphasized the importance of the emergence of new layers of workers "able to implement technically phrased instructions from above,"[9] sometimes called "pacemakers and taskmasters."

Socialization reached new degrees with the implementation of managerial capitalism at the transition between the nineteenth and twentieth centuries, ushering in the familiar forms of contemporary socialization in the global networks of transnational corporations and financial institutions. (To what extent and at what point in history should these managers be considered as forming a class will be discussed in the following chapter.)

The state at the intersect between the theories of sociality and class societies

Interestingly, in the sentences following the quoted extract from *Capital* earlier in this chapter, regarding the production process and the workshop, Marx extended the analysis of coordinating functions to the exercise of government:

> Just as in despotic states, supervision and all-round interference by the government involves both the performance of common activities arising from the nature of all communities, and the specific functions arising from the antithesis between the government and the mass of the people.[10]

(The sentence is, thus, an appositive, introducing the immediate comparison between workshops and states.)

The two facets of what we call the dual theory of societies were here vividly set out: (i) "common activities arising from the nature of all communities" defining sociality; and (ii) "specific functions arising from the antithesis between the government and the mass of the people" as in the theory of class societies. One can regret that, despite remarks such as the above, Marx was even less explicit regarding the conduct of common activities by states in capitalism than regarding the socialization of production. In both instances—production or government—the key notion was the "double nature" of the social process, as in Marx's quotation regarding the production process and the workshop.

The present discussion of Marx's views regarding the role of the state harks back to the brief reference to Marx's theory of the state in Chapter 4, in relation to the class location of bureaucracies. Was there in Marx's work an analysis of the state as central agent of sociality besides the strict functions of the state regarding the maintenance of the power of upper classes? Marx was never closer to the development of an explicit theory of the state than in *The Eighteenth Brumaire*. The notion of the organizational social functions of the state loomed behind, but Marx referred to "parasitic" administrative body, fully in line with his theory of class societies. (The appendix to the present chapter is devoted to Marx's analysis in *The Eighteenth Brumaire*.)

We do not see any contradiction in the acknowledgement of the "double nature" of the state. Why would Marx have denied or belittled the organizational functions of the state and their rising historical trend? As in the discussion of the historical socialization of production, the "common activities" must simultaneously be approached from the viewpoint of sociality and class societies. Like the capitalist in the workshop, the state acts as organizer, though not in just any fashion. There is no "pure form" of organization independently of the interests of upper classes, but the fact that the central tasks are conducted within a class society does not annihilate their social character and functions, which have to be deciphered as such. Whether Marx believed or not that this central action was capable of checking the chaotic course of the economy is a distinct issue.

The general conduct of economic affairs by governments is nowadays crucially important. There are, therefore, major state and para-statal aspects to the socialization of production. Governments are active in policies; legal and regulatory frameworks have been established and are recurrently reformed. Notably, a wealth of practices are devoted to the preservation of the stability of the macroeconomy; no market of any sort is up to the task. Institutions such as the International Monetary

Fund or the World Trade Organization are also components of the global institutional framework. Obviously, these institutions work in favor of the upper classes, as could be expected within class societies; this class character calls into question the way in which such institutions are managed, but not their existence as agents in charge of central organizational procedures.

The action of central authorities oversteps the management of the economy in the strict sense. A whole set of social functions must be performed regarding public transportation, education, research, health, and numerous familiar spheres of social organization. And much more is needed, specifically with the aim of the preservation of the earth from destruction.

And the emancipation from class dominations

The terminological parallelism between socialization and socialism is in no way coincidental. As already noted, in Marx's and Engels' minds, the prospects open to human emancipation were tightly linked to the progress of social organization and the advance of productive forces. Along such lines, Engels described capitalism as the anteroom of socialism:

> The possibility of securing for every member of society, by means of socialized production, an existence not only fully sufficient materially, and becoming day by day more full, but an existence guaranteeing to all the free development and exercise of their physical and mental faculties—this possibility is now for the first time here, but it is here.[11]

Two distinct tasks had to be simultaneously accomplished: (i) the mastering of production and more general social processes; and (ii) the implementation of the new world of freedom, democracy, or "de-alienation." The experience of managerial-capitalist countries as well as the countries of self-proclaimed socialism proved, however, that the coincidence between the two achievements, socialization and socialism, could not be taken for granted. On the one hand, a historical process of socialization is underway; on the other, no final term can be seen to the sequence of class patterns.

One can be of the opinion, as Marx and Engels were, that the attainment of an advanced degree of socialization is a precondition for socialism and emancipation. (There was no "looking backward" in Marx's and Engels' view of socialism-communism.) But emancipation is not a necessary product of socialization. Thus, the two following propositions must be clearly spelled out and distinguished:

1. A high degree of socialization is a prerequisite to the establishment of a society of emancipation (thus creating a "possibility," as in Engels' quotation above); and
2. A society of advanced socialization is a society of class emancipation.

The first proposition can be either questioned or supported, but the second cannot be defended. (This dual aspect of Marx's and Engels' prospects was a central theme in the book *Altermarxisme* by Jacques Bidet and Gérard Duménil.[12])

We obviously reach here a major limit of Marx's and Engels' analytical framework. Marx and Engels never contemplated the possible advent of a highly socialized class society beyond capitalism, that is, precisely what we call managerialism.

A dual theory of human societies

Although sociality and socialization in the limited sense here considered are simple notions, their joint treatment with Marx's and Engels' theory of class societies is in no way familiar. Elaborating on the distinction between the theories of socialization and class societies, this section briefly recalls basic conclusions:

1. There are two aspects to the functioning of human societies approached in terms of sociality, namely: on the one hand, the technical aspect of production and the corresponding division of tasks, within firms and among industries; and, on the other, the organizational role of central statal or para-statal institutions both domestically and internationally.
2. We denote as socialization the historical tendency toward increasing degrees of sociality in the above two respects.
3. Socialization as a trend toward increasing sociality is a "trans-mode of production" historical tendency.
4. The development of capitalist relations of production was a key stage in the historical process of socialization, but managerial classes are the agents of socialization par excellence.

5. The interpretation of the history of human societies in terms of sociality independently of its class character amounts to sheer ideology in the derogatory sense of the term. Marx's theory of history was built in refutation of this ideology. It is, nonetheless, the dominating ideology, in the past and within contemporary societies.

6. The above statement does not question the progressive potential (in the sense of the advance of what this book calls "social progress") inherent in the march forward of socialization, as expressed in the view that socialization creates the conditions required by the implementation of socialism as contended by Marx and Engels. High levels of socialization are, however, compatible with the preservation of class patterns and dominations. The importance of the notion of managerialism lies in this latter observation.

One can parenthetically notice that the distinction between sociality and class societies sheds some light on the proviso at the beginning of Chapter 3, qualifying Marx's analytical framework of modes of production as "a" theory "on" history rather than "the" theory. The succession of modes of production—subject to the dynamics of productive forces/relations of production, the sequence of class patterns, and class struggle—is unquestionably crucial to the interpretation of historical processes, but the broad notion of historical dynamics is blatantly larger than implied in the analysis of relations of production and classes in the strict sense.

At the close of this chapter, it is worth emphasizing that the distinction between the theories of class societies and sociality casts considerable light on the controversy between E. P. Thompson and what Thompson called "modern structural Marxists."[13] The section "The rule of law" of Thompson's *Whigs and Hunters. The origins of the Black Act*"[14] was a virulent attack against structuralist approaches, which directly echoes the dual pattern in the present chapter:

Thus, the law (we agree) may be seen instrumentally as mediating and reinforcing existent class relations and, ideologically, as offering to these a legitimation. [...] this is not the same thing as saying that the law was no more than those relations translated into other terms, which masked or mystified the reality. [...] the law, like other institutions which from time to time can be seen as mediating (and masking) existent class relations (such as the Church or the media of communication), has its own characteristics, its own independent history and logic of evolution.[15]

The first sentence signals Thompson's agreement with Marx's theory of class societies and superstructure while, in the last sentence, the mention of the "characteristics" and the "own independent history and logic of evolution" of the law straightforwardly matches our reference to the theory of sociality. One can, retrospectively, understand the uncertainty surrounding Thompson analysis of infra- and superstructures as recalled in Chapter 3. Although the required notions were not introduced, Thompson claimed the acknowledgement of the dual character of the theory of history.

APPENDIX TO CHAPTER 5: STATES AND BUREAUCRACIES IN *THE EIGHTEENTH BRUMAIRE.* THE VIEWPOINT OF FRANÇOIS FURET

The Eighteenth Brumaire of Louis Bonaparte[16] was published in 1852, after Louis-Napoléon Bonaparte's *coup d'état* on December 2, 1851, thus accomplishing a preliminary step toward the restoration of the empire one year later.

François Furet, the most sophisticated critic of Marx's political analysis and Marxist interpretations of the French Revolution, attempted to prove that, in *The Eighteenth Brumaire*, Marx had acknowledged some of the features of the state as an autonomous political entity (independently of class dominations). Furet, an earlier member of the French Communist Party (from which he resigned in 1959, as did other French scholars) joined the intellectual right. He had an exceptional knowledge of Marx's political work.[17]

Furet based his interpretation on two basic traits of the mid-nineteenth century in France, which Marx fully acknowledged:

1. The state apparatus had reached a high degree of development.
2. Louis-Napoléon in the conquest of power tactically "posited" himself above class divisions, and certainly not as the representative of bourgeois classes. Bourgeois leaders were jailed in the wake of the coup (typically for short periods of time), and many chose exile. (Louis-Napoléon was widely supported by French agrarian classes in relation to the image of his uncle.)

We have no a priori disagreement with the recognition that Marx had a clear insight regarding the march forward of sociality as manifested in the historical advance of government institutions. But *The Eighteenth Brumaire*, first of all, was one of the summits of Marx's analysis of class dominations in the strict sense.

Regarding Furet's first argument, the swelling of state institutions during the mid-nineteenth century (with its police and army) was described by Marx as less the continuation of the earlier process of socialization than the necessary response on the part of upper classes to the increasing strength of popular strife and the pending threat of a forthcoming revolution:

> The executive power with its enormous bureaucratic and military organi-zation, with its wide-ranging and ingenious state machinery, with a host of officials numbering half a million, besides an army of another half million— this terrifying parasitic body which enmeshes the body of French society and chokes all its pores sprang up in the time of the absolute monarchy, with the decay of the feudal system which it had helped to hasten. [...] All revolutions perfected this machine instead of breaking it.[18]

Furet's second argument is no more convincing. Louis-Napoléon was, obviously, the archetypal bourgeois leader. He governed in the name of the bourgeoisie and, increasingly, with the bourgeoisie. Concerning workers, Louis-Napoléon's book *The Extinction of Pauperism*,[19] published in 1844, inspired by Henri de Saint-Simon's or Saint-Simon's followers' ideas, belongs to what would nowadays be described as populism of the worst kind.

The Eighteenth Brumaire is famous for the analysis of what was later called "bonapartism," that is, structures of government in which upper classes abandon their favorite forms of governments—the bourgeois republic in which they can express their internal class contradictions—in favor of an authoritarian form of government in order to confront the violence of the struggle of popular classes. (And not much needs to be added to move to the theory of fascism or Nazism.) In this respect, there is no way of contending that Marx located Louis-Napoléon's government above class patterns and powers; rather the contrary.

Furet also based his interpretation on the view that, in the same text, Marx had acknowledged the basic features of the autonomy of the state in the analysis of the Ancien Régime. The specific traits of the monarchy were very well understood by Marx:

> The seigniorial privileges of the landowners and towns became transformed into so many attributes of the state power, the feudal dignitaries into paid officials, and the motley patterns of conflicting medieval plenary powers into the regulated plan of a state authority whose work is divided and centralized as in a factory.[20]

Marx's account of the historical process of formation of state institutions was directly evocative of the contemporary analysis by Alexis de Tocqueville in his book *The Ancien Régime and the Revolution*, published in 1856, for which Furet had a fascination. Tocqueville's thesis was that the Ancien Régime had already performed a significant proportion of the reforms of state institutions, the implementation of which was generally considered a major achievement of the French Revolution. Quite explicitly, Tocqueville's Chapter II.2 was entitled

"Why administrative centralization is an institution of the Ancien Régime and not, as some say, the work of the revolution or empire":[21]

> Just as the entire administration of the country was directed by a single body, all internal affairs were entrusted to a single agent, the *comptroller general.*[22]

Tocqueville's thesis must be moderated, but was not lacking actual foundations. Unquestionably, as noted by Furet, Marx was aware of the rise and transformation of state institutions during the Ancien Régime, and also conscious of the importance of the power of arbitration resulting from the transition between the remnants of feudal social relations and the emergence of the rising capitalist relations, but this did not place the state of the Ancien Régime above classes at all.

As contended in the main sections of this chapter, Marx was seeking interpretations "at the border" between his class theory and what we denote as the theory of sociality, leaning on one side or the other depending on circumstances. But this does not alter the fact that the viewpoint of class societies overwhelmingly dominated *The Eighteenth Brumaire.* Despite Marx's acknowledgement of the historical process of socialization, his main emphasis was on the theory of class societies (with the aim of the refutation of the apologetic character of pure theories of sociality, of which Furet's analysis was, much later, an additional expression on a long list).

6
Managerialism and managerial capitalism

As we will contend in Chapter 8, devoted to the transition between feudalism and capitalism, modes of production stretch over considerable periods of time, actually centuries. They have roots and shoots. The identification of a forthcoming mode such as managerialism is, thus, a challenging endeavor. The rising features of the new mode are strongly biased by their immature forms, the combination with capitalist traits, and the diversity of potential configurations depending on historical circumstances.

The viewpoint in the two first sections of this chapter is theoretical. The social structures of managerialism as an autonomous mode of production are first introduced, providing the foundations for the analysis of managerial capitalism as a combination of capitalist and managerial traits in the second section. The two latter sections are devoted to the historical emergence of managerial relations, namely: (i) the revolution in private management at the transition between the nineteenth and twentieth centuries; and (ii) the equally dramatic rise of government intervention, as expressed in its rising expenditure, during the twentieth century. In both instances, the analysis is centered on the United States.

Managerialism as mode of production-socialization

We recall that capitalism is a social structure based on the private ownership of the means of production. The capitalists, as owners of the means of production, are the upper class; they make decisions regarding the use of the means of production; ownership is transmitted within family relationships by inheritance or marriage.

An important thesis is that, in managerialism, a notion of contribution to the general activity of society must be substituted for the participation or absence of participation in production in the strict sense; the phrase "mode of production-socialization" must be preferred. Correspondingly, the criterion of the position vis-à-vis the means of production in the definition of classes must be extended to the consideration of the means of production-socialization, which also includes government assets. Beyond production in the strict sense, managers assume the leadership in the conduct of the primary tasks in which the main forms of sociality are grounded. Thus, the making of decisions regarding the use of the means of production-socialization is concentrated in the hands of a fraction of the population, defining its position as upper class.

The pattern of class relations can be symbolically represented as follows:

Managers as upper class
Popular classes or "managed classes"

(In the definition of this basic pattern, no mention is made of social categories that do not match managerial relations of production as such, for example independent workers who could survive the transition toward managerialism; and no separation is drawn between industrial and farm workers, other distinct industrial groups, or firms or government, etc.)

Membership of the upper class is transmitted by the privileges of education and social relations, the product of practices aiming at the preservation of the social position within families. Higher education is generally a necessary condition governing access to top positions, but the correspondence between knowledge per se and the location within the managerial pyramid is not rigid. The most efficient way of acquiring the necessary skills is often de facto access to elevated positions, strongly influenced by the membership of social networks. This is how classes are "reproduced." There is, however, no strict guarantee that the social status reached by one generation will be transmitted to the next and, in this respect, there is no radical difference from the ownership of capital in which wealth may also be dissipated. The role played by higher education supports the ideology of meritocracy substituted for the values of ownership in capitalism.

All aspects of production, investment, allocation of resources among firms and industries, the management of the macroeconomy, real and financial mechanisms, as well as the organization of social networks regarding transportation, education, health, research, the preservation of the environment, and the like, are involved. There is a division of labor among managers in these respects. Various fractions within the upper

class are, thus, defined, within stronger or weaker hierarchical configurations depending on historical circumstances. (A special mention can
be made of the division between firms and government managers.) The
allocation of powers and income among the various fractions of upper
classes is, obviously, the object of tensions.

Not only are the position vis-à-vis the means of production-
socialization involved in the determination of class patterns, but also the
channels of extraction and allocation of surplus-labor. To the traditional
channels typical of earlier modes of production, a new channel must be
added, inherent in the unequal distribution of wages and all forms of
supplements or advantages. Four such alternative channels may, thus, be
listed along the historical sequence of modes of production, namely the
extraction of the labor from:

1. slaves in what Marx called the "ancient" mode of production;
2. serfs in feudalism;
3. productive workers in capitalism;
4. managed classes in managerialism.

As within all modes of production, though to distinct degrees and
through distinct mechanisms, the extraction of surplus-labor is a collective process. A difficulty is that, in managerialism, there is no supposedly
simple empirical distinction between categories of income such as profits
and wages in capitalism.

The split between the higher wages of managers and the lower wages of
popular classes, as well as the hierarchies within each class, is determined
by the positions of the individuals vis-à-vis the means of production-
socialization. The analytical procedure of separation between classes
or fractions of classes must be based on the concrete analysis of tasks
and the positions along the obedience–authority spectrum. (A practical
way out is the reliance on empirical data, as illustrated with respect to
managerial capitalism in Chapter 2.)

It is important to understand that the reference to a process of extraction
of surplus-labor, common to all class-based modes of production, is not
premised on the definition of a labor theory of value. The labor theory of
value, as in Marx's *Capital*, is a component of the theory of commodity;
its explanatory power assumes a significant prevalence of commodity
relations, as expressed in "markets": products must be transformed into
commodities, as stated by Marx. Slaves and serfs were exploited in

societies in which commodity relations were still non-existent or hardly developed. The same would be true in a centrally managed managerial society, from which commodity relations would have disappeared. This does not mean, however, that the metabolism of "labor" could not be subject to theoretical analysis through mechanisms to be defined.

As we will contend in Chapter 17, "The economics and politics of managerialisms," various managerial configurations of social relations can be expected to prevail, depending on historical circumstances. For example, we interpret social relations within the countries of self-proclaimed socialism as managerialisms, while the contemporary trajectories of managerial capitalism also point to distinct forms of managerial relations. In this latter instance, assuming degrees of, at least, formal preservation (or hysteresis) of mechanisms inherited from earlier practices—notably the partial survival of market mechanisms (though possibly biased to large extents)—one can imagine that firms' managers would directly benefit from a fraction of the surplus extracted within their own firm; government managers would receive a fraction of the income flow transferred through taxation to government institutions (besides the allowance for the remuneration of lower-ranking employees and the other uses of government revenue); specific channels in the formation of the income of financial institutions might survive, with stronger or weaker degrees of similarity with the channels governing the formation of income in managerial capitalism, such as interest or dividends.

There are, however, important implications in the statement that managerialisms are modes of production-socialization. The limitations inherent in the above familiar mechanisms regarding the formation of incomes (including taxation), associated with managerialisms as modes of *production* in the strict sense, will be overstepped. Such mechanisms would follow from the existence of sets of prices that do not mirror the social "costs" actually involved (or only indirectly) or are thoroughly separated from cost relations. Already, within contemporary societies, significant segments of consumption are not or are only partially subject to the costs of production. This is the case regarding, for example, the use of infrastructures, education or health services, etc. One can surmise that it will be all the more so within mature managerialisms as modes of *socialization*.

There is, consequently, no way of defining the "political economy" of managerialism, generally speaking. One can surmise that such theoretical frameworks could be developed regarding historically specified configurations of managerialism.

Managerial capitalism

Contemporary societies are hybrid social formations, combinations of capitalism and managerialism, and, as such, are denoted "managerial capitalism." The hybrid character is manifested in all respects, regarding class patterns, the pervasiveness of market mechanisms, the formation of income, etc. And these traits are in constant evolution depending on the advance of socialization.

Returning to the analysis of social relations in capitalism as in Marx's *Capital*, the following threefold pattern was put forward in Chapter 4: (i) capitalists, (ii) productive workers, and (iii) unproductive workers (as profit-rate "maximizers"). To this first pattern, one can add the caste of bureaucrats. Due to the social polarization within each category, the definition of the class pattern typical of managerial capitalism requires the separation of profit-rate maximizers into managers and subaltern firms' employees such as clerks or trade agents; bureaucracies must also be broken down into government managers and subaltern employees. On this basis, the threefold class pattern is obtained, namely capitalists, managers (within firms and government institutions), and popular classes (production workers and all subaltern employees).

The class structure typical of early managerial capitalism in a social formation still close to traditional capitalism can, thus, be defined as the hierarchical three-tier configuration of the capitalist class as upper class, the managerial class as intermediate class, and popular classes:

Capitalist owners
Managers
Popular classes

An intermediate status is thus conferred on managers. With the progress of managerial traits, the location of managers within social relations gradually becomes more the status of an alternative ruling class, and it is more and more so within contemporary societies:

Capitalist owners ↔ Managers
Popular classes

The entrance into managerial capitalism I: The revolution in private management

Returning to the short history of the socialization of production outlined in the previous chapter, the progress of the new structures of ownership and management went hand-in-hand with the development of capitalism in Europe from its early stages. During the nineteenth century, the structures of ownership were transformed from one-man businesses to small partnerships.[1] Small partnerships were typically family units, though not necessarily; partners were also associated on account of their skills. Such new patterns of ownership and management developed throughout Europe during the nineteenth century, maybe with England in a leading role, and were reproduced in the United States. Besides these traditional institutions, there were already centralized private procedures underpinning the general functioning of the economy within institutions such as the stock market, clearing houses, or the like.

A striking feature of the history of the U.S. economy was, however, the dramatic transformation of the institutions in which the ownership and management of capital was expressed, at the transition between the nineteenth and twentieth centuries, to which the entrance into managerial capitalism in the U.S. can be dated.

We touch on here the key theme of the "separation between ownership and control," to which a vast literature was devoted in the United States.[2] The power of shareholders was gradually limited to the election of the members of the boards of directors in charge of the actual management. The sudden character and the dramatic scope of the transformation in the United States probably account for the specific interest U.S. scholars devoted to the revolution in private management during those years. The phrases "managerial revolution" and "managerial capitalism" were coined in relation to the transformation of U.S. capitalism or, at least, are mainly used in this context. The notions were later associated with Alfred Chandler's 1977 book *The Visible Hand*, whose subtitle is "The Managerial Revolution in American Business."[3] Strangely enough, these transformations were and are still widely overlooked in a country like France, whose managerial features were highly developed after World War II.

The rise of managerial traits was a long-term historical development, but the revolution itself was prompted by the structural crisis that occurred in the United States during the latter decade of the nineteenth century. The crisis was caused by a major decline in the profit rate.[4] The advance of industry and transportation had created unprecedented competitive tensions; the profitability crisis manifested itself as a crisis of competition and was interpreted as such. A network of agreements, pools, and trusts was implemented with the aim of the relaxation of these pressures. The antitrust legislation discouraged these agreements known as "loose consolidation" and instead stimulated the creation of new institutional frameworks in which firms were actually merging into larger units under collective ownership.[5] Around 1900, a major wave of incorporation occurred, known as the corporate revolution. The large corporations were backed ("dominated," one could say) by the large banks of the Morgans, Rockefellers, and others, defining a new financial system in which the ownership of capital in the strict sense was concentrated.[6] The third development was the specifically managerial revolution. The formation of large corporations pushed one decisive step further the process of separation between ownership and management and the delegation of management to salaried managers. Not only the transfer of the functions of the functioning capitalist to managers was involved, but also many of the tasks previously in the hands of workers—or rather, in the hands of already-privileged segments of the workforce on account of capacity or authority—were transferred to managers. A new institutional framework was thus established, whose cornerstone was the large corporation backed by the financial sector and managed by managers.

As more thoroughly discussed in Chapter 13, "Tendencies, crises, and struggles," the major institutional revolution and its gradual extension to the entire economy determined the course of the U.S. economy during the first half of the twentieth century, with outstanding achievements regarding technical change. These trends were maintained despite the occurrence of the Great Depression, actually a dramatic "side-effect" of the transition from one technical-organizational paradigm to the next. This course is too-often reduced to its spectacular manifestations in the workshop, as in Taylorism or Fordism; in fact it affected all aspects of management, such as trade, financing, or the management of the labor force.

The entrance into managerial capitalism II: The revolution in government

As in the case of private management, the ascending role of the government has a long history. Infrastructures, education, hospitals, etc.

were gradually developed during earlier centuries. There is, therefore, no strict dating of the origins possible. A common point with the rise of private management discussed in the previous section was, however, the sudden increase in the action of the government during the twentieth century, as strikingly depicted in Figure 6.1. More specifically, the New Deal and World War II were at the origin of a leap upward, and a sharper rising trend was established. Government expenses (the sum of local, state, and federal governments' expenses) amounted to only 7 percent of GDP before World War I. This rose to 21 percent during the New Deal and went on increasing to 34 percent in 1979, before entering into a period of quasi-stagnation around a plateau at 40 percent since

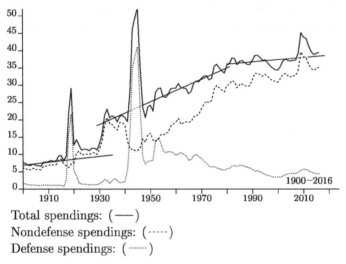

Total spendings: (———)
Nondefense spendings: (-----)
Defense spendings: (········)

Figure 6.1   Government spendings as a percentage of GDP

Total spendings are the sum of consumption, investment, current transfer payments, and interest payments. "Government" means "federal, state, and local governments."

The trendlines have been determined as follows: (i) the first trend, over the period 1900–13; (ii) the second, over the period 1932–79, excluding 1942–6, that is, abstracting from the impact of World War II; and (iii) the third, over the period 1980–2016 excluding 2008–11, that is, the impact of the crisis. One can notably observe the first leap upward of the percentage during the New Deal and the almost stagnating trend after 1980.

Defense spendings had a large impact during and after World War II, but a major declining trend was observed since the 1950s. The Korean and Vietnam wars are apparent, though less dramatically than could have been expected.

Source: usgovernmentspending.com.

2012. It is possible to date the entrance into "governmental managerial capitalism" to the occurrence of the "governmental revolution" associated with the New Deal.

Before closing this brief evocation of the break in the gradual extension of the social functions of the government, it is important to recall the new involvement of central authorities (the central bank and the government) in the management of the macroeconomy. As in the case of the progress of firms' management, a gradual historical process was underway, beginning with the intervention of the private banks of large financial centers such as New York and Chicago.[7] The revolution per se occurred later than the managerial revolution. It was also prompted by the occurrence of crises, notably the crisis of 1907, with its important financial component leading to the establishment of the Federal Reserve in 1913, and then the Great Depression, which paved the way to the Keynesian revolution after World War II.

7
A wealth of alternative interpretations

A broad literature has been devoted to the study of the managerial features of capitalism since the early twentieth century. Managers have been widely described as a new class, and the link was established with the rise of the countries of self-proclaimed socialism (to be considered in Chapter 16). In our opinion, two categories of developments account for the current diminished interest. A first factor was the entrance of the main economies and societies into the neoliberal phase of managerial capitalism, understood as a restoration of capitalist trends; a second, converging factor was the collapse of the alleged construction of socialism, including the dream of it. Contemporary tendencies in the distribution of income, notably the dramatic rise of higher-level wages might, conversely, be at the origin of a revival.

We will not address here the theories hinging around the transformation of the nature of labor itself, such as knowledge economics, the theory of information society, or cognitive capitalism.[1] There is no questioning the fact that economic transformations are underway in which the importance of knowledge and information is gradually increased. We consider, however, that there is no relevant approach to these tendencies independently of the earlier treatment of the separation between managerial and other forms of labor. The same is true regarding the radical revisionism of Michael Hardt and Antonio Negri, in which the shift to immaterial labor plays an important role and a broad notion of "multitude" is substituted for class analysis independently of rising managerial trends.[2]

"Streamlining" class analysis: The three classes of managerial capitalism

As could be expected, Marxist scholars attempted to interpret the rise of managers with reference to Marx's analysis of class patterns. In symmetry with the consideration of managers as members of the proletarian class, a straightforward interpretation was Nicos Poulantzas' analysis of managers as capitalists during the 1970s. Poulantzas' assessment was based on the view that managers perform the tasks of the active capitalist, as stated by Marx (see Chapter 4 of this book):

> This enables us to conclude that the managers, who belong to the capitalist class by virtue of the place of capital that they occupy, cannot constitute a distinct fraction of this class, e.g. a fraction distinct from the owners.[3]

In the frameworks listed in the remainder of the present section, managers are rather located in an intermediate class location and a reference is more or less explicitly made to the reassignment of one fraction of surplus-value to the benefit of managers. It was so in the analysis by Christian Baudelot, Roger Establet, and Jacques Malemort.[4] The title of Alain Bihr's 1979 book *Between Bourgeoisie and Proletariat: Supervision within capitalism* [*Entre bourgeoisie et prolétariat: L'encadrement capitaliste*], speaks for itself.[5] Managers were described as the agents of "the subaltern functions of capital reproduction."[6] Bihr was specifically concerned by political implications: "[...] in its struggle for emancipation, the proletariat must simultaneously confront not a single but two enemies."[7]

In his book *Class, Crisis, and the State*, published in 1978, Erik Olin Wright rejected the analysis making managers a fraction of the bourgeoisie, be it petty or large, and developed a framework hinging around the notion of contradictory class location.[8] "Contradiction" can be interpreted in a dialectical fashion as dual in nature:

> Instead of regarding all positions as located uniquely within particular classes and thus having a coherent class character in their own right, we should see some positions as possibly having a multiple class character; they may be in more than one class simultaneously.[9]

The emblematic example of such contradictory locations is the group of small employers, simultaneously capitalist and workers. In a similar manner, Olin Wright defined the class of managers as a hybrid of the bourgeoisie and the proletariat.[10] These views were later confirmed in his subsequent book, *Classes*, published in 1985. A common criticism was made to all other approaches, "namely, that every position within a class structure falls within one and only one class."[11] For all practical purposes, however, there is not much difference between a contradictory (or hybrid) and an intermediate class location, "intermediate" meaning displaying some of the features of each group. The relationship with our views is straightforwardly expressed in the difference between the simple representations in Chapter 6 regarding class structure in managerial capitalism (page 57). The first arrangement is in line with Olin Wright's making of managers an intermediate class; the second highlights the distance from our own view.

One can also mention Luc Boltanski's book *The Making of a Class: Cadres in French society*, in which the term *cadres* is used in the French broad sense of the term, that is, managers, senior officials, political leaders, and the like.[12] The object of Boltanski's analysis is, however, much less the "making of a class" than the making "of the notion" of cadre. The constellation of cadres is deemed rather heterogeneous and there is no autonomous well-defined analysis of the class location of the group within the French society.

More recently, one can also mention Simon Mohun's study of class structures in the United States based on Thomas Piketty's and Emmanuel Saez's income data since World War I (also the empirical foundation of our analysis in Chapter 9).[13] Three classes, the capitalist class, the working class, and managers, are distinguished. Members of the capitalist class are set out as individuals or households that may act as wage earners but do not need to do so, given the size of the income they derive from their wealth. The opposite is true regarding those who are workers as well as managers. The difficulty of separating the two latter groups is solved empirically by the specification of the income of a particular group as borderline (actually, the overseers). Below this borderline income, wage earners are classified as workers; above it, as managers. The technical procedures used are rather difficult to disentangle. A puzzling result is that the percentage of tax units belonging to the class of managers diminished from 28.8 percent of total tax units in 1918 to 14.2 percent in 2012 (Mohun's Table 1). This finding is telling of the fundamental divergence between Mohun's approach and ours regarding the historical dynamics of managerial trends.

To the limits of Marx's framework and beyond

As contended in Chapter 4, there is no genuine analysis of the class location of managers in Marx's *Capital*. Correspondingly, the chapter also suggested that any derivation of this class location required the extension of Marx's framework beyond the limits of its explanatory power ("Stretching explanatory powers" as in the title of the last section of that chapter.)

We recall that within the analytical apparatus of Marx's *Capital*, the class location of managers can be approached in relation to what Chapter 4 ("Managers in Marx's analysis") called "salaried workers as profit-rate maximizers" (as secretaries or salespersons). Along such lines, managers are an upper fraction of wage earners in charge of a number of capitalist valorization or circulation tasks aiming at the improvement of firms' performances and, thus, distinct from productive workers. In this respect, managers are also distinct from subaltern profit-rate maximizers. The basic function of managers is the maximizing of the profit rate to the benefit of capitalists, specifically from the top of the hierarchies of wage earners, that is, with particular competence and authority, and this latter specification is not indifferent. They are rewarded by the transfer of a fraction of the surplus-value, like subaltern profit-rate maximizers, but on distinct hierarchical foundations. The making of managers a fraction of the bourgeoisie on such grounds, as in Poulantzas' analysis, or a petty bourgeoisie, only required the accomplishment of one further step. That this bourgeoisie be termed petty or not is secondary.

Gérard Duménil's analysis during the 1970s was built along such lines, but under the key provisos that this interpretation was defined within the strict confines of Marx's analytical framework in *Capital* and that the ongoing transformation of production relations would imply the accomplishment of a theoretical revolution:

> One can contend that managers and lower-rank employees form a new petty bourgeoisie, quite distinct from traditional fractions; this is probably, nowadays, the most appropriate manner of giving a specifically capitalist expression of their social location.
>
> An adequate formulation of the problem here considered, beyond a "static" approach, requires, however, the consideration of the metamorphosis of production relations within capitalism and even from this stage of historical development to another stage, since these transformations most likely foreshadow a fundamental alteration of production relations. Would it not be beyond the concept of capital itself that the analysis should thus be conducted?[14]

Two appendices followed, regarding, respectively, James Burnham's *Managerial Revolution* and the USSR, suggesting this necessary extension.[15] The crucial point was there, and this analysis foreshadowed the program of the previous chapters (following decades of further research and publication): The limits of Marx's political economy had to be overstepped as an effect of the transformation of relations of production. Managers, as a class within managerial capitalism, must be understood in relation to the emergence of the new mode of production.

Beyond capitalism: Schumpeter, Burnham, and Galbraith

Within a quite distinct brand of literature, the emphasis was actually placed on the transformation of relations of production (even if the phrase was not used), thus creating a tight link with our own analysis. The key difference with the studies in the first section above is that when managerial trends are approached along such lines, managers are no longer seen as the agents of capitalist classes but as an autonomous group in pursuit of its own objectives. The dilemma was, thus, well set out, namely whether managers must be understood as new actors in a more advanced stage of capitalism or as the promoters of a new society beyond capitalism? We recall that our own answer is "Both."

One can quote here Alan Hughes' convincing assessment in his contribution to the *New Palgrave Dictionary*:

> That the financial and organizational structure of the modern corporation has changed and is still evolving, is without dispute. The same cannot be said for the view that this has led to either a more soulful or socially responsible capitalism, or to a socio-economic structure in which a distinctly identifiable social group of "managers" has come to exercise power in its own sectional interests.[16]

One can first recall here the now-forgotten theories of the convergence of the "two systems," namely capitalism and self-proclaimed socialism. The theme was still widely discussed during the 1960s and 1970s, after which time the interest vanished.[17] These analyses pointed to new developments beyond the limits of capitalism, in sharp contrast with the present ideology of "neoliberal capitalism as the end of history," which superseded such analytical frameworks in the wake of the failure to reform the countries of self-proclaimed socialism.

The first name to mention in this context is obviously Joseph Schumpeter, with his famous *Capitalism, Socialism, and Democracy*, published in 1942. The book must be understood as having been written about a decade after the Great Depression and in the context of the war economy. (One can anecdotally recall that Schumpeter detested Roosevelt policies.) Two preliminary remarks must be made. First, the Marxian interpretation is explicit, as the four chapters forming the first part of Schumpeter's book were devoted to Marx's analysis. Second, the book was later understood as anticipating the convergence of the systems. Very tellingly, the following statement was inserted by the publisher at the beginning of the book in the 1976 edition: "The mixed economy has become established in North America as well as in the countries of the European Community, while in the socialist countries there has been a move towards various forms of decentralization and of a market economy."

Schumpeter's thesis was unambiguously stated in the Prologue to the second part of *Capitalism, Socialism, and Democracy*, entitled "Can capitalism survive?"

> The thesis I shall endeavor to establish is that the actual and prospective performance of the capitalist system is such as to negative [*sic*] the idea of its breaking down under the weight of economic failure, but that its very success undermines the social institutions which protect it, and "inevitably" creates conditions in which it will not be able to live and which strongly point to socialism as the heir apparent. My final conclusion therefore does not differ, however much my argument may, from that of most socialist writers and in particular from that of all Marxists.[18]

Very interestingly, Schumpeter's interpretation did not prolong the early Marxist "catastrophist" prognosis regarding the future of capitalism, elaborating on the *Communist Manifesto* (as celebrated by the German social-democracy of Karl Kautsky or Rosa Luxemburg, to which we will return in Chapter 16, devoted to self-proclaimed socialism), but was much more in line with what we have in the previous chapters denoted as the historical process of socialization. This is confirmed by Schumpeter's description of the reasons accounting for the acceptance of socialism by broad sectors of the population.[19]

One must also recall the simultaneous publication of Burnham's *Managerial Revolution*.[20] The difference is that Burnham's analysis hinged around the shift from private to state ownership, with the rise of a class of state officials rather than the managers of private corporations.

The best-known such framework elaborating on an actual transformation of relations of production (even if the phrase was also not used) was, however, the analysis of John Kenneth Galbraith. The point of departure was the separation between ownership and management. The notion of technostructure is so familiar that it is hardly necessary to recall it. The emphasis was on the broad character of the group, explicitly not limited to top executives:

> This [*management*] is a collective and imperfectly defined entity; in the large corporation it embraces chairman, president, those vice presidents with important staff or departmental responsibility, occupants of other major staff positions and, perhaps, division or department heads not included above. It includes, however, only a small proportion of those who, as participants, contribute information to group decisions. [...] It embraces all who bring specialized knowledge, talent or experience to group decision-making. This, not the narrow management group, is the guiding intelligence—the brain—of the enterprise. There is no name for all who participate in group decision-making or the organization which they form. I propose to call this organization the Technostructure.[21]

Galbraith was clearly dealing with a new phase in history, and it is hard to imagine that a reversal toward earlier forms was envisioned. Galbraith was fundamentally right but, as we will contend in Chapter 10, historical dynamics are multifaceted mechanisms, and the remainder of the story was more complex than could be expected.

Sociologies and historical philosophies

There is an obvious link between Marx's framework and the analyses hinging around "power elites" in the United States. The reason is straightforward: Powers are concentrated at the top of social hierarchies, and wealth is an obvious criterion besides managerial capacities. One can mention the works of Charles Wright Mills and William Domhoff.[22] "Power elite" refers to social groups at the top, typically families or cronies, in charge of key social functions, as opposed to the rank and file. For example, a family can be basically classified among capitalist families while some of its members are large landowners or important managers, and others hold high positions within the government or the army.

One feature of the research conducted along such lines was the attempt to pin decisions on individuals or particular groups of people interacting within networks of social relations, instead of broad social categories, typically classes or fractions of classes, as in "structuralist" Marxism. (One can cite here the interesting work by Maurice Zeitlin confronting structuralist approaches, notably of French inspiration, during the 1970s.[23]) Correspondingly, the emphasis on power elites was criticized on behalf of the individual treatment of social processes, whose paroxysmal form is conspiracy theory.

The fact that the members of the same family within the highest tiers of social hierarchies may be active within distinct spheres of power is not only unquestionable but, in our opinion, a basic feature of class societies and an important aspect of the analysis of the relationship between classes and states. Regarding government, the involvement within government institutions has always been a central aspect of social relations on the part of the members of upper classes. Regarding ownership and management, the merger between capitalist and managerial relations at the top is a fundamental character of the current transition between the two modes of production, as had been the case at the transition between feudalism and capitalism (see Chapter 8).

As could be expected, sociologists and philosophers identified the new managerial features of contemporary societies, thus necessarily entering into the fields of private and government management. Two prominent illustrations are briefly addressed below, namely the works of the sociologist Pierre Bourdieu and the philosopher Michel Foucault.

During the heyday of academic Marxism, there was a pervasive tendency to reduce all forms of dominations to a category of exploitation in Marx's sense, for example regarding sexual repression, genders, or "races." This was, very understandingly, interpreted as an outraging exaggeration of the explanatory power of Marx's analysis by elements of activists on the left. Marx's theory of history should not be mistaken for a general theory of domination. The new frameworks emerging in rebuttal of this inclination to overstep the limits of the explanatory power of Marx's framework were perceived as breaths of fresh air.

Bourdieu's sociology is a theory of autonomous "fields" and "metafields" (military, police, juridical, economic, linguistic, cultural, symbolical, etc.). A capital is defined as a "power over a field" (economic, social, and cultural capitals, and the like, including symbolic capital).[24] The members of the ruling classes concentrate the capitals of various kinds in their hands, like the members of power elites. The power of upper classes is primarily based on economic capital, and this is the main link with Marx's analysis.[25] The focus of Bourdieu's analysis is not, however, on historical dynamics, despite recurrent inquiries into the history of fields.[26]

A disappointing observation regarding a potential contribution of Bourdieu's sociology to the analysis of managers is that firms are not considered a field and, consequently, private managers are not a central component in the analysis. This is surprising in a framework in which the existence of cultural or social capital besides economic capital is emphasized.[27] Regarding the topmost layers of wage earners, Bourdieu's interest was mostly on senior officials, described as the members of a state nobility.[28]

As in the case of Bourdieu above, not much interest was devoted by Foucault to firms' managers. The contrast is, however, sharp between Bourdieu's sociology and Foucault's philosophy, in which historical dynamics are conferred a key role. Foucault's central concept is "power-knowledge." The term is self-explanatory: Domination is an obvious feature inherent in all forms of social relationship in which the monopoly of knowledge is implied, and there is no questioning the existence of such asymmetrical social relationships and their potential importance.

The notion of power-knowledge establishes an unquestionable link between Foucault's framework and the analysis of managers. Jacques Bidet's most recent publications attempt an ambitious synthesis between Marx's and Foucault's theoretical frameworks, specifically based on Foucault's book *Biopolitics*.[29] What we denote as managers had already been called "leaders" by Bidet, and the new term is quite adequate to the new Marxian-Foucauldian perspective.[30]

A careful separation must, however, be maintained between Foucault's framework and any reading of history based on Marxian foundations. A short appendix to Chapter 10 is devoted to the damages caused to social analysis by Foucault's contribution to the so-called "deconstruction" of Marxist analysis regarding "government rationality" and the application of the notion to neoliberalism.

8
Hybridization as analytical challenge

The vindication of the thesis of the gradual establishment of managerialism as a new mode of production-socialization is a challenging endeavor. Marx provided the theoretical foundations but probably never thought his analysis could be extended to the consideration of a new class society: For Marx and Engels, the transition underway in the mid-nineteenth century was between capitalism and a society freed from all forms of exploitation and domination.

Taking at face value the list in the Preface to *A Contribution to the Critique of Political Economy*—the Asiatic, ancient, feudal, and modern bourgeois modes of production[1]—three transitions were a priori implied. The ambition of the present chapter is limited to the consideration of the transition between feudalism and capitalism, or what can be, more rigorously, called the genesis of capitalist production relations (equivalently bourgeois relations). The potential benefit is the skill acquired in the deciphering of social patterns in constant transformation and the resulting hybrid configurations. (The explanatory power of Marx's framework regarding the transitions between earlier modes of production, for example between the ancient and feudal modes of production, is very questionable.)

The choice of cases included as illustration in this chapter is highly selective. No attempt is made at the "general" interpretation of an issue as complex as the dissolution of feudal relations and the emergence of capitalist production relations—a theme still in debate among historians. In any instance, the emphasis is on the emergence of the new relations of production rather than the "crisis" of feudalism.[2]

In this analysis, we use the epithet "capitalist" in relation to the valorization of a capital advance, that is, in a broad sense. Early forms are involved, notably, in agriculture, the capital invested on farmed land in particular by merchants active in the commerce of agricultural products, and in foreign trade. Regarding the manufacture, production during the seventeenth, eighteenth, and early nineteenth centuries was mostly performed by small masters and their journeymen,[3] under the sway of the new class of merchants. There were, however, already large manufactories gathering several hundreds of employees, and gradually more so. One could also mention financial capital as a new sector, though the link with the economy remained weak. But credit relations, specifically as implied in the reference to usurers' capital (often the capital of merchants themselves, when producers were not able to comply with their commitments), played a key role.[4]

There is no questioning the fact that a more restrictive use can be made of the term "capitalism," limited to the consideration of social relations after the establishment of the factory system, in which the channel of extraction of surplus-labor was grounded in the wage relation. A more profound discussion would, however, be required, since, regarding early stages, small masters already hired journeymen and, regarding more advanced configurations, important fractions of labor within factories were subcontracted and not based on an actual wage relation.

"Capitalist social relations" is subject to a broader use than full-fledged "capitalism" and, in our opinion, is the most appropriate way of referring to the early stages of capital accumulation.

From feudalism to the genesis of capitalist relations of production: The French Ancien Régime

There is no possible discussion of the transition between feudal and capitalist relations of production independently of the preliminary definition of feudalism. (The substantive was coined at the beginning of the nineteenth century and, thus, could be used by Marx.)

The "feudal society," as historians put it, is generally dated to the half-millennium between the ninth and fifteenth centuries in Europe. A lord or "overlord"—who held the land on the basis of an alleged form of ownership inherited from the period of the great invasions in Europe (or the Norman conquest in England)—granted the benefit of one fraction of this land, including the local inhabitants, as a fief to a vassal in exchange for military service. At the top of the pyramid was the monarch, second to God. (The benefit of the fief became de facto hereditary in 868 under Charles the Bald, with regional differences.) This is, at least, the traditional content given to the notion.[5] These definitions have a broad consensus, but leave aside the medieval communes which began to develop during the tenth century, fighting to obtain charters guaranteeing their "liberties" in front of the bishops, abbots, or secular lords. The notions and dates remain, however, controversial. An extreme example of diverging views is the work of historians seeking to establish a direct link between the European nobility and the Roman antiquity, the nobility being the emanation of the Roman senate.[6]

These approaches hinge around what Marx would have classified among superstructures rather than the economic infrastructure, that is, the channels of extraction of surplus-labor from the peasants and the population of the communes. The emblematic lever of feudal exploitation was serfdom, but a much broader institutional framework was involved, such as the corvée and many forms of taxation. ("Free" segments, that is, non-serf components of the peasantry, were liable to the corvée.) In discussion below are the chronological limits to be set to feudalism as a mode of production in Marx's sense. Both origins and ends are at issue.

Regarding the origins, it would be necessary to consider the mechanisms allowing for the extraction of surplus-labor during the earlier half-millennium between the unraveling of the Roman empire(s) and the ninth century, marked by the withering away of the traditional forms of estates (the Roman villas of the late empire) and slavery.[7] What were the channels of extraction of surplus-labor under the Merovingians and Carolingians within what is now France and Northern Europe? What forms of hybridization were observed with the earlier mode of production?

More relevant to the present analysis is the discussion of the "end of feudalism," supposed to coincide with the emergence of capitalist relations, an equally difficult issue when feudalism is approached as mode of production instead of a set of political institutions. Serfdom disappeared in Western Europe in the fourteenth or fifteenth centuries. (Due to the broad diversity of status, reference is, however, often made to an earlier or much later date, also reflecting early de facto abolition or late formal abolition.[8]) In Eastern Europe, serfdom lasted longer and was even strengthened in a number of instances. The corvée survived to serfdom, even in France, where the royal corvée, as unpaid labor in the construction of roads or canals, still existed during the eighteenth century.

We focus here on the French experience and, more specifically, the nature of the French society during the Ancien Régime. (The period is dated from the beginning of the reign of Henri IV in 1589 to the French revolution in 1789, thus strictly two centuries.) The phrase was coined to avoid the anachronistic reference to a feudal society. Many feudal traits were still there, but the society is not described as such by historians since the lord–vassal relationship had disappeared.

The situation regarding land ownership can be summarized as follows. Two broad forms of property had to be distinguished. At the top of social relationships, as typical of the structures of manorialism, one found the land directly controlled by the lord, namely the demesne. (The head of the manor was not necessarily a member of the nobility, but bishoprics and monasteries, or rich commoners.) Abstracting from a very small fraction of the land owned in full property, most of the remaining lands were the villein holdings of the *censives*, on which peasants had to pay the *cens*—defined in the seventeenth and eighteenth centuries as a given sum of money—to the lord. A specific feature of the French society was the comparatively low percentage of land in the demesnes (about one third). In order to preserve their income, the lords farmed their demesnes, typically to merchants from the cities, or gave the land in *métayage*. *Métayage* became the main form of tenancy of the lands of the lords (as the *cens* had been highly depreciated by inflation). In addition to the *cens*, the peasants had to pay to the lord taxes and duties, in addition to the rising taxes to the central government.

On the eve of the French revolution, the lords were acting with the aim of the restoration of their earlier privileges. The famous Gracchus Babeuf, to which we will return in Chapter 14 in the analysis of bourgeois revolutions, began his career as "feudist," digging into the archives of manors (the *terriers*) in search of forgotten documents allegedly supporting the claims of the nobility. (And this is how Babeuf became a diehard revolutionary.)

The French revolution was quite adequately described as a bourgeois revolution finally won by the bourgeois class, while the lords lost their remaining privileges besides the mere property of land. Thus, the night of August 4, 1789 is commonly referred to as the "Abolition of feudalism in France" by The National Constituent Assembly, and this was the terminology used in the decrees. Not only was the nobility affected but also the clergy. Were the privileges of the nobility and clergy still significant? The answer is "Yes."

The ambiguous character of the terminology is, however, disappointing. Nobility, fiefs, and feudal rights survived the feudal society! The conundrum is well illustrated by Albert Soboul's statement at the beginning of his famous work *The French Revolution* [*La Révolution*

Française]. (Soboul was the most famous Marxist historian of the French revolution.) The remaining unquestioned privileges of the nobility were described as follows by Soboul:

> [...] the nobility owning the fiefs perceived feudal rights on the peasants. (One could, however, belong to the nobility without owning a fief, and be a commoner and own a noble fief: All link had disappeared between nobility and the feudal system.)[9]

During the eighteenth century, the heirs of the former feudal nobility, transformed into a class of landowners and gradually more engaged in other categories of businesses, still benefited from feudal rights and privileges. In addition, they still assumed local functions regarding law and public administration. Year after year, these tasks had, however, been deprived of real content. The actual functions had been gradually transferred to a new highly centralized and growing administrative body under the direct control of the central government. The new administration unambiguously worked in favor of the progress of the rising capitalist features in the new society. Turgot's physiocratic program of 1774 (Anne Robert Jacques Turgot), to which we will return below, just at the transition between the reigns of Louis XV and Louis XVI, was manifestly in favor of the development of capitalist relations of production (so demanding that it failed). In addition, the strength of the central government was on the rise. The position of arbitration of the central administration between the old nobility and the rising capitalist class during the Ancien Régime had conferred on the monarchy a high degree of autonomy and, as is sometimes erroneously contended, allegedly established the state apparatus above class patterns and struggles. (These themes are discussed in the appendix to Chapter 5 in relation to François Furet's use of Alexis de Tocqueville's work.)

Only one step forward had been accomplished on August 4, 1789. It was actually the National Legislative Assembly which, during its last weeks immediately prior to the establishment of the National Convention in September 1792, voted for the genuine reform of ownership of land in the countryside, marking the actual break with the structures inherited from feudal ownership relations. The new legislation was only applied in 1793. Notably, the commons usurped by the lords during the previous 40 years were returned to the communes; all rights on the *censives* were

abolished and the land was given to the peasants without financial com-
pensation to the lords, including segments of farmed land.[10]

Regarding the survival of feudal relationships, the question can finally
be raised: Was there a common aspect between the Merovingian elites
within social relations still partly embedded in the structures of the late
Roman Empire and features inherited from the German tribes, on the
one hand, and the nobility during the Ancien Régime up to the outbreak
of the revolution in the France of the late eighteenth century in which
the basic traits of an agrarian and merchant capitalism were progressing
rapidly, on the other? The question might be judged absurd.

There is an answer, however. *Mutatis mutandis*, in both instances,
fractions of political and straightforwardly economic privileges were
still based on legal (written or customary) foundations rooted in the
alleged inheritance of the nobility from the German invaders. When
Louis XIV decided, in 1669, that the nobility could take hold of one
third of the commons in the French countryside (in what was called
triage), this was performed on the basis of the principle that these lands
had been generously given to village communities by lords as legitimate
owners of all land since the conquest! More generally, there were no
other foundations than this reclaiming of the remaining privileges of
the nobility prior to the revolution. Emmanuel Joseph Sieyès' pamphlet,
published in 1789, had huge success, stating that the reliance on the
German conquest only showed that the invaders had to be sent back to
their Eastern forests:

> Third Estate need not fear examining the past. It will betake itself to
> the year preceding the "conquest"; and as it is nowadays too strong
> to be conquered it will certainly resist effectively. Why should it not
> repatriate to the Franconian forests all the families who wildly claim
> to descend from the race of the conquerors and to inherit their rights
> of conquest.[11]

An English "Ancien Régime"

Similar hybridization processes were observed in England, probably
earlier than in France though there is nothing obvious in this respect.
A thorough comparison lies beyond the limits of the present study. The
following comments can, however, be made:

1. *The politics of emerging capitalist relations.* In his book *The English Revolution 1640*, Christopher Hill, the leading Marxist historian of the English revolution, stated that "something like an industrial revolution took place in the century before 1640."[12] Following Hill, the relationship between the Tudor monarchy and the rising bourgeoisie was one of alliance, since the emerging bourgeois class looked forward to the stabilization of the political situation. This analysis rests on at least three assumptions: (i) the occurrence of an "industrial" revolution in the sixteenth century, though the term "industrial" might not be the most appropriate; (ii) politics in which the new bourgeois class was involved; and (iii) a role of "arbitration" in the hands of the monarch, evocative of Marx's analysis of the French Ancien Régime (see the appendix to Chapter 5, devoted to *The Eighteenth Brumaire*). This alliance between the Tudor monarchy and the bourgeoisie must be contrasted with the social strife during the seventeenth century between the Stuart monarchs and the Parliamentarians (manifesting the joint interests of the "progressive" section of large landowners and the rising bourgeoisie, in Hill's terminology, that is, supporting the advance of the new relations of production).[13] The confrontation between the Parliamentarians and the Stuarts led to the Civil Wars and the revolution (see Chapter 14). Reference was recurrently made by Hill to the aristocracy and backward segments of the gentry acting in favor of the preservation of the old forms of ownership and privileges, but no return to actual "feudal" relations of production was implied.

And here we learn something very relevant to the analysis of the emergence of capitalist relations of production and the inheritance from feudal relations. Like in France, the survival of feudal rights remained an important feature of social relations in the England of the seventeenth century, notably in the system of copyholds, which can be traced to the decline of serfdom, that is, documents stipulating the duties and rights of tenants, which formally survived up to the nineteenth century. But Hill actually emphasized the burden the old classes and primarily the Crown placed on the development of capitalist relations of production, living like social parasites on the emerging capitalist relations. Besides taxation, Hill mentions the establishment of monopolies, "in the attempt to control certain industries and obtain a rentier's rake-off from that control."[14] In our opinion, a broader use of this notion of "burden" placed by the fractions of the old classes and the Crown on the new classes should be made in the analysis of the French Ancien Régime in comparison with the survival of old relations of production in this strict sense, than is actually expressed within the French historiography.

2. *The political economy of emerging capitalist relations.* Independently of Marx's analysis, to be discussed in the following section, there is also a "history of economic thought" aspect underlying the comparison between the French Ancien Régime and English society during the same period. It is probably not superfluous to recall that Turgot's *Réflexions sur la Formation et la Distribution des Richesses* [*Reflections on the Formation and Distribution of Riches*] was written in 1766 (and published in 1770), that is, a decade or so before Adam Smith's *The Wealth of Nations*.[15] Smith had met Turgot in Paris and knew his work, and the relationship between the two analyses is obvious.[16] One should also recall that Smith used the terminology "masters" and "merchants" to refer to capitalists, in a manner directly evocative of the early stages of capitalist accumulation. But who would deny that Smith was a theoretician of capitalist relations of production? Despite the likely advance of relations of production in England, the view that Smith was the analyst of capitalist relations of production and Turgot of pre-capitalist relations would be a rough simplification: in both countries a process of transition was involved.

A more detailed analysis reveals a wealth of common aspects between the two countries, sometimes anecdotal but nonetheless quite telling. For example, a similar objection to the demands of the nobility regarding commons in France (in the reference to *triages* in the previous section) had, much earlier, been expressed by the Levellers during the English revolution with respect to the descendants of the Norman invaders at the root of the English nobility, instead of to the German invaders in Sieyès' pamphlet.[17]

Marx and the economics of emerging capitalist relations

The survival of feudal relationships must also be discussed with respect to basic economic mechanisms as analyzed by Marx. As clearly expressed in the extract of *Capital* regarding usurer's and merchant's capitals in the third section of Chapter 3 of this book, Marx limited the use of the notion of "capitalism" to the period following the rise of the factory system. This was also the option generally taken by Marxist economists, for example Maurice Dobb in his famous *Studies in the Development of Capitalism*.[18] In any instance, the criterion earmarking capitalism in the strict sense should not be mechanization per se but the factory system in which the extraction of surplus-labor was based on the wage relation.

A first issue is the determination of rents on farmed lands. During the transition, a process of polarization was apparently underway between, on the one hand, "progressive" landowners and farmers, still in the sense given to the notion by Hill, that is, landowners and farmers deliberately involved in the emergence of the new relations of production and, on the other, traditional, passive, owners and tenants, with the comparative progress of the former. Marx's notion of "differential rent" in Part Six of Volume III of *Capital* assumed the development of capitalist relations of production and is of no help in this analysis; a form of what Marx denoted as "absolute ground rent" could be the expression of the continuing monopoly of large landowners on the traditional desmesnes, but we do not know of studies allowing for such quantitative assessments.

Clearly, Marx had remarkable insights regarding the early forms of capitals during the long period of emergence of capitalist relations of production. One can, notably, consult Chapter 36 of Volume III of *Capital*, promisingly entitled "Pre-Capitalist Relations." Unfortunately, Marx never truly addressed this difficult issue in its complexity. *Capital* is the theory of the capitalist mode of production in the paradigmatic form of the factory system and, later, the large industry. Correspondingly, the analysis of the "primitive accumulation" in Chapter 25 of Volume I of *Capital* is the analysis of the historical process of formation of a population available for exploitation in the new context of the wage relation, so dramatically illustrative of the violence of all class societies.

The reference to usurer's capital and merchant's capital suffered from the lack of explicit "articulation" with social relations within the countryside, without mentioning foreign trade and slave trade. We have not been able to locate developments in Marx's work in which the link would be established between the various components of these emerging social relations, namely, the specific role of merchant capitalists in the farming of the lands of large landowners and the practice of lending to small masters, though references to these mechanisms can recurrently be found in the works of historians. Overall, from what we know of the work of historians, the empirical and theoretical analyses of the French

Ancien Régime or its equivalent in England remains uncertain. Is there a theory of Anciens Régimes?

The conclusion from the above historical survey in the present and previous sections is straightforward: Modes of production have long histories, with economic and political roots and shoots. Hybridization is in no way specific to the current transition between capitalism and managerialism. In the same way that the current relations of production within contemporary societies are termed "managerial capitalism," the Anciens Régimes could have been called "capitalist feudalism" if the emphasis had been placed on the economy rather than on traditional feudal political superstructures, since "feudal" levers of extraction of surplus-labor were still in place in combination with new channels, as well as old costly and inefficient superstructures, while the economic forces of capitalist relations of production were moving ahead. And the comparison with the contemporary hybrid forms of managerial capitalism is here highly relevant, as we will show in Part II.

There is no standstill, only dominations of one aspect over the other— sequentially, more feudalism than capitalism, more capitalism than feudalism, more capitalism than managerialism, and more managerialism than capitalism.

The genesis of a class contradiction: Bourgeois and proletarians

Given the homology between relations of production and classes, the same hybridization process as in the previous sections is obviously inherent in the dynamics of class patterns. A broad set of correspondences and mismatches was already at the center of previous chapters regarding the distinctions between capitalist owners and managers on the one hand, and managers and popular classes on the other. The present section contends that the same was true during the early progress of capitalist relations of production, obviously with specific content.

The merger at the top of social hierarchies during the sixteenth, seventeenth, and eighteenth centuries between the rising segments of bourgeois classes and the aristocracy—declining as such, but involved in a process of reconversion—has often been described. Very early, the nobility engaged in new forms of business in the aim of enhancing its income. Mines were exploited on the demesnes and ironworks in the forests, money was invested in foreign trade, and the like. At the same time, capitalist entrepreneurs were gaining access to the nobility by various devices, such as weddings, services to the Crown, and the purchase of land.

Even in the middle of the nineteenth century in England, that is, in the wake of the Industrial Revolution, the wealthiest were still landowners, and the emblematic feature of access to the top of social hierarchies was the ownership of large estates, paving the way to the access to nobility for rich industrialists. William Rubinstein, in his study of the society of the mid-nineteenth century in England, strikingly described the reshuffling of social positions: "the early industrialists, as is well known, operated on a comparatively small scale."[19] Referring to the 1879 agricultural depression, when industrial wealth became dominant, Rubinstein emphasized that "businessmen were still purchasing land," though "it was apparently during this period that ownership of land ceased to be the automatic prerequisite of new peerage creations."[20] And we would add "only during this period." In every country, under similar circumstances, high officials were acquiring hereditary or nonhereditary titles.[21]

Up to the early nineteenth century, the basic class divide was still between, on the one hand, the idle segments of the nobility and the clergy at the top of social hierarchies and the new class of merchants; and, on the other, a population of producers at the bottom. The small masters worked with workmen (journeymen), usually living within the house of the masters, and the link was tight. The main split was not there.

The particular forms of this emerging capitalist pattern were reflected in the conduct of popular struggles. The famous struggles of the *canuts* in Lyon in 1831 and 1834 were led by small masters. A few hundred merchants provided the raw material to about 8,000 masters, each employing a handful of journeymen in the silk industry.[22] The product was handed to the traders at a given price. The struggle followed from the joint deterioration of the situations of masters and workmen, confronting more advanced forms of capitalist relations of production. The organization of production in Paris was strikingly described by Maurizio Gribaudi under the name "collective manufactory" [*fabrique collective*]. Numerous independent workers and their employees produced various parts of the same luxury goods, which were then purchased and finally sold by merchants.[23] These were the workers on the barricades in 1830 and 1848.

During the same years, the main component of the Chartist movement in England (1838–58) was a population of small masters, surrounded by journeymen. The Chartists considered that "labor is the source of all wealth"; the crowd acclaimed speakers denouncing the confiscation of labor by a small minority of rich people.[24] The general strike had to be jointly conducted by the small master and his journeymen against the same common enemy. One can only recall here the history of the movement from its early steps, the beginning of a long fight: notably, the earlier disappointment with the Reform Act of 1832—still only 20 percent of the population could vote[25]—the continuous meetings, strikes, and riots, the People's Charter of 1838, the National Convention in London in early 1839 (the "General convention of industrial classes"), the presentation of the gigantic petition to the Parliament, the insurrection in Newport and its terrible repression at the end of 1839.

To these examples it would be necessary to add, at least, the uprising of the Silesian weavers in 1844, with similar features.

As is well known, the pattern of class confrontation changed progressively, though in a dramatic fashion, with, economically, the development of the factory system and the rise of the proletariat and, politically, the new course of alliance between the emerging middle classes and upper classes. The establishment of the new class contradiction and its manifestation in the conduct of social confrontation was paralleled by the so-called "liberal turn," as the expression of the alliance between the middle class and the bourgeoisie in England in the middle of the nineteenth century. One can cite here John Foster's fascinating Marxist study of three English industrial towns, notably Oldham (in the countryside, near Manchester).[26] In a thoroughly distinct spirit, one can also mention Eric J. Evans' converging diagnosis in his book *Britain before the Reform Act*.[27] The development of the two categories of transformation—the new class contradiction and the shift of the middle class to the right—was obviously not coincidental. As is also well documented by Foster, in parallel with these political trends, the early local forms of social organization and the corresponding balance between social powers were dismantled and new patterns of much more "efficient" repression of social movements implemented nationally.[28]

In France, in about the same years as Ricardo's *Principles* were published, the person of the capitalist was approached by Henri de Saint-Simon—who was nothing of an economist—as the pivotal actor in a broad historical vision of social progress of which the organization of production was the key aspect. (Saint-Simon was writing at the end of the second decade of the nineteenth century.[29]) The application of knowledge to production was the pivotal notion, and the scientists were described as the auxiliaries of businessmen (a fraction of the same social category). The "capacity" involved in the conduct of business enterprise was central in Saint-Simon's analysis and, strangely enough, ownership was hardly mentioned. The skills and toil of the active *industriel* (a substantive in French) were praised, while the siblings of a capitalist family passively benefiting from the income derived from inherited wealth, that is, the owners in the strict legal sense of the term, were objects of contempt. In the course of hundreds of pages, Saint-Simon urged Louis XVIII to found his power on this class of industrialists instead of relying on the parasitic classes of ecclesiastics and nobility. Correspondingly, no clear distinction was made between active capitalists and workers, the unifying criterion being the involvement in economic activity, though Saint-Simon began to use the word "proletarian" and encouraged upper classes to alleviate the suffering of the poor as a basic virtue of the new Christianity of which he was the apostle.[30]

The actual course of social change and class struggle was gradually deciphered. A central role was played by the disciples of Saint-Simon, as in the set of conferences published under the heading *The Doctrine of Saint-Simon*, in which a strong and painful shift was manifested away from the original analysis of the master.[31] During those years, a large number of periodicals were published in Paris, expressing a broad range of opinions from republicanism to socialism and, explicitly, communism.[32]

It is in this context that the clear divide between capitalist owners and the proletarian class was first set forth. A key figure was Jean Reynaud, unambiguously defining the proletarian class:

I call proletarians the people who produce the wealth of the nation, who only own the daily wage of their work, whose labor is subject to causes beyond their control, whose everyday reward amounts to only a weak fraction of their toil, constantly reduced by competition, whose future rests on the wavering promises of the uncertain and hectic course of industry, and who have no other hope for their old age than a place in hospitals or a premature death.[33]

Then, the bourgeois class:

I call bourgeois the people to which the fate of proletarians is subjected and fettered, people owning capitals and living on their annual yield,

who hold under their sway the course of industry whose enhancement or regress is subject to their consumption, who fully benefit from
present circumstances, and have no other wishes for the future than
the prolongation of their fate as enjoyed in the previous day and the
continuation of a constitution that give them the first rank and the
best share.[34]

The course of social change and struggles had finally revealed the fundamental transformation of class patterns. This is how Marx discovered
the new social antagonism, as well as communism, during his exile in
Paris.[35] When Reynaud wrote the above lines, Marx was 14 years old.
We also recall that the nature of capitalist economies had already been
identified and analyzed by Adam Smith and David Ricardo, in, respectively, 1776 and 1815—to become the basis of Marx's study of political
economy.

It took several decades before these views regarding the fundamental
class antagonism within capitalism actually spread within the worker
movement. As more thoroughly discussed in Chapter 15, devoted to
utopian socialisms and anarchisms, when the First International was
created in 1864, the leaders were master craftsmen, not workers as
members of the proletarian class, and the dominating ideology was correspondingly Proudhonian.[36] A twofold difficulty was thus expressed.
On the one hand, an adequate analytical framework had to be defined;
on the other, struggles had to be conducted along such lines. The clarifi-
cation came simultaneously in the two respects.

Returning to contemporary developments, the relationship between
the painstaking identification of changing class patterns in the early
nineteenth century and the difficult identification of the rise of
managerial traits in managerial capitalism is all too obvious. While the
main social split is nowadays between lower and higher wage earners, and
increasingly so in conformity with the rise of managers, the resistance
to the development of a new analytical framework remains very strong
in the left, with the almost exclusive emphasis on capital income. The
malaise is felt in one way or another, and reference is made to "corporations" as social entities in which the capitalist and managerial traits are
intertwined, thus avoiding the explicit mention of managers. There is
no clear perception of the class divides underlying traditional political
institutions such as political parties—one can even assert that there is
"no perception at all."

PART II

Twelve Decades of Managerial Capitalism

The object of the present part is no longer the transition between modes of production but rather the distinction between various periods in the course of managerial capitalism, that is, since the late nineteenth century. The key notion is "social order" as specific configuration of class dominations and alliances between the three classes—capitalists, managers, and popular classes—of managerial capitalism. A clear separation must be maintained between the two categories of mechanisms: (i) the dynamics of productive forces and relations of production underlying the succession of modes of production-socialization, including hybrid social formations, as in Part I; and (ii) the sequence of social orders as the expression of the changing class dominations and alliances within a given mode or social formation, as in the present part.

There is a formal analogy between the approaches in Chapters 2 and 9, as the two chapters are based on the consideration of income data. However, in Chapter 9 the identification of income patterns is no longer at issue; rather the variation over time of income and wealth inequalities.

Chapters 10 to 12 are straightforwardly devoted to social orders. Chapter 10 introduces the three such configurations that punctuated the course of managerial capitalism; Chapter 11 specifically accounts for the institutions of class dominations in neoliberalism, that is, the global institutions of ownership and control of corporations under the sway of the upper sections of managerial classes (notably their financial component); Chapter 12 analyzes the social forces that governed the succession of social orders, namely traditional governments and the agents at the top of the institutions of ownership and management above.

Chapter 13 harks back to Marx's theory of historical dynamics in Part I, relocating the sequence of social orders in the broader framework of productive forces, relations of production, class patterns, and class struggle as manifested during the twentieth and early twenty-first centuries. Special emphasis is placed on the tendencies of technology and distribution.

9
Varying trends of inequality

Hierarchies of income and wealth are certainly not the decisive criteria in the study of class relationships, but the dramatic changes observed regarding inequalities in the course of managerial capitalism testify very tellingly to the alteration of class dominations, alliances, and struggles (as income hierarchies manifested in class patterns in Chapter 2).

The new drill in statistical inquiry in the present chapter must be understood as a preliminary step toward the analysis of social orders in Chapter 10.

Inequality: Total income

The investigation below draws from the data collected by Thomas Piketty, Emmanuel Saez, and Gabriel Zucman, without which the present research would have been impossible. The presentation and interpretation are ours.

All tables and figures are for the United States. We begin with the total income of U.S. households. Seven groups are distinguished, from the lowest to the highest incomes (seven income fractiles without overlap): (i) the great mass of households forming the fractile 0–90 (between 0 and 90 percent); (ii) the upper decile (the 10 percent at the top) broken down into six categories, as explicit in the top line of Table 9.1. The table provides figures for the year 2015, emphasizing now-familiar features of income inequalities. (The three tables in the chapter have been prepared for the last years, 2015, 2011, and 2012, for which data are available in each respect.)

Beyond the evidence of inequality in 2015 directly illustrated in Table 9.1, the present analysis focuses on the changing patterns observed since 1913. This is the object of Figure 9.1. Since a considerable period of time is considered, a correction must be made for inflation: The variables are, thus, estimates of the yearly average income of households in each fractile, that is, the average nominal income of a household as in the bottom line of Table 9.1 for 2015, deflated by the Consumer Price Index (CPI). Given the amplitude of income inequalities, no comparison of historical profiles between fractiles would be possible in the original form of the data. For this reason, indexes were used instead of the original values of deflated incomes: For each fractile, the series was rescaled to 100 for the average of the period 1960–73. The choice of this elementary period is based on an actual property of the series, namely that the income of all fractiles grew at approximately the same rate during these 14 years (as evident in the figure). This treatment provides a striking picture of the changing patterns of inequality, to which we now turn.

Table 9.1 Income hierarchy among households: Seven fractiles as of 2015

Fractile	0–90	90–95	95–99	99–99.5	99.5–99.9	99.9–99.99	99.99–100
Fraction of all households (percent)	90%	5%	4%	0.5%	0.4%	0.09%	0.01%
Number of households (1,000 units)	150,583	8,366	6,693	837	643	151	17
Average yearly income ($1,000)	33	143	242	485	901	2,907	18,863

Source: T. Piketty and E. Saez. "Income inequality in the United States, 1913–1998." *The Quarterly Journal of Economics*, CXVIII(1): 1–39, 2003, Table A4: "Top fractiles income levels (excluding capital gains)."

Considering the fractile 0–90, the index grew from about 23 (the lowest point) prior to World War II to 111 in 1974, that is, was multiplied by 5, ushering in a phase of stagnation. Similar observations can be made for each fractile, though revealing distinct profiles. Two vertical continuous lines have been drawn in 1933 and 1974, separating three distinct periods. The following commentaries can be made:

1. *Prior to the New Deal.* A first ample pattern of inequality was manifest.
2. *From the New Deal to the mid-1970s or early 1980s.* Beginning with the New Deal, new trends were established expressing a sharp reduction of inequalities up to about 1960 (with the vertical dotted line). The rise in the income of the less-accommodated fraction of households was spectacular. Comparing the incomes of the various fractiles in

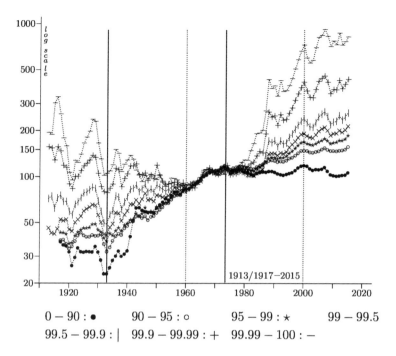

$0 - 90 : •$ $90 - 95 : ○$ $95 - 99 : ⋆$ $99 - 99.5$
$99.5 - 99.9 : |$ $99.9 - 99.99 : +$ $99.99 - 100 : -$

Figure 9.1   Average yearly income per household in seven fractiles (constant dollars, 1960–73=100)

For each fractile, the series was rescaled to 100 for the average of the period 1960–1973. The fractiles are listed below the figure. Vertical lines have been drawn in 1933, 1960, 1974, and 2000.

Source: as in Table 9.1.

1960 and their average values prior to 1929, a striking difference is observed between the fates of the upper and lower categories. The contrast is specifically sharp between the upper fractile, 99.99–100, whose income was divided by 2, while the income of the bulk of households in the fractile 0–90 was multiplied by 2.5. As already stated, after 1960 the incomes of all fractiles grew at about the same rate up to the mid-1970s, thus defining a second subperiod.

It is important to recall that the available series are pretax incomes. As an effect of the large rates of taxation of high incomes during those years (to be shown in Figure 10.2), the diminished income inequality during the second period would be much more spectacular if approached in after-tax measures.

3. *Since the mid-1970s or early 1980s.* At least up to 2000 (as indicated by the second vertical dotted line), the new course of rising inequality was dramatic. The income of the fractile 0–90 stagnated, while the income of the top fractiles skyrocketed. Comparing the average income of the top fractile, 99.99–100, since 2000 to its value in 1973, a multiplication by more than 7 was observed.

The conclusion of this analysis of income inequality is unequivocal: Three broad periods can be distinguished since World War I, namely (i) a period of strong inequality up to the New Deal, which marked a sharp break; (ii) up to 1960, a period of reduction of inequality followed by 14 years of constant degrees of inequality; and (iii) after 1973, a period of restoration. Assessed between 2000 and 2015, the rise of inequality was as spectacular as the reduction during the first part of the second period, up to a level of inequality similar to the average level during the first period.

Inequality: Wages

Given the general emphasis on classes in the book, there will be no surprise in the discovery that we interpret the historical profile of inequalities in the previous section in relation to the alteration of class patterns. But the object of analysis is even more specific regarding the respective roles conferred on managers and other wage earners, hence the emphasis on wage hierarchies.

Table 9.2 Wage hierarchies among wage-earners: Seven fractiles as of 2011

Fractile	0–90	90–95	95–99	99–99.5	99.5–99.9	99.9–99.99	99.99–100
Average yearly wages ($1,000)	48	144	220	399	669	1,867	10,334

Source: T. Piketty and E. Saez. "Income inequality in the United States, 1913–1998," Table B3: "Average salary for each fractile (in 2011 dollars)."

The average wages for one household in each fractile in 2011 are shown in Table 9.2, built along the same lines as Table 9.1 for total income. Likewise, the same methodology is used in Figure 9.2 as in Figure 9.1 (though only three fractiles are considered, for clarity). The three same basic periods are observed. The wages of the fractile 0–90

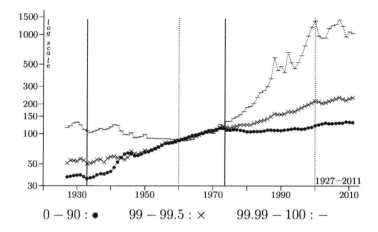

Figure 9.2 Average yearly wage per household in three fractiles (constant dollars, 1960–73=100)

The figure is built along the same lines as in Figure 9.1.

Source: as in Table 9.2.

rose from the Great Depression to the 1970s in about the same proportions as the total income of the fractile, which is not surprising since the capital income garnered by this segment of the population is very small. Thus, wage inequality was considerably reduced during the first period. The same parallel growth in the wages of the various fractiles is apparent between 1960 and 1973 as for total incomes. After 1974, wage inequality was dramatically restored: (i) the shape of the figure, evocative of an opening fan, is even broader than for total income; and (ii) the movement began earlier. Contrary to what is often thought, the comparatively faster growth of higher wages since the end of the 1970s was the main component of the upward trend of income inequality in Figure 9.1.

This latter observation immediately raises the issue of the comparative role played by capital incomes (or wealth) and higher wages in the historical trends of inequality. We turn to the consideration of wealth.

Inequality: Wealth

The same approach is repeated in Table 9.3 and Figure 9.3 as for wages in the previous section. The variable is the average wealth of one household in each fractile, deflated by the GDP deflator. The same three periods are again set out.

Table 9.3 Wealth hierarchies among households: Seven fractiles as of 2012

Fractile	0–90	90–95	95–99	99–99.5	99.5–99.9	99.9–99.99	99.99–100
Wealth ($1,000)	100	993	2,248	5,759	12,329	47,254	442,236

Source: E. Saez and G. Zucman. "Wealth inequality in the United States since 1913: Evidence from capitalized income data." *The Quarterly Journal of Economics*, CXXXI(1): 519–78, 2016, Tables: (i) "Top wealth shares, estimates obtained by capitalizing income and household wealth as a fraction of national income," and (ii) "Household wealth as a fraction of national income."

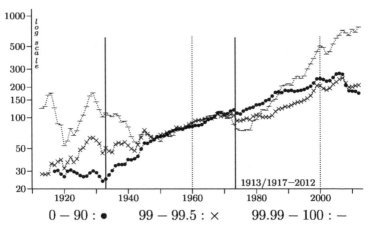

$$0 - 90 : \bullet \qquad 99 - 99.5 : \times \qquad 99.99 - 100 : -$$

Figure 9.3 Average wealth per household: Three fractiles (constant dollars, 1960–73=100)

Sources: as in Table 9.3.

The wealth of the upper fractile was taken into ample fluctuations prior to the New Deal. After a period of stabilization at a still comparatively high level after the stock-market crash in 1929, an important decline occurred during World War II. Simultaneously, the wealth held by the fractile 0–90 rose even more than the incomes of the fractiles, up to the 1970s. A significant decline was then observed during the crisis of the mid-1970s (a "structural crisis," to be analyzed in Chapter 10). This was specifically true of upper fractiles, more engaged in financial investments. (Between 1972 and 1975, the fall suffered by the top fractile, 99.99–100, amounted to 26 percent of the wealth of the fractile.) New upward trends were finally established whose degrees were similar to those from which the top fractile benefited regarding total income in Figure 9.1. Due to the rise of housing prices, the wealth of the fractile

0–90 went on increasing up to the 2007–9 crisis, with a final return to about the value which had been reached in 1985. (Since 1980, there was an important upward trend of pensions as component of the wealth of households, but we do not have the necessary information to separate between the various fractiles.)

Levels of inequality

Before closing the empirical analysis of inequality in the present chapter, it is important to emphasize the distinct average *levels*, as opposed to *trends*, during the three same periods. To this end, we compare the variables for the top fractile, 99.99–100, and the fractile 0–90. We recall that the first group is made up of 17 thousand and the second of 150 million households.

The degrees of inequality can be assessed by the calculation of the ratios between the two fractiles regarding income, wages, and wealth, as in Tables 9.1, 9.2, and 9.3. The results of the comparison are shown in Table 9.4.

Considering incomes in the first column and comparing the periods prior to the Great Depression and after 2000, the ratios were respectively 365 and 533, revealing an increased inequality; during the period 1960–73, of lower and stable inequality, the ratio amounted to 73. The

Table 9.4 Income, wages, and wealth hierarchies between two fractiles

Ratios	$\dfrac{99.99\text{–}100\text{ Income}}{0\text{–}90\text{ Income}}$	$\dfrac{99.99\text{–}100\text{ Wages}}{0\text{–}90\text{ Wages}}$	$\dfrac{99.99\text{–}100\text{ Wealth}}{0\text{–}90\text{ Wealth}}$
(1) 1917–29	365	86	3264
(2) 1960–73	73	27	1001
(3) 2000–12	533	238	2781
Increase in inequalities (3)/(2)	7.3	8.8	2.8

Due to the deficiency of data, the averages for wages have been determined for the periods 1927–8, 1960–73 and 2000–11.

The variable "Increase in inequalities (3)/(2)" is the quotient between the ratio during the third period and the ratio during the second period, for example, 7.3=533/73, in the first column.

Sources: as in Tables 9.1, 9.2, and 9.3.

ratios for wages and wealth can be read in the similar manner, respectively in the second and third columns. The same threefold pattern is apparent. An additional observation is that the degrees of inequality are much lower for wages and higher for wealth.

Summing up

The three variables—total income, wages, and wealth—provide converging images of the variation of inequalities in the U.S. economy since World War I. Invariably, the same periods were identified: (i) prior to the Great Depression; (ii) since the depression and to the mid-1970s or early 1980s; and (iii) since then. The main findings are the declining trend of inequality after the Great Depression up to 1960 and the restoration of that trend after the mid-1970s or early 1980s.

In terms of trends as well as levels, these transformations are not minor changes. There is no surprise in the observation that capitalism or managerial capitalism, as a class society, is always unequal, but the profiles described in the above sections reveal spectacular variations. A society in which 10 or 20 thousand households among the best accommodated earn, on average, 500 times more than the bulk of the population is not the same as a society in which the ratio amounted to 70. Wealth inequality remained, however, very strong during all periods, including the intermediate period, with a ratio larger than 1,000 (Table 9.4, third column). The wealth of the fractile 0–90 was consistently very low.

Within a study specifically devoted to managerial capitalism, that is, social formations in which high wages are the main channel in the process of extraction of surplus-labor, the rise of specifically wage inequality takes center stage. The finding that the rise of wage inequality was significantly larger than the increase of income or wealth inequalities during the third period is crucial (as shown in the bottom line of Table 9.4): Regarding wages, the quotient of the ratios between the two fractiles was 8.8 (second column), compared with 2.8 for wealth. This observation matches the no-less-dramatic finding in Chapter 2 regarding the rise of the share of wages in the income of the top 1 percent (the fractile 99–100), reaching 80 percent of total income (Figure 2.2): The dynamics of income within contemporary managerial-capitalist societies, inasmuch as they reproduce or will reproduce the model that prevailed in the United States, are not those expected from strictly capitalist societies.

The basic principles underpinning the theory of history within the first chapters suggest a first synthetic interpretation: The gradual transformation of productive forces and relations of production, as expressed in the continuing progress of socialization, propelled social relations further along the transition from one mode of production to the next, to the benefit of higher-wage-earners. But the course of class dominations and alliances bent the march of history along the winding road identified in the previous sections. How to account for the stubborn pattern in three stages?

10
The sequence of social orders

We denote as "social orders" political configurations of domination and alliance among classes (possibly fractions of classes). These configurations are prominently expressed within state institutions and, to that extent, determine the course of reforms and policies. But much more is involved, notably regarding firms' management or income distribution.

Since the beginning of the twentieth century, the interaction between the classes of managerial capitalism—capitalists, managers, and popular classes—was expressed within three such social orders: (i) the first financial hegemony of large capitalist owners up to the Great Depression; (ii) the post-depression/post-World-War-II compromise between managers and popular classes under managerial leadership, up to the 1970s; and (iii) the second managerial-capitalist financial hegemony in neoliberalism from the 1980s onward, gradually more under managerial leadership.

For brevity, we often denote the post-depression/postwar compromise as "postwar compromise"; we also use the phrase "social-democratic" compromise, thus stressing the welfare features typical of this social configuration (in particular regarding Europe). We term the first and third social orders as "financial hegemonies" by virtue of the pivotal role played by financial institutions.

Social orders are separated by episodes of structural crisis, that is, macroeconomic perturbations of broader amplitude than the recessions punctuating the course of the business cycle. The duration of structural crises is about a decade; the latest erupted in 2007.

The link with the empirical analysis in the previous chapter is straightforward. The sequence of three periods in Chapter 9—prior to the Great Depression, since the depression up to the mid-1970s or early 1980s, and since then—was the expression of the changing socio-economic conditions resulting from the succession of the three social orders:

High inequalities	↔	First financial hegemony
Diminishing and lower inequalities	↔	Postwar compromise
Rising and high inequalities	↔	Second financial hegemony

While the focus in the present chapter is on the succession and features of the three social orders, Chapter 12 attends to the class strategies that governed the switches from one social order to the next.

The emphasis in the main sections of this chapter is on the United States. The first appendix is devoted to the specific features of the entrance into managerial capitalism and the sequence of social orders in Europe. The second appendix discusses Michel Foucault's analysis of liberalism (and neoliberalism) in his set of lectures entitled *Biopolitics*.

The first financial hegemony up to the Great Depression

The domination of the new segments of the class of large capitalists associated with the corporate, financial, and managerial revolutions was established in the United States at the beginning of the twentieth century (see Chapter 6). We denote this first social order as a capitalist financial hegemony, on two grounds: (i) the financial features of ownership resulting from the corporate revolution; and (ii) the power of large banks and their often famous owners such as the Morgans and the Rockefellers over the new corporations, supported by the financial revolution.

In parallel with the rise of the new large economy, an important aspect of social relations during those years was the existence of a traditional lower segment of capitalist classes protected by the package of antitrust legislations, whose pillar was the famous Sherman Act.[1] Thus, besides popular classes, three social groups could be distinguished: (i) large capitalists in control of the advanced sector of the economy (nonfinancial corporations and large banks); (ii) traditional capitalists (notably small owners); and (iii) the class of managers in formation. The relationship between large capitalists, on the one hand, and the heads of small businesses and the class of managers, on the other, were the expression of a form of unequal social alliance under the leadership of large capitalists.

In the general context of the rise of the worker movement worldwide, the end of the nineteenth century and the early twentieth century were periods of intense class confrontation in Europe and the United States—not only in Russia or Germany—at least up to World War I. It is not possible to do justice here to the heroic episodes of popular strife during those years. Regarding the United States, one can recall the Colorado coal strike of 1913–14 and the Ludlow massacre, pitting the Rockefellers against workers in a dreadful warfare. But this was only one episode among many.[2] A major development was the occurrence of World War I, which created circumstances favorable to the repression of social unrest under the banner of patriotism. Nonetheless, during the ensuing decades, the strength of the worker movement worldwide and within the United States remained a prominent factor in the dynamics of social transformation.[3]

The various aspects of the analysis in Part I are here tightly inter-twined, namely the historical evolution of class patterns as expression of the transformation of production relations in managerial capitalism, to which the new network of class power relations in the present chapter must be added. One can easily recognize the Marxian analytical complex productive forces/relations of production, class patterns, and class struggle.

The post-depression/postwar compromise

In the United States, as within most industrial countries, the effects of the depression were devastating and paved the way to World War II. This was notably true of Germany, with the rise of Nazism, and Italy, with the already-fascist government. Conversely, progressive political regimes were established in the United States and France, during the New Deal and the Popular Front respectively.

Focusing on the course of events in the United States, the responsibility for the crisis was, at first, pinned on excess competition. During the first New Deal, senior officials in the government, known as "new dealers," stepped center stage in an attempt at the central organization of the economy with the aim of calming competitive pressures. The crisis was further blamed on financial mechanisms. Binding packages of measures were taken against finance, as in the Glass-Steagall Act and Regulation Q. Fiscal deficits were still not welcome, at least up to the new recession in 1937 that interrupted the first phase of the recovery.[4] The preparation of World War II, with the involvement of the government in the financing of investment and strong policies, allowed for the full restoration of the economy. This chain of events paved the way to the Keynesian revolution after World War II. (At the same time, an important portion of the traditional sector of small owners had been eliminated, as manifested in the rise of the share of wages in total income at the end of the depression.)

All aspects of socio-economic relationships were involved in the new course of the economy after World War II: (i) limits placed on international trade and the international flows of capital in the context of the Bretton Woods agreements of 1944; (ii) a new management of corporations targeted at the growth of output and technical innovation, in which the interest of shareholders were given a secondary role; (iii) macro policies, institutional reform, and regulation targeted at the control of the stability of the macroeconomy and growth; (iv) policy actions in favor of purchasing powers, education, health, and retirement; and (v) the struggle against inequalities by the implementation of minimum wages and the heavy taxation on high income and inheritance. And the list does not end there. The contrast is specifically sharp when the postwar decades are assessed in comparison with the ensuing neoliberal decades, as will be shown below.

Two basic features were involved in the new course of income distribution, both testifying to the new social trends: (i) the comparative decline of capital income in the income of top fractiles as expression of the transformation of relations of production (Figure 2.2); and (ii) the reduction of inequality as the expression of the new social order (Figure 9.2). This was the period during which the reduction of inequality in the distribution of total income, wages, and wealth documented in the previous chapter was manifested (Figures 9.1, 9.2, and 9.3). The purchasing power of the great mass of wage earners (that is, within the fractile 0–90) was sharply increased in only a few years during World War II. The most striking development was, however, that the new upward trend in the purchasing power of popular classes was maintained from 1933 to the mid-1970s, that is, over four decades.

A historical shift of such size cannot be imputed to any well-identified and precisely dated policy measure or institutional change. It testified to the action of new underlying social forces, typical of what we denote as the second social order, that is, the post-depression/postwar "social-democratic compromise," supporting the new hierarchy of class powers. The new social order was the expression of a political compromise between popular classes and the rising classes of private and public managers in the context created by the depression and the war, and was maintained during the three first postwar decades.

Both government managers in the conduct of policies and managers in the management of private corporations gained a new autonomy vis-à-vis capitalist classes. The earlier hierarchy between financial institutions and nonfinancial corporations during the first social order was destroyed, to the benefit of a much more balanced arrangement. Nonfinancial corporations differentiated their activity within large firms known as conglomerates. Large degrees of cooperation held between nonfinancial managers in the framework of interlocking directorship.

The phrase "financial repression" has sometimes been used to refer to the regulation of financial mechanisms after the Great Depression and the fight against the concentration of income and wealth at the top of social hierarchies. The term may be judged excessive, but it is hard to overstate the size of the transformation.

The first variable in Figure 10.1 is the share in the total income of all U.S. households garnered by the top fractile, 99.99–100. A division by a factor of almost 4 is revealed (from about 2 to 0.5 percent between

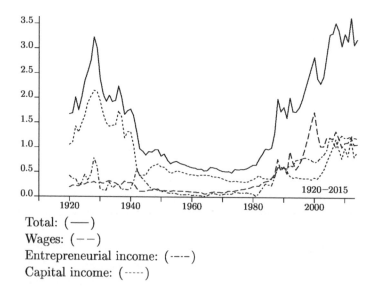

Total: (——)
Wages: (— —)
Entrepreneurial income: (----)
Capital income: (-----)

Figure 10.1 The share of the income of the fractile 99.99–100 and its three components in the total income of households (percent)

Source: T. Piketty and E. Saez. "Income inequality in the United States, 1913–1998." *The Quarterly Journal of Economics*, CXVIII(1): 1–39, 2003, Tables A1 and A7.

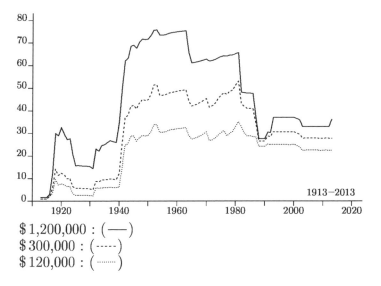

$ 1,200,000 : (———)
$ 300,000 : (-----)
$ 120,000 : (·········)

Figure 10.2   Average tax rates for three levels of yearly income (percent)

Source: "Tax Foundation," U.S. Federal Individual Income Tax Rates History, 1913–2013 (inflation-adjusted brackets) and calculations by the authors.

the pre-World-War-I levels and the 1970s). We recall that the series depict pretax measures; given the large rates of taxation charged on high incomes after World War II, the reduction of the share in total income received by the top fractile must have been even more impressive. (The remainder of the information in Figure 10.1 will be discussed in the following section.)

Figure 10.2 shows the average tax rates charged for three values of yearly incomes, in constant dollars of 2012. The figure reveals the dramatic increase in tax rates during World War II, from about 10 to almost 50 percent for income amounting to 300,000 dollars, and up to 70 percent for top incomes. (Again, the analysis is limited here to the left-hand part of the figure.)

We recall that the most spectacular development was the reduction of inequality among wage earners. As shown in Table 9.4, the range of wage inequality—comparing the top segment, that is, the fractile 99.99–100, to the bulk of wage earners, the fractile 0–90—was divided by 3 (from 86 to 27).

Overall, even if there was no radical elimination of capitalist classes, one can refer to an ongoing process of "euthanasia" of capitalists as such (not as human beings), gradually affecting the incomes, wealth, and powers of these classes.

From the mid-1970s onward: The second financial hegemony in neoliberalism

The transformation of social relations in the mid-1970s and early 1980s was no less spectacular than the sudden reconfiguration in the wake of the Great Depression. The income trends observed in the United States, as discussed in Chapter 9, provide the clearest possible answer to the famous question "Who benefits from the crime?", the answer being: Upper classes.[5] Who was the victim? Equally unquestionably: Popular classes.[6]

As a preliminary to this investigation, it is important to stress that the present section does not address the important social transformations that occurred in parallel with the implementation of neoliberalism. A dramatic example was the rise of the incarcerated population in the United States. Between 1925 and 1957 this population doubled, from 100,000 prisoners to 200,000, and remained at this level up to the 1970s; then, from the mid-1970s, the figure exploded, reaching almost 1,600,000 persons in 2014.[7]

One may wonder what destabilized a more-than-four-decade long social trajectory. At least four categories of factors converged:

1. The establishment of neoliberalism was the outcome of the offensive of capitalist classes in alliance with upper management against labor and the left, that is, an episode of class struggle in which upper classes had the edge over popular classes. The struggle on the part of upper classes under the neoliberal banner began even prior to World War II (as discussed in Chapter 12); it culminated during the 1970s and 1980s. The previous compromise was broken to the benefit of a new alliance within the upmost layers of class hierarchies.

2. The worker movement worldwide—the single force which could have stopped the offensive of upper classes—was gradually unraveling. Two mechanisms combined to this effect, namely the inability of the countries of self-proclaimed socialism to establish standard forms of "democracy" and accomplish basic reforms and, domestically, the narrow perspectives of left forces within the main capitalist countries.

3. A third important factor was the conflict between class determinants and imperial rivalry worldwide, with the United States arbitrating

to the benefit of the preservation and enhancement of the international hegemony of the country, in particular when the measures also worked in favor of upper classes. This is what we denote as the "national factor." For example, at the end of the 1950s, the United States allowed the development of the Euromarkets, in which banks developed their activity outside of their own country in order to escape from the constraints of national regulations, thus accomplishing the first steps of financial globalization.

4. The structural crisis of the 1970s created the necessary underlying economic conditions, with the wave of two-digit inflation within major countries and the failure of Keynesian policies to restore the macroeconomic situation in the context of a profitability crisis. The inflation wave finally led to the 1979 coup,[8] with the rise of interest rates to dramatic levels, marking a sudden step forward in the implementation of neoliberalism.

Beginning with Margaret Thatcher in the United Kingdom, followed by Ronald Reagan in the United States, the neoliberal (counter)revolution had devastating effects both nationally and internationally, first of all with the debt crisis in Latin America. A major financial crisis also occurred within the United States and Northern Europe during the 1980s.

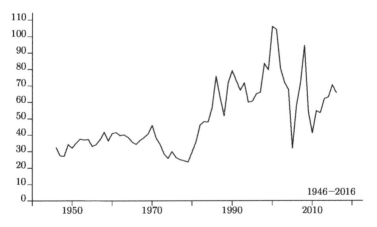

Figure 10.3   Net dividends as a share of profit (percent)

Profits after tax (without adjustments); Corporate business.

Source: National Income and Product Accounts Tables (NIPA), Tables 1.14 and 7.10.

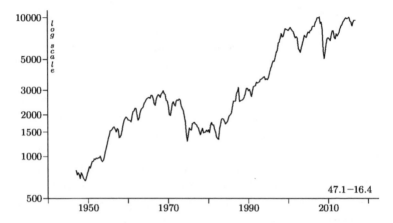

Figure 10.4 New York Stock Exchange composite index
Deflated by the GDP deflator.

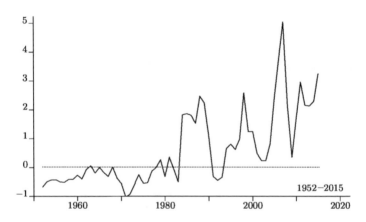

Figure 10.5 Buybacks minus new issuances of stock shares (percentage of tangible assets)

The unit of analysis is the nonfinancial corporate sector. A negative value of the variable means that corporations are issuing a net flow of stock shares as a source of financing. A positive value can be interpreted as the mark of a process of negative accumulation. For example, a value of 3 on the vertical axis shows that, during the year, corporations were repurchasing their own shares (thus, disaccumulating capital) for an amount equal to 3 percent of the value of their tangible assets.

Source: Flows of Funds accounts, Tables F.103 and B.103, "Nonfinancial corporate business" (flows and balance sheets).

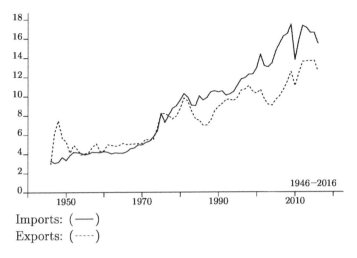

Figure 10.6 Imports and exports of goods and services (percentage of GDP)
Source: NIPA, Table 1.1.5.

Three aspects of the new course of management must be stressed: (i) the maximizing of rates of return on corporate own funds or, equivalently, the maximizing of shareholder value, thus nullifying the autonomy gained by nonfinancial managers during the postwar compromise; (ii) the increased distribution of dividends; and (iii) the hike in the remuneration of high managers in wages and supplements (notably the exercise of stock options).

The sudden shift toward the lavish distribution of dividends between 1980 and 2000 is illustrated in Figure 10.3. As shown in Figure 10.4, in parallel with this development, stock-market indices corrected for inflation skyrocketed. Beginning with the minimum in 1982, in 1987 the index had been multiplied by 2; in 1995, by 3; in 1996, by 4; in 1999, by 6. (Between the maximum in 1965 and the minimum in 1982, the index had been divided by 2, as an effect of the crisis of the 1970s.) Corporations engaged in new practices of repurchase of their own shares with the aim of bolstering their stock-market indices. As shown in Figure 10.5, the degree reached by repurchases is hard to believe (see the commentary below the figure).

At the same time, the framework of economic international relations was transformed, in what is known as neoliberal globalization. The first aspect was the liberalization of international trade in goods and services. It is sometimes contended, with reference to the early progress of international trade negotiations in the wake of World War II, that globalization was a continuous phenomenon since the end of the war. Figure 10.6 emphasizes, however, the break in the rise of international trade during the 1970s (with a step forward during the 1970s reflecting the increase in the price of oil). A similar transformation occurred for international capital flows, with the rise of U.S. direct investments abroad and foreign direct investment in the United States.[9] Neoliberal globalization can be interpreted as a deliberate move placing all workers worldwide in a situation of competition and, thus, considerably weighing on the wages of production workers within the most advanced countries.

One can return here to the outstanding benefits the top fractions of households drew from the new circumstances, as shown in Figure 10.1 (using the right part of the figure). The exploding percentage of total income garnered by the top fractile, 99.99–100, speaks for itself. The figure further shows that during the neoliberal decades the wages received by the members of this group at the top of income hierarchies reached about one third of the total income in the group. The channel "entrepreneurial income" underwent a dramatic upward shift. The members of this extremely well-off fractile did not discover the beauty of small business: Entrepreneurial income accounts for the income of S-corporations (not subject to corporate taxes, and whose income is taxed with the income of the individual). Similar configurations were also apparent within the fractile immediately below, 99.9–99.99. (The sum of the two fractiles defines the top one-thousandth of households, that is, 167,000 households in 2015.) Within this fractile, wages amount to one half of the total income, and capital and entrepreneurial incomes for the other half. These observations prolong the general shift of high income toward wages described in Figure 2.2, in which we see an expression of rising managerial trends.

In a similar manner, returning to the tax rates shown in Figure 10.2 (using the right part of the figure), one can observe the simultaneous decrease in tax rates regarding high incomes. Considering top incomes, two steps downward are revealed, from 66 to 48 percent between 1981 and 1982, and from 48 to 28 percent between 1986 and 1988. The combination of Figures 10.1 and 10.2 emphasizes the benefits the topmost layers of social hierarchies drew from neoliberalism. None of these dramatic shifts was ephemeral.

Not only high incomes in general, the sum of wages and capital incomes, benefited from the new course of the economy in neoliberalism.

A specific feature of the new social order was the new power acquired by financial managers (and their key role, to which we will return in Chapter 11). We do not know of any source allowing for the separation between the wages of specifically financial managers and other managers. It is, however, possible to distinguish between the average wage (and salary) in the financial sector and the average wage for all wage earners in the private sector. The result is shown in Figure 10.7. The variable is the ratio of the average wage by employee within, respectively, the financial sector and the total private sector.

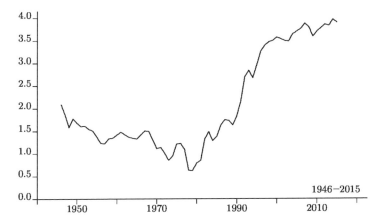

Figure 10.7   Ratio of average wages: Finance and insurance versus private industries

A ratio of 2 on the vertical axis indicates that the average wage in the financial sector was double the average wage for the entire private sector.

Source: NIPA, Table 6.6: "Wage and salary accruals per full-time equivalent employee by industry."

The ratio fluctuated around a declining trend between 1946 and 1978, from about 2 to 0.7. The restoration was spectacular. In less than two decades, a plateau was reached at about 3.5. One can surmise that upper wages played a crucial role in this rise, thus emphasizing the favorable fate of financial managers in neoliberalism. Not only wage inequality is involved: These trends illustrate the more general alteration of the formation of sectoral incomes to the benefit of the financial sector (as in fees, interest, and dividends), allowing for the payment of high wages.

Here is not the place to analyze the process that led to the crisis of neoliberalism in 2007–8, to which we have devoted other studies.[10] Two categories of factors can be mentioned: (i) the general features of neoliberalism regarding financialization and globalization (notably financial globalization), and deregulation; (ii) the imbalance manifested in the course of the U.S. macroeconomy, in particular the growth of the debt of households, the deficit of foreign trade, and the rise of foreign debt (the three mechanisms being obviously linked).

The heydays and decline of Galbraith's and Chandler's analyses

Before closing the analysis of the postwar compromise and neoliberalism, it is useful to return to the work of John Kenneth Galbraith, as discussed in Chapter 7. The concept of technostructure implied not only the transformation of relations of production but also the abandonment of profit-rate maximizing as the pivotal criterion in the conduct of management.[11] Alfred Chandler, in his *Visible Hand*, written before the implementation of neoliberalism, also clearly pointed to the secondary role played by profitability in managerial capitalism, at least in the short term. This was Chandler's seventh general proposition: "[...] in making administrative decisions, career managers preferred policies that favored the long-term stability and growth of their enterprises to those that maximized current profits."[12] On the one hand, advanced forms of managerial capitalism had been reached; on the other, managers had conquered high degrees of autonomy in the management of corporations and the conduct of policies.

The social circumstances described by Galbraith and Chandler were the combination of (i) the historical trends of relations of production pushing managers to the fore; and (ii) the social leadership of managers during the postwar compromise. The coincidence between the two sets of developments marked the apex of these theoretical frameworks. In retrospect, a clear confirmation of Galbraith's and Chandler's statements regarding the abandonment of profit maximizing during the postwar decades is that one of the pillars of the neoliberal alliance between capitalists and managers was the symmetrical pegging of the remuneration of top managers to profits and, even more straightforwardly, to stock-market performances.

Treating the crisis—Preserving the social order. A fourth social order after 2008?

The crisis of neoliberalism of 2007–8 was a structural crisis, as such suggesting the entrance into a new social order, as was the case after each of the three earlier crises. The crisis was unquestionably "the crisis of neoliberalism," deeply rooted in the inner mechanisms of the new social order. Almost ten years after the crisis, it is still difficult to formulate a diagnosis regarding the new course of events. One thing is clear, that the continuity with the earlier class foundations of neoliberalism is ensured: The alliance at the top of social hierarchies was not dissolved.

The treatment of the crisis required a strong intervention on the part of central institutions, notably the government and the central bank, at odds with free-market economics. As during the transition to neoliberalism, the national factor played a central role given the rising concerns regarding the decline of U.S. international hegemony, but the memory of the Great Depression was, in itself, a sufficient motivation supporting a strong intervention. The action of government officials had been a basic component in the treatment of the previous structural crises, and there was nothing truly specific regarding the 2007–8 crisis in this respect. In the United States as well as worldwide, the action of central authorities avoided the repetition of a catastrophe similar to the Great Depression, and this explains how the course of neoliberalism was not basically unsettled.

As of 2017, it is clear that no full return to pre-crisis dynamics has been accomplished regarding financial regulation and macro policies (notably with the passage of the Dodd-Frank Act in 2010). The intervention of central authorities remains stronger than prior to the crisis. In each instance there was, at least, a degree of hysteresis, as new policies were prolonged to at least the following decade. An important piece of legislation was passed in 2010, namely the Foreign Account Tax Compliance Act (FATCA), targeted at the repression of tax evasion.[13] U.S. citizens must report their holdings of accounts in the rest of the world. Foreign financial institutions, under the threat of sanctions, must inform the Internal Revenue Service of the existence of these assets. Many countries, including tax havens, have signed agreements with the United States.

Whether contemporary policy orientations will be ephemeral or be consolidated during forthcoming decades remains a pending issue. A first option could be described as "administered" neoliberalism, that is, neoliberalism combined with stronger policies. If the new trends are prolonged or even enhanced, the reference to administered neoliberalism will become less appropriate, and the use of a notion such as "neomanagerialism" gain relevance as a new social order.

The set of measures taken in the wake of the crisis does not demonstrate that the trajectory of the U.S. economy will be sustainable. The stable pattern of slow growth observed after the crisis is supported by very low interest rates and a broad set of measures. Despite shale gases and the low price of oil, the deficit of foreign trade still amounted to 2.5 percent of GDP in 2016. (The same is true of the United Kingdom, where the average deficit reached 2 percent GDP during the period 2010–16, and 6.5 percent if services are excluded.) When a country suffers from such lasting imbalances, compensating measures must be taken to support domestic demand. There are no choices other than an increase in fiscal deficits or in households' flows of borrowing. Prior to the crisis, arbitration was made in favor of households' borrowing, with well-known devastating consequences. Since 2008, the new instrument became the flows of borrowing on the part of the government, while the debt of households was slowly diminishing.

The election of Hillary Clinton should have ensured the harmonious preservation of earlier trends, to the benefit of upper classes. A new and unexpected situation was, however, created by the election of Donald Trump, with the alleged offensive against free trade and the uncertain orientation of foreign and military policies. As of 2017, it is still too early to make a reliable forecast. One can, however, risk the prognosis that deviations at odds with the interests of the upper segments of capitalist and managerial classes will not be tolerated.

Any progress along the sequence of neoliberalism—administered neoliberalism—neomanagerialism must be understood as a step forward in the gradual establishment of relations of production beyond capitalism, in the march towards full-fledged managerialism. Sensible assessments require, however, much historical distance.

The state; Social orders to the right and left

The key notions in the analysis of social orders in the previous sections are "class dominations" or "alliances." The contrast is sharp with the terminology used within political spheres, academia, and the media, which jointly lost the sense of class analysis. The present section establishes the link between the notions of current use and their content in relation to social orders. A set of broader issues, such as the theory of the state and the political orientations to the right or left, are involved.

Our analysis of the state (and para-statal institutions) is of basic Marxian inspiration. The consideration of social orders in the present chapter suggests, however, a reassessment of Marx's theory. We see in this adjustment an important supplement to the revision or "specification" of Marx's analytical framework. The main point is straightforward, namely that the state is not merely the agent of ruling classes: Within a sufficiently sophisticated class society, the state is the institutional framework in which the dominations and alliances among classes or fractions of classes are formed and, at the same time, by which the corresponding power relations are enforced.

The configurations of dominations and alliances within a social order (as conveyed by the state) define the political orientations to the right or left. For example, the unequal alliance between capitalist classes, smaller capitalist owners, and the rising class of managers during the first social order must be understood as an alliance to the right. The same is true of the alliance between capitalist classes and managers in neoliberalism, also to the right. (The transformation from the first to the second financial hegemony was the rising leadership gradually assumed in neoliberalism by managers along the historical road leading to their full hegemony, instead of the leadership of capitalist classes during the first social order.) Conversely, the alliance between managers and popular classes during the postwar compromise was an alliance to the left, though also under the hegemony of managers.

APPENDIX TO CHAPTER 10 (1): MANAGERIAL CAPITALISM AND SOCIAL ORDERS IN EUROPE

European countries were early participants in the general progress of the institutions of ownership and management as well as the new forms of technical change during the nineteenth century. The contrast was obviously significant between a country of early industrial revolution, namely the United Kingdom; France, which underwent a major process of industrialization during the nineteenth century with forms of large ownership; and the comparatively late but spectacular industrialization of Germany. The main difference with the United States was probably the sudden and far-reaching institutional revolution from the nineteenth century to the next, which conferred on the U.S. its economic and political international hegemony, as described in Chapter 6. It is not that social conflicts were not dramatic in the United States but, as recalled earlier in the main body of this chapter, a stricter control of the political situation was ensured between the late nineteenth and early twentieth centuries.

A huge difference between Europe and the United States was the general political structure at the beginning of the twentieth century. Arno Mayer, in his analysis of the determinants of World War I, elaborating on Joseph Schumpeter's early work,[14] pointed to the alliance at the top of social hierarchies between the capitalist class and the descendants of European dynastic families within the European empires, namely the United Kingdom of the Hanoverians, the Germany of the Hohenzollerns, the Austria of the Habsburgs, the Hungary of the Esterházys, and the Russia of the Romanovs. In each country, the leading positions in diplomacy and the army were held by members of the nobility, and the French Third Republic was no exception. The power of these classes was still based on major concentrations of wealth, notably but not exclusively landed property.[15] Getting rid of the remnants of feudal society with its imperial inclinations was a long and appalling endeavor to which the United States was never subjected, despite the earlier violence of the Civil War that finally confirmed the capitalist trends in their most advanced configuration in the North.

One can parenthetically note that this interpretation was fully at odds with Karl Polanyi's symmetrical reading of history in his much celebrated *Great Transformation*, written during World War II. The world wars were pinned on the strange features of "markets," Polanyi's substitutes for capitalism, in a puzzling interpretation that found a strong echo in the left:

> Our thesis is that the idea of self-adjusting market implied a stark utopia. Such an institution could not exist for any length of time without annihilating the human and natural substance of society; it would have physically destroyed man and transformed his surroundings into a wilderness. Inevitably, society took measures to protect itself, but whatever measures it took impaired the self-regulation of the market, disorganized industrial life, and thus endangered society in yet another way. It was the dilemma [*between the destructive character of markets and the disorganizing potential of their control*] which forced the development of the market system into a definite groove and finally disrupted the social organization based upon it.[16]

Following Polanyi, the main social force capable of ensuring peace in Europe was the *haute finance* (in French): "The Rothschilds were subject to no *one* government; as a family they embodied the abstract principle of internationalism" since "their business would be impaired if a general war between the Great Powers should interfere with the monetary foundation of the system"[17] or "The influence that *haute finance* exerted on the Powers was consistently favorable to European peace."[18] Thank god that the *haute finance* is in power nowadays within neoliberalism, and formal empires belong to the past!

Even leaving aside the two world wars and the revolutions in Russia, dramatic and mostly dreadful events marked the course of history in Europe: with the failure of the revolution in Germany; the rise of social-democratic parties in the Second International and Communist parties in the Third; the Fascist regime in Italy in 1922; Nazism in Germany in 1934; the Anarchist upheaval, the Popular Front, and the civil war in Spain in 1936; and similar tragic developments. Relevant to the present analysis is the acute degree of social confrontation reached in Europe during the first half of the twentieth century.

As a consequence of the chaotic chain of events, the contours of the transition to managerial capitalism are more difficult to delineate regarding Europe than the United States. Europe was a laboratory of socio-political experiments exacerbated by social tensions, notably regarding the new course of the second social order. In this respect, the contrast was sharp with the United States: The relationship between the postwar social order and the worker movement was much more spectacular in Europe.

As in the United States, the role of managers, in particular government officials, was crucial during the two world wars and the Great Depression in all countries, including Nazi Germany. Besides the role played by managers within these various configurations, a crucial factor was the struggle of popular classes, notably the worker movement in the strict sense.

A first example of the impact of the worker movement in Europe was the ephemeral French Popular Front in 1936–38. Léon Blum declared that the Front was not the outcome of a victory of the proletarian class but the expression of a compromise between this class and the middle classes of small employers and subaltern employees. (Interestingly, in these debates, no mention was made of managerial classes.[19]) The new orientations were denoted as "social-democratic," with the preservation of the private ownership of the means of production within major sectors of the economy, and the nationalization of significant segments of the large economy. A broad welfare program was implemented, including paid leaves, the 40-hour labor week, the collective agreements within firms [*conventions collectives*], etc. These political trends were the cradle of the postwar compromise in France, with a powerful Communist Party.

The genuinely social-democratic compromise was reestablished after World War II, in the framework of the Fourth Republic, in the so-called Tripartism (from the end of the war to 1947) within the coalition between centrists (MRP), socialists (SFIO), and communists (PCF), first with Charles de Gaulle, then without him. A broad program of nationalization was again conducted regarding banks, insurance, transportations, and energy; the economic action of the state was guided by indicative planning; a far-reaching welfare system was implemented in what is known as Social Security. The departure of the powerful Communist Party from the government in 1947 ushered in a period of alternation between the left and the right, up to the creation of the Fifth Republic, in what could be called a mixed economy. The policy of de Gaulle, the first president of the Fifth Republic, can be interpreted as a "stabilized" form of social compromise regarding both welfare programs and economic policies, with a continuing strong intervention of the government in the economy.

In the United Kingdom, after Winston Churchill, Clement Attlee rose to power in 1945 as Prime Minister, establishing a new configuration of social consensus similar to the course of events in France, with programs matching what we denote as the social-democratic compromise in the new context of Keynesianism and the Beveridge plan. The basic features were nationalization, welfare programs, education, housing, and the like.

In the wake of the Nazi episode and given the confrontation with the Communist Popular Republic in the East, a specific feature of the postwar compromise in Germany was the framework of the *Mitbestimmung* [co-management]. The ambition of the first law, the Montan-Mitbestimmungsgesetz of 1951, was to give balanced weights to the delegates of wage earners and shareholders within a number of sectors such as mining and iron. The Betriebsverfassungsgesetz of 1952 extended similar measures to all sectors, though under moderate forms, thus restoring the preeminence of shareholders.

The case of Sweden is even more emblematic of the new course in Europe. It shed considerable light on the spectacular features of the postwar social order on the continent. The Social Democratic Workers' Party of Sweden (SAP) reached power in 1932 and remained in power to 1976. The Swedish Trade Union Confederation (LO) was a key component of the new institutions. The explicit objective was a gradual transition to socialism. At the same time, policies of active Keynesian macro stabilization were implemented. "Social-democracy," in a strict sense, can be defined as typical of the Swedish experiment.

Overall, the use of the phrase "social-democratic compromise" appears much more appropriate regarding Europe than the United States. It must, however, be emphasized that, given the repression of communist inclinations during McCarthyism in the United States, there was a significant degree of similarity between the social courses on both sides of the North Atlantic Ocean. It is hard to imagine that the new trends in the United States after World War II could have prevailed in the absence of the political orientations in Europe and the Bolshevik revolution in Russia. Time was ripe for social compromise, and upper classes had to yield. Similarly, the distinct courses of history also explain why the extension of welfare measures in the United States never measured up to the levels reached in Europe.

Still in relation to the dynamics of the worker movement, the transition was sudden in France after the election of François Mitterrand, leader of the Socialist Party in alliance with the Communist Party, with a stark program of nationalization and state interventionism. The entrance into neoliberalism under the aegis of Jacques Delors was almost immediate, culminating in the Maastricht Treaty in 1992, establishing the new rules of financial globalization and paving the way to the launching of the euro in the Madrid European Council in December 1995.

One can parenthetically emphasize that the simultaneous opening of Europe to international trade and the free movement of capital worldwide as in the Maastricht Treaty, on the one hand, and the subsequent establishment of the common currency, on the other, was a major blunder whose consequences are now blatant; the blunder was not the creation of the euro *per se*: The monetary unification of Europe had to be established prior to the opening of trade and financial borders, and well ahead, thus making of the less-advanced European countries a favorite field of trade and investment for the more advanced, and contributing to the strengthening of European internal networks.

Given the rigors of financialization and globalization, it would be erroneous to deny the neoliberal features of Europe since the members of the European Community signed the Maastricht Treaty: There was, indeed, a neoliberal turn in continental Europe. But it might, actually, be more appropriate to refer to a specific form of "financial orthodoxy," centered in Germany. France attempted to make headway within international finance, but with disappointing results.[20]

APPENDIX TO CHAPTER 10 (2): MICHEL FOUCAULT'S NOTION OF "GOVERNMENTAL RATIONALITY"—ITS APPLICATION TO (NEO)LIBERALISM

Michel Foucault's 1978–9 lectures at the College de France were published under the title *The Birth of Biopolitics*.[21] The main object was liberalism. At the time the lectures were presented, the new features of what is now known as "neoliberalism" were just beginning to emerge, but Foucault had already used the term (it had been coined before World War II). The link with the analysis in the present chapter is straightforward: Foucault put forward an interpretation of neoliberalism fully at odds with the interpretation in the main body of this chapter. At a more general level of analysis, Foucault's "deconstruction" of Marx's analytical framework must also be addressed.

The word "biopolitics" is absent from Foucault's book, with the exception of the mention of the project of treating the issue. (The definition has to be sought in a later publication, to be introduced below.) The main object of the lectures was governmental practices under the name "governmental rationality," with the following definition: "Governmental *ratio* is what will enable a given state to arrive at its maximum being in a considered, reasoned, and calculated way."[22] "Governmental ratio" (governmental rationality) means a set of principles and rules, but in using this term Foucault apparently did not mean the practice per se but rather the "reflection" on the practice:

> I have not studied and do not want to study the development of real governmental practice [...]. I have tried to grasp the level of reflection in the practice of government and on the practice of government. In a sense, I wanted to study government's consciousness of itself, if you like [...][23]

What Foucault had in mind was made explicit by the ensuing example that "in the Middle Ages the sovereign was commonly defined as someone who must help his subjects gain their salvation in the next world,"[24] that is, what we would denote as sheer ideology.

Two main fields of application of the notion of governmental rationality were considered. Regarding first the new governmental rationality during the Ancien Régime, Foucault interpreted the impact of "political economy" (the physiocrats, say, Turgot, in France) on the French monarchy during the eighteenth century (even the seventeenth century), as a process of "self-limitation" of the power of the Crown, that is, a change in governmental rationality.[25] Was Foucault dealing with the "self-consciousness" of the king, in line with the above statement, or was he dealing with the actual transformation of government practices? In both instances, the most striking feature of Foucault's analysis was the total absence of link with the ongoing transformation of relations of production, class struggle, and ideologies, signaling a U-turn away from a Marxian approach to socio-economic mechanisms, including ideologies.

To put the matter very simply, and focusing on the main development during the Ancien Régime, the control of the trade and price of corn had been the object of tight regulations (so tight that they are hard to imagine[26]). The purpose was the prevention of the recurrent *jacqueries* (that is, upheavals in the country-side) resulting from the speculation on the price of corn. Besides the action of the monarch, practices were governed by important customary rules (a "pater-nalistic model") targeted to the preservation of social peace for being more or less in line with peasants' views regarding local social relationships. The so-called economists persuaded the king to rule out all limitations hampering the rise of capitalist relations of production. The consequences were so devastating that the measures, hardly taken, were repealed (and this occurred repeatedly).

The monarch was in no sense (actually or in his consciousness) self-limiting his own power, which did not exist in this respect, but cooperating with rising social forces (specifically, supporting the new capitalist class interests). The success of the endeavor would have manifested in the strength of the monarch, as the physiocrats had contended, but the policies failed (actually they were delayed).

A similar story should be told regarding English classical economists and the rise of capitalism, as convincingly expressed in E. P. Thompson's work.[27]

In the above analysis, Foucault was paving the way to his interpretation of neoliberalism as a form of government rationality, rallying the conventional and highly questionable interpretation of economic liberalism as the self-limitation of the action of the government—with the sudden leap forward into biopolitics, though the word was not used. The definition of biopolitics is given at the end of *Biopolitics* in the *Course Summary*, originally published elsewhere:[28]

> The theme [*of the lectures*] was to have been "biopolitics," by which I meant the attempt, starting from the eighteenth century, to rationalize the problems posed to governmental practice by phenomena characteristic of a set of living beings forming a population: health, hygiene, birthrate, life expectancy, race [...][29]

We see in this interpretation a major misreading of social dynamics, which prolongs Foucault's identification of Keynesianism with the control of prices and planning as opposed to market mechanisms. It is, in particular, hard to see the least link between the German Ordoliberalism (to which Foucault devoted a long development) or Valéry Giscard d'Estaing's and Raymond Barre's policies and politics, on the one hand, and biopolitics on the other, contrary to what was suggested by Foucault.[30] Given the list of aspects in the above quotation, the reference to biopolitics would appear more relevant if applied to the rising welfare mechanisms typical of the social-democratic compromise in Europe during the first decades after World War II, rather than neoliberalism.

Foucault repeatedly referred to Gary Becker's economic analysis of human capital (later the economics of the family or crime) as an expression of the grasp of economic rationality on the life of individuals.[31] Becker's appalling applications of general equilibrium economics do not prove that individual behaviors were subject to any form of rationality à la Becker, and that would have been the height of absurdity!

There might be a philosophy of power relations, but there is no theory of history—facts as well as ideologies—without relations of production, class patterns, and class struggle.

As could be expected, the second pillar of Foucault's rebuttal of the basic principles of Marx's framework was his contemptuous rejection of dialectics:

> And it is precisely in this case, in this kind of analysis, that we emphasize, and must emphasize a non-dialectical logic if we want to avoid being simplistic. For what is dialectical logic? Dialectical logic puts to work contradictory terms within what I would call a strategic logic.[32]

Pierre Dardot and Christian Laval in their book on neoliberalism elaborated on Foucault's notion of governmental rationality, defending the thesis that neoliberalism extended the rationality governing firms' management to the conduct of the life of individuals.[33] We would rather straightforwardly contend that, within neoliberalism, the private life of individuals has been subjected to the class objectives of neoliberalism (in the same way that the socialists in the nineteenth century contended that capitalism had destroyed family life). Unquestionably, families must adapt to the new socio-economic rules of neoliberalism, as expressed, for example, in the accommodation of unemployed children otherwise of age to build a life of their own, or the separation of couples in line with the requirement of professional mobility, but this does not question the family's "governmental rationality": Quite the contrary, it sets it in motion in opposition to firms' neoliberal rationality.

11

Class and imperial power structures

This chapter is devoted to power configurations within contemporary neoliberal managerial capitalism, namely class and international hierarchies.

We resort to the same expositional device as used in the sequence of Chapters 9 and 10, that is, beginning with the introduction of technical materials as a preliminary to general interpretations. The technical aspect is borrowed from studies realized by a group of econophysicists (distinct from those in Chapter 2), devoted to the global networks of ownership, control, and management. The dramatic picture drawn emphasizes the central role played by large financial institutions, the leadership of managers (notably, the managers of these institutions), and the hegemony of the United States worldwide. In this latter respect, the link is obvious with what used to be called imperial relationships.

Ownership and control

The analysis of the structures of ownership and management in neoliberal managerial capitalism harks back to two distinct sets of mechanisms, namely the specific traits of relations of production at the present stage of managerial capitalism and the features of neoliberalism as contemporary social order. The complex interaction of the two categories of determinants is sometimes difficult to disentangle; additional complexity is created by the existence of significant differences among countries.

The work of the group of economists and physicists to which we refer here is now rather well known.[1] The data set is the *Orbis 2007 marketing database*. Thirty-seven million economic actors, from 194 countries in 2007, are identified, namely corporations, rich individuals, and a number of institutions holding stock shares, such as mutual funds or, more generally, institutional investors. These agents are linked by 13 million ownership links. An ownership link is defined by the holding of the shares of a corporation. The notion is given a broad sense, including the management of stock shares besides the direct ownership of the shares.

Only a subset of agents is considered in the study. The selection is based on the preliminary identification of all transnational corporations worldwide, that is, a total of 43,000 corporations located in 116 different countries. To these transnational corporations, 500,000 other corporations and 77,000 individual shareholders are added, with which the transnational corporations have direct or indirect ownership relations (one holding the stocks of the other).

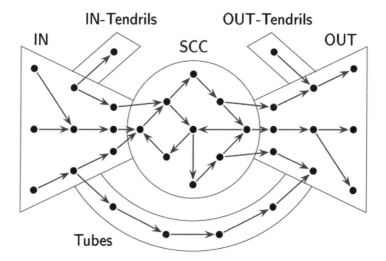

Figure 11.1 A schematic representation of the structure of the "largest connected component" of the network of ownership and control

Economic agents are represented by dots, and ownership relations by arrows. An arrow going from one agent to another indicates that the former holds shares of the latter. The circle at the center, the "strongly connected component" (SCC), denotes the core of the "largest connected component," manifesting a tight interplay of reciprocal ownerships. The core owns the agents located to the right within the OUT, itself a hierarchical network where the agents closer to the core hold shares of others further off from the core. Symmetrically, a number of agents are located upstream, to the left, holding shares of the core. A number of ownership relations circumvent the core within "tubes," and a few "tendrils" are grafted on the basic structure, but they are much less important than the previous channels of ownership.

Source: S. Vitali, J. Glattfelder, and S. Battiston. "The network of global corporate control." *PLOS ONE*, 6 (10): 1–6, 2011 (https://doi.org/10.1371/journal.pone.0025995), Figure 2, A.

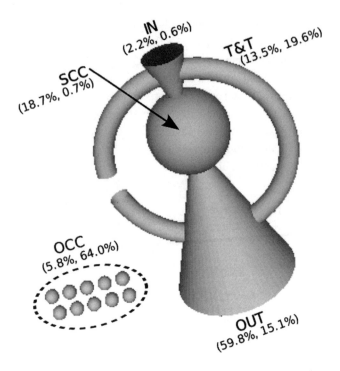

Figure 11.2 The global network of ownership and control: The "largest connected component" and the "other connected components"

The commentary of the figure is given in the text.

Source: Vitali et al., "The network of global corporate control," Figure 2, B.

Figure 11.1 provides a schematic representation of the main component of the network. The construction is explained in the commentary below the figure, with the "strongly connected component" (SCC) at the center, the IN to the left, and the OUT to the right (and the "tube" and "tendrils"). The diagram introduces the interpretation of the actual network in Figure 11.2. The following fascinating findings are revealed:

1. A huge connected structure, the "largest connected component" (LCC) dominates, supplemented by small components, separated among themselves, within the "other connected components" (OCC). As documented in Figure 11.1, the LCC consists of the in-section (IN), the out-section (OUT), the "strongly connected component" or core (SCC), and the "tubes" and "tendrils" (T&T).

The pairs of percentages in Figure 11.2 are important. The percentages to the right indicate the proportion of transnational corporations (TNCs) belonging to a component. One can, thus, observe that 64 percent of TNCs belong to the OCC worldwide, thus leaving 36 percent for the entire LCC. But the second percentage reveals that the TNCs belonging to the OCC realize only 5.8 percent of total TNC profits (the operating revenue), while the TNCs belonging to the various components of the LCC realize the other 94.2 percent of total profits. The towering position of the main body must thus be emphasized. It accounts for what can be called the great economy.

2. The SCC component, the core of the network, is made up of 1,318 corporations, that is, a tiny minority of all corporations. They are mainly large financial institutions. An important feature is that they form a network of almost exclusive mutual ownership.[2] (They own one another.)

Figure 11.3 provides a more explicit image of the financial core (still for the year 2007). The darker arrows denote the main ownership relationships. Many of these institutions look familiar. Lehman Brothers was still there. BlackRock, the largest asset manager in the world, nowadays pools together Barclays and Merrill Lynch. With own funds and assets of, respectively, only 29 and 220 billion dollars in 2016, BlackRock managed 5,700 billion dollars of securities.[3] Despite the small number of corporations, the SCC realized 18.7 percent of the profits of the entire network.

3. The OUT accounts for the large transnational corporations and their affiliates. 59.8 percent of total profits are realized within this component.

4. The IN is made up of a number of individuals or corporations holding shares of the SCC or, indirectly through tubes, of the OUT. There is no ownership relation going upward from the SCC to the IN.

Besides the holding or management of shares and the benefit of profits, the studies emphasize the concentration of controls. (As in the title of the Vitali et al. study, "The network of global corporate control.") Full control is defined by the holding by a group of agents of more than 50 percent of the shares of a corporation. Using this criterion, various assessments of the degrees of concentration of controls are supplied: (i) 737 corporations or individuals (belonging or not to the SCC) control 80 percent of the economic value of transnational corporations worldwide;

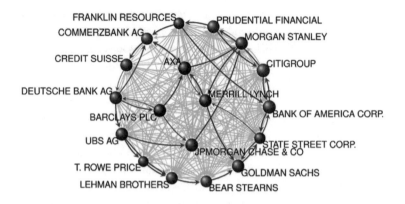

Figure 11.3 The main institutions of the financial core in 2007
Source: Vitali et al., "The network of global corporate control," Figure 2, D.

(ii) a "super-entity" of 147 financial corporations belonging to the SCC controls 40 percent of the value of transnational corporations. The following important conclusion is reached: "This means that network control is much more unequally distributed than wealth."[4]

To the above observations, one can add that: "Individual people do not appear as multinational power holders very often."[5] This statement seems to contradict the spectacular concentration of wealth in the hands of a small group of billionaires. A very shocking figure is that, in 2016, the 100 richest billionaires worldwide owned the equivalent of the wealth of the poorest half of the world's population.

The object of the present analysis, however, is not inequalities but the power to control the economy, in particular the large economy. The wealth of the 100 at the top (equal to the wealth of the poorest half of humankind) amounted to "only," if one may say, 1 percent of global wealth. Even more relevant to the present investigation is the observation that the wealth of the 100 was equal to 3.5 percent of the total stock-market capitalization worldwide, and the wealth of the 2,043 billionaires in the world, equal to 11.4 percent of stock-market capitalization.[6] These figures recall that contemporary societies are neoliberal managerial capitalisms and that the wealth is concentrated at the top of social hierarchies, as contended in Chapter 10. This does not change the key observation in the present chapter that the management of the ownership of the large economy is basically in the hands of top financial management. The management of the wealth of billionaires oversteps the limits of the capacity of individuals, and may be managed by the large financial institutions of the financial core of the SCC or by "private" financial institutions created to this end by individual billionaires, and as such is also in the hands of financial managers.

Anglo-Saxon hegemony

The previous section deliberately left aside all considerations related to international power relations. The unequal role conferred on various countries in the network described in Figure 11.2 is, however, blatant.

The question must therefore be raised of the national anchorage of the LCC. The issue can be addressed from three distinct viewpoints. What are the countries of nationality of, respectively, individual capitalist owners, financial institutions, and top managers? There are relationships between the three categories of membership, but no strict correspondence. A manager from Germany may work in a U.S. financial institution and manage the assets of a rich Chinese family.

In the study supporting the analysis in the previous section, basic information was provided regarding the nationality of the 50 largest control-holders.[7] Among these control-holders, 24 are U.S. corporations, to which one can add 8 from the United Kingdom. Other studies confirm the domination of the two countries. These studies use a notion of "community."[8] A community is a set of economic agents, individuals or corporations, linked by a network of ownership relations tighter than with other agents. Two important properties are revealed: (i) The common trait linking the corporations within a same community is their location within particular countries, much more than their fields of activity (the categories of industries or services); and (ii) The spatial reach of these communities is considerably reduced if financial corporations are taken off, and this finding demonstrates that financial institutions play a major role in the definition of communities. One can parenthetically notice that the few capitalist individuals or families among the large control-holders belong to the communities of their own countries.

Figure 11.4 depicts the general configuration of the network, limited to the eight most important communities. (Technical explanations are provided below the figure.) The main feature of this spatial network is that it is centered around the United States and the United Kingdom. The United Kingdom plays the role of transmission belt between the

United States and other regions of Europe. The relationship is tight between the two leaders, then irradiating from the United Kingdom toward continental Europe.

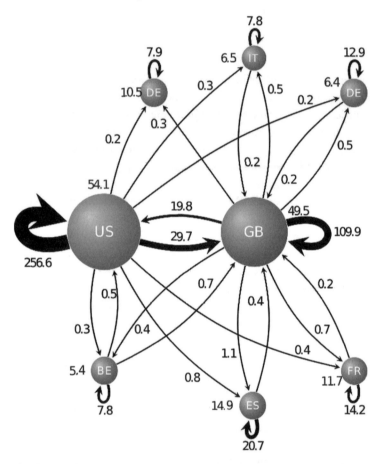

Figure 11.4 The network of the eight largest "communities" of ownership

Each sphere denotes one community: US for the United States; GB for the United Kingdom; DE for Germany (Deutchland); IT for Italy; BE for Belgium; ES for Spain (España); and FR for France. The figures next to the spheres are the numbers of corporations in thousands. The arrows denote the holding of shares, and the figures next to the arrows the number of links in thousands (that is, the number of corporate ownership relations). The closed-loop arrows show the ownership relations within a community. Arrows are drawn only when the number of holdings is larger than 50.

Source: S. Vitali and S. Battiston. "The community structure of the global corporate network."*PLOS ONE*, 9 (8), 2014 (http://dx.doi.org/10.1371/journal.pone.0104655), Figure 5.

The conspicuous positions of the communities of the United States and the United Kingdom are notable at the center of the diagram. At the top, in the middle, is Italy, and on both sides Germany. (It is a puzzling feature of Germany that two communities are defined for this country, testifying to the existence of a dual pattern of ownership and control.) In the lower part of the diagram, one finds Belgium, Spain, and France. The U.S. and U.K. communities are very large, with, respectively, 54.1 and 49.5 thousand corporations, compared with the other countries, for which the number of corporations is equal to or less than 15 thousand. The position of the United States and the United Kingdom is also manifest in the number of relationships towards other communities. The tight character of the reciprocal relationship between the two countries is also impressive. The Anglo-Saxon network of ownership and control is very dense, and all the more so when compared to the links with the main countries of continental Europe.

Another striking feature is the very small number of links between the countries of continental Europe, always less than 50 and thus not represented in the diagram. After almost seven decades of European integration, the intra-European network of ownership and control remains very weak. The financial institutions of the United States and the United Kingdom still enjoy the position of final arbiters between the corporations of the various countries of continental Europe. Anglo-Saxon financial institutions may sanction the management of the corporations and, indirectly, the policies of the various countries, to a greater degree than the potential reciprocal control between countries within the continent.

The web in Figure 11.4 depicts the main network of ownership-control of the eight major communities in the world, and it is unquestionably a North-Atlantic network. Considering the 100 largest communities worldwide, they are almost exclusively dominated by a single country located in North America or Europe. The first Asian community is ranked in the twelfth position. The two largest communities, the U.S. and U.K., are dominated by a powerful and dense kernel of corporations; conversely, the structures of the other communities are less dense, and weaker hierarchies are observed.

The Anglo-Saxon network of ownership and control is unquestionably at the root of a process of "neoliberal financial socialization" worldwide. The resulting configuration must, however, be understood as a quite specific form of interaction, actually reduced to a strictly financial aspect based on the comparative assessment of profit rates.

The establishment of the network was realized at the cost of the destruction of earlier networks, as in the direct interaction between the directors of nonfinancial corporations or through the coordinating roles of states. Not only the holding of securities but also variegated forms of direct interaction are involved in the new structures, as documented in the following section.

The interface between ownership-control and management

The institutions belonging to the super-entity are in the hands of top managers, notably the managers of financial institutions, interacting with the top managers of nonfinancial corporations. This privileged position is extended towards lower levels of hierarchies, though to diminishing degrees, as within any pyramidal system of social relations.

The collective control by financial institutions of nonfinancial corporations is performed by three broad categories of means. First, financial institutions purchase or sell the shares of corporations, depending on the ratio between the profits made and the capitalization of the firm on the stock market. When the performances are judged deficient, the financial institutions sell the stock shares, thus sanctioning top managers (the beneficiaries of stock options), or straightforwardly take hold of the corporation with the aim of its restructuring. Second, a number of specialized hedge funds carry out the function of activist shareholders or financial police. Corporations enjoying excess fundings will be forced to repurchase their own shares. Thus, financial institutions govern the allocation of funds among corporations and stimulate market prices. A third device is the direct contact between the financial managers from financial institutions and the managers of nonfinancial corporations within boards of directors. This is what we denote as the interface between the "financial ownership-control" and the "management of nonfinancial corporations."

The directors delegated by financial institutions to the boards of nonfinancial corporations are known as outsiders, and the top managers active within the nonfinancial corporations they manage, insiders. The boards of directors are the key institutions in which information is shared, decisions made, and the discipline of financial institutions imposed; not the shareholders' meetings, though the directors are named during these meetings. The requirements regarding profit rates are formulated within boards of directors. Decisions are made regarding the allocation of profits between the self-financing of investment (domestically or abroad) and the distribution of dividends, as well as the wages and supplements paid to high managers. It is in these institutions that the trends regarding incomes and management depicted in Chapters 9 and 10 are determined.

The relationship between the financial managers from financial institutions and the insiders is, simultaneously, one of cooperation and domination of the latter by the former. Financial managers sitting within large sets of distinct boards enjoy a towering position, but there are also bridges, as individuals may switch from one category of institutions to the other.

Managerial national and transnational elites

The description of the global network of ownership and control in the previous sections suggests the existence of an international framework of collective control and management by a global elite. Available studies depict, however, a significantly more complex situation.

A first observation is that strong national networks of managers still exist. The coincidence between the nationalities of the CEOs of large transnational corporations and their corporations remain stricter than could be imagined. Eight countries are considered in one study: Germany, China, Spain, the United States, France, the United Kingdom, Italy, and Japan, for the period 1996–2006.[9] The conclusion reached is that it is impossible to refer to a global elite, at least without further qualification.

A stronger concentration of power seems, however, to have been realized at the summit of the pyramid. We are dealing here with a very small world of top members of the power elite, with now-significant international characters, though originating mainly from North-Atlantic countries. A study is devoted to the boards of directors of the 500 largest corporations in the world, also over the period 1996–2006.[10] The directors sitting within at least two boards are considered. A group of "transnationalists" is set out, whose number rose from 142 to 200 over the decade considered. These transnational directors "have gained prominence within the global corporate elite and are firmly embedded in the network, through extensive ties to each other and to various national components."[11] And further on: "But what is perhaps most striking about the distribution of the global elite is its Euro–North American centrism."[12] A number of corporations from the rest of the world entered into the group of the top 500, but very few individuals of corresponding nationality penetrated the so-called "corporate super-elite": "the rise to economic prominence of several semiperipheral states means an increase in the number of directors of firms based in the global south. However, most of that increase is among the non-interlocking directors."[13]

Upper classes of all countries unite under an imperial banner!

Recent controversies developed around the possible formation of a global ruling class.[14] The issue is whether it is still relevant within contemporary societies to refer to distinct national ruling classes, or would a reference to a single global ruling class be more appropriate? The issue of the coexistence of two ruling classes as in managerial capitalism is generally not raised; we doubt it is possible to reach convincing conclusions on such grounds.

The question is actually twofold. First, is there a merger of capitalist owners worldwide? Second, is a similar mechanism underway regarding managers, notably top managers? The answer to the latter question is not necessarily the same for the managers of financial institutions and of nonfinancial corporations.

The analyses in the previous sections suggest a number of potential answers. To the extent that the holders of stock shares worldwide entrust the management of their securities to the same financial institutions, their interests as capitalist owners are convergent; to the extent that they lose the control of these securities, their position is one of passive rentiers. On these two grounds, the reference to a global capitalist class might be judged moderately relevant, though such a class would anyhow lack institutional identity and actual power. The case of large capitalist owners is distinct. As contended, they scarcely act as actual controlholders, and their action is typically confined to a specific community; the opposite of what would be expected of a global capitalist class.

As contended in the previous section, the national identities of financial institutions are still anchored within denser geographical elementary networks, in sharp contradiction with the notion of a global ruling class. A similar conclusion is reached regarding top managers still rather tightly linked to geographical communities, with the important exception of the summit of the pyramid.

The march forward of the Anglo-Saxon network is manifest in the progress of the managers of the large financial institutions, namely the outsiders sitting within the boards of directors of nonfinancial corporations. Their power is already well established and still in progress. This elite is the main agent of the formation of a global ruling class but, to date, it is more the expression of the international hegemony of the United States, or a North-Atlantic ruling class, than an actual global ruling class, since the members of this super elite mostly work within Anglo-Saxon corporations.

This approach still basically suffers from the lack of consideration of state relationships and international rivalries. On an international scale, states are the vectors of historical, social, cultural, and political identities and, to this extent, actors in a global network of cooperation and strife. In the past, the various processes of unification which led to the formation of nation-states have been accomplished under the aegis of hegemonic nations. One can think here of the formation of nation-states in Europe, in China, or probably anywhere.

Considering jointly the two latter traits—the domination of Anglo-Saxon institutions and the international hegemony of the United States—the available information suggests the possible strengthening of a North-Atlantic community under the leadership of the United States, but the outcome is still a long way off. This is what was meant by the title of the present section. The slogan is obviously not ours, as it should go without saying!

Relations of production and international hegemony

At the close of this chapter devoted to class and international dominations, it is important to return to the framework of historical trends of productive forces/relations of production, class patterns, and class struggle as in Part I.

There is a close relationship between the advance of a country (leading or lagging behind) regarding the above historical dynamics and the international hegemony of the country. In our opinion, the root of the domination of the United States worldwide during the twentieth century must be sought in the transformation of the institutions of ownership and management at the transition between the nineteenth and twentieth centuries. The occurrence of the corporate, financial, and managerial revolutions during those years allowed for the advance of the country during the following decades and the dramatic course of productive forces during the first half of the twentieth century, as documented in Chapter 13.

Although the United States had engaged in the imperial race toward the establishment of a formal empire at the end of the nineteenth century (notably in the Philippines), this traditional route was abandoned to the benefit of the Wilsonian march forward of informal (though, obviously, not non-violent) imperialism as the expression of the new international economic domination of the country.[15] Correspondingly, as convincingly demonstrated by Alfred Chandler in his book *Scale and Scope,* failure of the United Kingdom to transform its own institutions of ownership and management, as the expression of the adherence of upper classes to traditional social structures, was dramatically manifested in the lost international hegemony of the country.[16]

The United States marched first along the path of managerial capitalism and dominated the world.

12

The politics of social change

The reference to class strategies assumes that the actors of historical processes know what they want, with what purpose and what effects. Even if the weight of earlier experiences and current circumstances was immense, one cannot, for example, deny that the reforms and policies in the United States in the wake of the Great Depression and World War II were the outcomes of innovative actions on the part of government officials, with a large degree of consciousness. It would be equally difficult to contend that, half a century later, the dramatic transformations in income distribution, institutional-regulatory frameworks, and management in neoliberalism were not the outcomes of "premeditated" undertakings. The question raised in the present chapter is straightforward: Who decides and in whose interest? A last section is devoted to economic theory in relation to the conduct of policies in the previous sections.

Economic and political governing cores

Within contemporary societies, the powers in the hands of managers in alliance with capitalist classes within financial institutions and boards of directors has reached dramatic proportions, rivaling the powers of traditional governments. We thus contrast two institutional centers, namely a "political governing core" and an "economic governing core," both placed under managerial leadership:[1]

1. By "political governing core," we mean traditional statal and parastatal institutions;
2. By "economic governing core," we refer to the institutions of ownership and control and the interface ownership-control/management in the previous chapter, in particular the so-called "super-entity."

The distinct professional activities and the corresponding networks of social relations mold the specific identities of the components of managerial classes—private and government managers—active in either one or the other core. Distinct assessments of ongoing developments are induced by professional practices, and the agents in the two components see society and the world in possibly significantly divergent ways. The channels of access to surplus-labor are different: Government officials do not have, for example, the same interests as financial managers in the deregulation of financial mechanisms. The separation is, however, an intraclass divide, not an interclass opposition. The sociological features of the individuals belonging to the two groups do not fundamentally differ; a number of persons may share the two categories of positions; and family bonds will typically straddle such social boundaries, as in the notion of power elite.

The discussion of the politics and ideology of social orders in Chapter 10 already pointed to a complex of cooperation and strife. Depending on circumstances, the influence of the members of the economic core on senior officials or members of parliaments may be strong, and likewise under other circumstances. For example, the comparative social weight of senior officials is enhanced during structural crises, while during periods of prosperity the managers of the economic core see to it that the course of reforms and policies does not set too-strict limits to their action or straightforwardly serves their interests.

The World Economic Forum in Davos is the emblematic institution in which the cohesion of the two cores is expressed. International senior officials, economists, and journalists meet annually around top business executives. A broad range of publications emphasize the requirement of new forms of global government or "governance," overstepping the boundaries of traditional political institutions and countries.

Flipping between right and left?

Three social orders were defined in Chapter 10: (i) the first financial hegemony of large capitalist owners up to the Great Depression (from which we abstract in the present chapter); (ii) the post-depression/ postwar social-democratic compromise between managers and popular classes up to the late 1970s; and (iii) the second managerial-capitalist financial hegemony in neoliberalism. As contended at the end of Chapter 10, these social orders can be located on the political spectrum, respectively to the right, the left, and the right: The postwar alliance between popular and managerial classes was an alliance to the left, while the alliance between managers and capitalists in neoliberalism was an alliance to the right.

The question must therefore be raised of the correspondence or mismatch between the usual classification of governments between the left and the right, and the above classification defined in relation to social orders. Two theses are put forward: (i) In the United States, the entrance into the postwar compromise (a social order to the left) and neoliberalism (a social order to the right) can be clearly imputed to Democrat or Republican administrations, traditionally located to the left and right (at least, comparatively); and (ii) Conversely, during each social order, an alternation was observed between Democrats and Republicans.

A specific treatment must thus be given of the administrations that governed the United States during the first steps of the postwar compromise and neoliberalism, namely the Democrats of Franklin Roosevelt and the Republicans of Ronald Reagan. In both instances, the link between the left and right along the usual political spectrum and the underlying class alliances (in our treatment of social orders) was straightforward. When we refer to the postwar compromise as a social-democratic compromise, we obviously do not mean that social-democratic parties were in power in the United States but that the reforms and policies enacted testified to the underlying alliance between popular classes and managers independently of the alternation between the right and left in the traditional sense; similarly, an alternation between the Democrats and Republicans was observed during the neoliberal decades despite the permanent alliance between the managerial and capitalist classes.

The political circumstances that led to the establishment of the postwar compromise are familiar. The switch from the Republican administration of Herbert Hoover to the Democrat administration of Franklin Roosevelt had dramatic consequences. Reference is typically made to the New Deal coalition of labor unions, blue-collar workers, farmers, retired people, intellectuals, and minorities supportive of the New Deal and the Democrat administrations up to the 1960s. The social compromise was, however, significantly redefined after the war, and new trends initiated, although, in important respects, the continuity with the New Deal was ensured. The Employment Act was passed in 1946, originally devised to establish the Keynesian course of economic affairs. As a result of the action of the so-called Conservative coalition, the more radical and explicit measures tending to the management of the macroeconomy and the enactment of welfare programs were excised, while the financial regulation implemented during the New Deal was basically preserved.

The key aspect in the postwar deal was, however, the separation between the functions conferred on the private sector and the tasks delegated to government officials: Private corporations were in charge of production and investment, and the management of the macroeconomy was placed in the hands of central authorities. To this one can add that, abstracting from possible temporary actions of central authorities, the determination of prices and wages was basically in the hands of firms. Important functions were also conferred on governments regarding the fight against inequality (notably by taxation) and welfare expenses. It is this allocation of functions that fundamentally defines Keynesianism, besides the distinction between the specific macro policies used in the management of the macroeconomy.

The 1960s of the Kennedy and Johnson administrations is known as the heyday of Keynesianism;[2] the methods used by the Republican administrations of Richard Nixon and Gerald Ford (between 1969 and 1977) in the fight against inflation remained, however, in line with the Keynesian reliance on government intervention. The Economic Stabilization Act was signed in 1970, allowing the president to impose wage and price controls. Although Nixon in his memoirs charged these policies of "tampering with the orthodox economic mechanisms," they were used in 1971 and 1973.[3] With the return of the Democrats to power during the Carter administration (1977–81), the Humphrey-Hawkins Full Employment Act of 1978 confirmed the reliance on Keynesian stimulative policies in the context created by the crisis of the 1970s.

The sudden shift toward neoliberal policies after the election of Ronald Reagan at the end of 1980, prepared by the "1979 coup" at the end of the Carter administration, has often been described, given, in particular, the new trends toward deregulation. As indicated in the name of the Deregulation and Monetary Control Act of 1980, earlier regulations inherited from the New Deal, such as the Glass-Steagall Act and Regulation Q were abrogated (respectively in 1999, and 1986 and 2011.) The entrance into neoliberalism was, however, not associated with a relaxation of monetary policy but with a strengthening of the grasp of the Federal Reserve on financial institutions, as also indicated in the name of the Act.

Again, the crisis of 2007–8 led to a spectacular return of government intervention and, as of 2017, the end of it is not in sight (see Figure 6.1).[4]

A similar alternation between left and right governments was observed in Europe. In particular, in France, the United Kingdom, and Germany, there was an approximately balanced sequence of right and left governments during the postwar compromise.

One can recall the paradoxical course of the transition to neoliberalism in France under the banner of a left government, marking a major exception to the second thesis above. During the late 1970s, a preliminary inclination of policies to the right had been observed. The first "austerity plan" was implemented in 1976 in order to fight inflation, the main measures being the control of wages, the pegging of prices, and increased taxation. Although Raymond Barre was praised for having been the "best French economist," the policy failed. The failure paved the way to the election of François Mitterrand in 1981 on a "socialist" program in alliance with the Communist Party (the *Programme Commun*), supporting a wave of nationalizations and a strong intervention of the government. In 1983, a sudden U-turn was accomplished with the switch toward neoliberalism as advised by Jacques Delors.

Social orders and administrations in basic economic variables

The two theses at the beginning of the previous section were already clearly supported by the course of the main economic variables in Chapter 10: The changes in the profiles of basic economic variables from one social order to the next were spectacular, while the recurrent flips between right and left administrations (between Republican and Democrat administrations) within each social order remained invisible in the data. One can return here to Figures 10.1 to 10.7, regarding notably income distribution, income taxes, dividend payouts, buybacks, and foreign trade. In Figure 10.3, the share of dividends in the profits of corporations oscillated between 30 and 40 percent up to the crisis of the 1970s, that is, during the postwar compromise, and then rose to 60 or 70 percent; buybacks in Figure 10.5 were negative prior to 1980 (that is, stock shares were issued contributing to the financing of corporations) and turned positive and large during neoliberal decades, the expression of a process of negative accumulation. One can also return to Figure 6.1, showing total government spendings (with or without defense spendings) as a percentage of GDP. The growth rate of government spendings during the postwar compromise was rapid and slower during neoliberal decades. No significant differences were observed regarding the alternation between Republican and Democrat administrations.

Regarding specifically social spendings, which might be considered an expression of the right or left characters of administrations, the growth in Figure 12.1 was steady over the entire period. Again no relationship is apparent with the succession of governments. For example, during the Republican administrations of Nixon and Ford, the variable fluctuated above its historical trend.

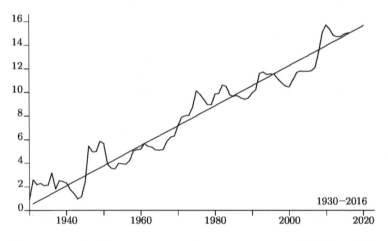

Figure 12.1   Social government spendings as a percentage of GDP and their trend

A single trendline has been determined over the entire period.

Source: National Income and Product Accounts Tables (NIPA), Table 3.1: "Government current receipts and expenditures."

As shown in Figure 12.2, the main difference regarding growth during the two social orders is that the postwar compromise was a period of sharply fluctuating but rapid growth up to the crisis of the 1970s, while the neoliberal decades were a period of lower and declining growth rates, in particular during the 2000s. During the Eisenhower administrations, there was a concern about price stability and fiscal orthodoxy: It was the duty of the government to pay the war debt in a currency supporting actual purchasing powers. But this policy did not have clear negative consequences on growth rates.[5] Besides rather large growth rates, the 1960s were an exceptionally long period of steady growth without recession. The following downward trend of growth rates (including the revival during the 1990s) was caused by the general course of neo-liberalism (the management of corporations, globalization, etc.) and the underlying trends of technical and organizational change, and cannot be imputed to macro policies of given governments.

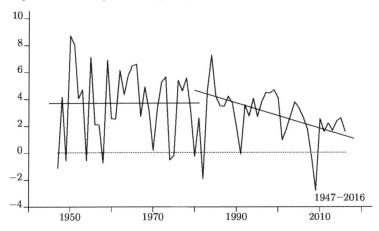

Figure 12.2   The yearly growth rates of GDP (percent)

Source: NIPA (as in Figure 12.1), Table 1.1.6: "Real Gross Domestic Product."

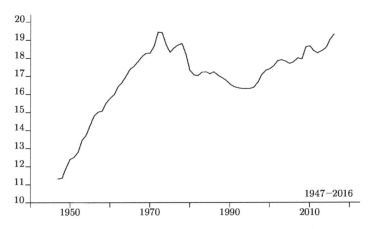

Figure 12.3   Hourly earnings of production workers (2009 dollars)

The hourly nominal wage of production workers has been deflated by the consumer price index. The number of production workers amounted to 88 percent of employees in 1947 and 82 percent in 2016.

Source: Bureau of Labor Statistics (BLS), Employment, Hours, and Earnings from the Current Employment Statistics survey.

The distinct courses of the purchasing power of production workers in Figure 12.3 during the two social orders is spectacular. The movement downward–upward during the neoliberal decades did not mirror the changing policies of successive administrations but rather the longer-term dynamics of technical and distributional changes. More research would be required.

Cooperation and strife between the two governing cores

The connection between the two cores is strong. The relationship between, for example, Margaret Thatcher and the pundits of London's City is a well-known phenomenon. Multiple studies point to such relationships, stressing the position of top managers as influential members of think tanks, their active role in lobbying, and their impact on the management of universities and as advisers of governments, if not directly as members of those governments. As recalled, the World Economic Forum at Davos, created in 1987, is the Vatican of the new neoliberal church.

The field of U.S. international hegemony defines a major common ground on which the convergence between the political and economic governing cores has always been firmly grounded. This was true much prior to the entrance into neoliberalism, as an expression of U.S. imperialism in defense of U.S. transnational corporations, notably in Latin America and Europe. Many of the trends paving the way to neoliberal globalization, regarding international trade and financial mechanisms, have long histories. From the start, the Bretton Woods agreements, as conceived by Keynes, were biased by the abandonment of the bancor in favor of the dollar, allegedly "as good as gold." Limiting the analysis to the post-World-War-II decades, negotiations were conducted by governments within the General Agreement on Tariffs and Trade in 1947, with the explicit aim of promoting free trade. In 1957, a new breach was opened in the Bretton Woods framework by the development of the so-called Euromarkets along the New York–London axis. The term referred to financial activities performed outside of the country of origin of banks, thus freeing the banks from existing regulations. The resistance was strong on the part of U.S. governments, but the go-ahead was given to the encroachment on the rules defined at Bretton Woods. The faithfulness of governments to the principles enacted in the wake of the Great Depression was far from complete, thus paving the way to the transition to neoliberalism. These trends culminated in neoliberal globalization, and governments were at the helm, not "self-limiting" their actions.

The link between the power of U.S. financial institutions worldwide and the international hegemony of the country is well known and vividly asserted in the publications of the National Defense University, for example:

> President Obama's vision for U.S. foreign policy is that national interests are based upon a strong domestic foundation and emphasizes the integration of all elements of national power. [...] The elements of national power can never be separated from one another. Military and economic power must go hand in hand [...] In today's world, DoD's missions in Iraq and Afghanistan are as equally important to national interests as Wall Street's ability to provide capital markets.[6]

Or, in the same vein:

> The financial services industry is the foundation of the United States' prosperity and global economic power.[7]

Regarding the dissolution of the postwar compromise and the neoliberal (counter)revolution, our interpretation is, however, that the economic governing core played the key role:

1. International relationships are crucial to the action of the economic core, given its international reach.
2. The neoliberal features of corporate management regarding the stock market and capital income, notably the promotion of the maximizing of shareholder value, can be straightforwardly imputed to the network of ownership and control and the interface between ownership-control and management (see the role of the boards of directors in Chapter 11).
3. Last but not least, the decisions regarding the wages and bonuses of top managers are made within boards of directors. Indirectly this impacts on the entire income hierarchy of upper management. Thus, the dramatic break in the dynamics of upper wages, as discussed in Chapter 9, also a dramatic aspect of the entrance into neoliberalism, can be straightforwardly pinned on the class dynamics of the economic governing core.

One can stress here the convergence with Michael Useem in his book *The Inner Circle*, subtitled *Large corporations and the rise of business political activity in the U.S. and U.K.* The book was published in 1984, that is, well before the works used in Chapter 11 regarding the global institutions of ownership and control became available. In our opinion, the research of econophysicists confirms Useem's analysis but, above all, stresses the accomplishment of important steps forward within new configurations.[8]

The members of Useem's inner circle were the top managers engaged in the network of interlocking directorates. The circle was described as "the forefront of the business outreach to government, nonprofit organizations, and the public."[9] The interference of the inner circle with traditional political affairs was, very convincingly, dated to the 1970s, as an effect of the profitability crisis:

> Evidence we shall examine indicates that the 1970s and early 1980s were a period of unprecedented expansion of corporate political activities, whether through direct subvention of candidates, informal lobbying at the highest levels of government, or formal access to governmental decision-making processes through numerous business-dominated panels created to advise government agencies and ministries.[10]

Useem emphasized the sharp increase in the financing of conservative parties at the end of the 1970s.[11]

At a more general level of analysis, a sharp difference with our viewpoint is that Useem understood the new stage of capitalism as a form of "institutional capitalism," that is, in Useem's opinion, a stage located beyond managerial capitalism.

Economic theory in the political turmoil

In general, the reference to theoretical tenets plays a subsidiary role as buttress-wall in the architecture of new social orders. But more than sheer ideology is involved. There is unquestionably a neoliberal theoretical framework, as there was a Keynesian framework.

Beginning during the interwar period in the United States, the Great Depression questioned the foundations of free-market economics. As contended, the ensuing compromise was supported by the Keynesian principle of the separation between the management of private firms and the central management of the economy.

Within academic circles, two alternative economic frameworks were available after World War II, fundamentally supporting the autonomous functioning of markets or government intervention, namely the traditional theory of general equilibrium and the Keynesian framework. An alleged synthesis was expressed in what was denoted as the "neoclassical synthesis" in the Hicks-Hansen model (the IS-LM model), actually a formal treatment of Keynes' analysis. Only the management of the macroeconomy in the strict sense was involved, when much broader socio-economic options were at stake in the definition of economic principles after the war. The failure of the countries of self-proclaimed socialism was not anticipated, and the theories of the convergence between the two "systems" used to be taught within universities.

A form of practical compromise between free markets and state intervention was advocated. One can cite, for example, the comfortable statement by John Kenneth Galbraith:

> There are some things where the government is absolutely inevitable, which we cannot get along without comprehensive state action. But there are many things—producing consumer goods, producing a wide range of entertainment, producing a wide level of cultural activity—where the market system, which independent activity is also important, so I react pragmatically. Where the market works, I'm for that. Where the government is necessary, I'm for that. I'm deeply suspicious of somebody who says, "I'm in favor of privatization," or, "I'm deeply in favor of public ownership." I'm in favor of whatever works in the particular case.[12]

Nonetheless, a gradual shift occurred in economic thinking in which Keynesian economics was gradually channeled more into the framework of general equilibrium. One line was the consideration of rigid prices, keeping the economy away from its alleged optimal position; a second track was the introduction of market imperfections, for example the so-called asymmetries of information as within new Keynesian economics. (For example, regarding credit mechanisms, the lender is not fully informed of the situation of the borrower.) This latter framework, nowadays, defines a form of mainstream thinking among macroeconomists within central institutions such as the Federal Reserve and the Bank for International Settlements, with names such as Joseph Stiglitz and Ben Bernanke. The contrast is sharp with academic free-market economics.

Looming in the background, aggressive neoliberal ideology had a long history: The intellectual currents that finally prompted the return of upper classes had remained constantly active. The term "neoliberalism" was used as early as 1938 in Paris, and the Mont Pelerin Society, the cradle of neoliberal ideology, was created by Friedrich von Hayek and Wilhelm Röpke in 1947.[13] The role played by the Chicago school is well known, notably the link with dictatorships in Latin America, notably Augusto Pinochet as Thatcher's "true friend."

One can parenthetically recall that a degree of confusion is created by the reference to the specific traits of ordoliberalism in Germany, in which a central role was conferred on the state as guarantor of social discipline against the alleged threat inherent in social-democracy:

> [...] ordoliberalism as a specific continental European current was largely formed in Germany—and also in Turkish and Swiss exile—from the 1930s to the 1950s. Its distinctive characteristic is an elaborately developed theory of the state, which is held to be indispensable for the constitution and stabilization of the continuously aspired competitive order. German ordoliberal concepts entail a strong authoritarian element, which is displayed in a fundamental skepticism toward democracy.[14]

Independently of the ambiguous character of the notion and its murky historical foundations, the social forces that supported the rise of neoliberalism proved insuperable. (The ordoliberal reliance on the state must, obviously, not be mistaken for the Keynesian intervention of the state in the macroeconomy, at odds with ordoliberal ideology.[15])

With the arrival of Reagan at the presidency, the emphasis was on supply-side economics ("trickle-down" economics) and an ephemeral return to monetarism. At the same time, what remained of Keynesian-Marxian economics was brushed aside.

Within traditionally left parties, the actual class foundations of the ideological turn from the social-democratic compromise to neoliberalism were obviously never acknowledged. The march toward financialization and globalization is described as an expression of "modernity," not in the sense prompted by the philosophies of the enlightenment but as supported by ongoing historical trends pointing to a future of alleged progress for being located further on in time.

Within government circles, notably in Europe, the transition from one social order to the next had to supersede serious political tensions within public opinions. The theories of the "third way" were put forward, as ideological buttress in the justification of the participation of alleged left governments to the neoliberal endeavor.[16] Instead of a synthesis or intermediate path between diverging currents, an alternative way—the third way—had been supposedly found. The campaign was orchestrated in the media with the aim of occulting the true nature of the political U-turn of government elites that echoed the managerial reshuffling of alliances to the right.

13

Tendencies, crises, and struggles

The analysis of managerial capitalism since its origins in the late nineteenth century to the present in the previous chapters led to the distinction between three successive configurations of class dominations and alliances, termed "social orders." The emphasis was on the specific features of each social order, that is, periods of three or four decades. The present chapter is devoted to the historical tendencies underlying the secular sequence of social orders, the chain of crises separating the various episodes, and the impact of class struggle in the same long-term perspective. By "historical tendencies" we mean the trends of technology and distribution, as commonly defined, but also the transformation of relations of production.[1]

Despite the progress of organization and central controls in managerial capitalism, capitalism remained prone to recurrent structural crises. Four such crises occurred since the late nineteenth century, namely during the 1890s, 1930s, 1970s, and in 2007–8. The three social orders were separated by these crises. (As contended in Chapter 10, it is presently still unclear whether the crisis of 2007–8 marked the entrance into a fourth social order.)

Two brands of structural crises

Structural crises are episodes of macroeconomic perturbation whose duration is about ten years, distinct from (and combined with) the recessions punctuating the traditional business cycle. (Since World War II, ten such cycles were observed in the United States instead of two structural crises.)

The four above structural crises were not caused by the same categories of mechanisms. The crises of the 1890s and 1970s were profitability crises, that is, the outcomes of actual declines in firms' profit rates. No major financial disruptions were involved, although in both instances the rearrangement of financial institutions was part of the transformation occurring in the wake of the crisis. Conversely, we denote the crises of the 1930s and after 2007–8 as crises of financial hegemony. The use of the term "financial" in this context may be questioned, since in both instances much more than financial mechanisms was involved. The reason is twofold. On the one hand, upper classes engaged in unsustainable practices supported by their outstanding power within financial institutions (hence the reference to financial hegemonies); on the other, financial turmoil was part of the two crises, contrary to profitability crises.

Profitability crises were the consequences of the historical tendencies of technical and distributional change, ushering in phases of actual decline and low levels of profit rates. Deficient profit rates interfere with the usual functioning of firms and are the causes of the crises. Conversely, crises of financial hegemony hark back to the type of disruption Marx and Engels described in *The Communist Manifesto*, in which capitalist classes behave as apprentice "sorcerers." Ambitious and perilous strategies are conducted by capitalist classes beyond the limits of existing social controls, and major crises follow, as was the case in 1929 and 2007.

Specifically relevant to the present analysis is the relationship between the occurrence of structural crises and the rise of managers. As contended in Chapter 6, the crisis of the 1890s dramatically stimulated the transition to managerial capitalism, introducing the managerial revolution. The same was true of the Great Depression. The depression simultaneously ushered in a new age in the management of the macroeconomy in the Keynesian revolution after World War II and strengthened the dominance of large corporations under the leadership of managers. In both respects, the managerial features were further consolidated after World War II.

The enhanced action of managers within central institutions was the main countertendency to the potentially increased instability of the macroeconomy; and, as we will show, the progress of firms' management (as expressed in technico-organizational trends) was the main counteracting tendency to the falling profit rate during the first half of the twentieth century.

Profitability trends

It is not possible to do justice here to Marx's analysis of the historical tendency of technical and distributional change. The first important development can be found at the end of Volume I of *Capital*, in the analysis of the so-called Law of capitalist accumulation.[2] When the rythm of capital accumulation reaches such degrees that a shortage of available labor force is felt by firms, stimulating the rise of wages, capitalists use more equipment (additional fixed capital) in comparison with labor, thus, relaxing the pressure on labor costs. Only in Volume III, Marx addressed the fact that the cost of additional capital may be elevated and, thus, strongly limit the efficiency of the remedy. Marx had an outstanding insight regarding the features of available technical innovation governing the outcome of such confrontations: The stimulation to invest in more costly equipment resulting from rising wages typically leads to what we denote as "trajectories à la Marx", whose main feature is a declining profit rate, instead of thoroughly remedying the consequences of the increased cost of labor.

Rather than the profit rate (profits/capital), Figure 13.1 shows the "productivity" of capital in the United States since the Civil War. The productivity of capital is the ratio of output (the Net Domestic Product,

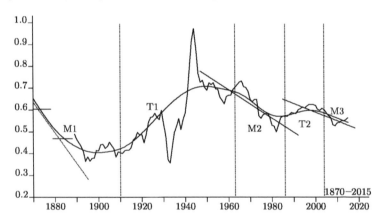

Figure 13.1 The productivity of capital and its trend

The downward-sloping straight lines describe the trajectories à la Marx. Four vertical lines have been drawn in, at 1910, 1963, 1986, and 2004. Five periods are thus distinguished and denoted, with the letters M for Marx (during periods of declining trend) and T for Traverse (during periods of rising trend). Only decennial averages are available during the first two decades (hence the small horizontal segments in this figure and in Figure 13.2).

Source: G. Duménil and D. Lévy. "The historical trends of technology and distribution in the U.S. economy since 1869. Data and figures." (www.cepremap.fr/membres/dlevy/dle2016e.pdf, 2016.)

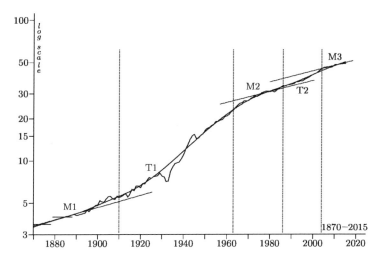

Figure 13.2   The productivity of labor and its trend (2009 dollars per hour)

The interpretation is similar to that in Figure 13.1, with the exception that the difference between a period M and a period T is not the decline or rise of the variable but the lower or higher growth rates.

Source: As in Figure 13.1.

NDP) and the stock of fixed capital, that is, the ratio NDP/stock of fixed capital, both in nominal terms. The stock of fixed capital is the sum of equipment and structures. The historical profile of this variable is very similar to the profile of the profit rate when a broad measure of profits is used in the numerator. (By "a broad measure of profits," we mean profits prior to the payment of taxes and interest, and prior to the distribution of dividends to shareholders.) The productivity of capital is equal to the profit rate under the assumption that the share of profits remained constant (with an obvious notation, $r=P_K\pi$). A downward trend in the productivity of capital signals that gradually more equipment and structures are used in comparison to output. The decline of the productivity of capital is the most straightforward indicator of a pattern of technical change conforming to Marx's insight (a trajectory "à la Marx").[3]

The productivity of capital and the profit rate are subject to business-cycle fluctuations. (They decline when the economy becomes less active, and vice versa.) Relevant to the present analysis of historical tendencies is, thus, the trendline in Figure 13.1, abstracting from fluctuations. The downward-sloping straight lines symbolically depict the three trajectories à la Marx, M1, M2, and M3, with declining productivities of capital. In between, the profiles manifested during T_1 and T_2 are oriented upward, that is, in a direction contrary to the tendency (the countertendency dominating over the tendency).

Both downward trends, during M_1 and M_2, were at the origin of profitability crises during the 1890s and 1970s. The third tendency à la Marx, M_3, at the end of the period, has not yet materialized in a declining profit rate, due to the tight control of the purchasing power of wage earners (with respect to the bulk of wage earners, and not those at the top of wage hierarchies, obviously).

Managers and technical change

Returning to the main object of the chapter, namely the disentangling of directions of causation in the complex of social relations, the present section points to the link between the managerial revolution (a major development in the dynamics of relations of production) and the trends of technico-distributional change. We supplement the account of the profile of technical change in the previous section by the consideration of the productivity of labor, that is, the ratio of the NDP in constant dollars and the number of hours worked, as shown in Figure 13.2.

Regarding the first traverse, T_1, in Figures 13.1 and 13.2, the main findings are, respectively, the upward trend of the productivity of capital (and, correspondingly, the profit rate) paralleled by the exceptionally steep rise of labor productivity, jointly defining a very favorable course of technical change. A wave of technico-organizational change gathered momentum during the first decades of the twentieth century, reaching spectacular degrees from the 1920s onward. The Taylorist workshop ("scientific management") and the Fordist assembly line are two well-known aspects manifested in these trends. The assembly line was developed around World War I. The growth rate of the trend of labor productivity rose from the earlier yearly value of 1.25 percent during M_1 to 3 percent during World War II. The new technico-organizational paradigm obviously meant heavy investments in fixed capital, such as those which would have traditionally led to a trajectory à la Marx, but the gains regarding output were so large that the productivity of capital increased.[4] At the same time, the growth rate of real wages reached exceptional levels, but this upward trend did not result in a decline of the profit rate, due to the simultaneous hikes in labor and capital productivities.

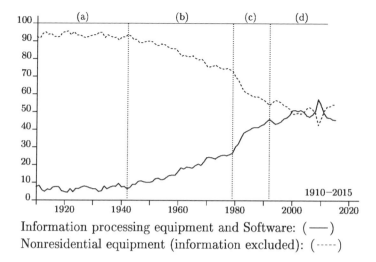

Information processing equipment and Software: (——)
Nonresidential equipment (information excluded): (-----)

Figure 13.3   The share of investment in information technologies in the total investment in equipment and software (percent)

Information technologies are the sum of information-processing equipment (one component of equipment) and software (one component of intellectual property products). Other nonresidential investments are the sum of industrial equipment (machinery, electrical apparatus, engines, etc.), transportation equipment (trucks, buses, autos, aircraft, ships, railroad equipment, etc.), and other components.

Three vertical dotted lines have been drawn in, at 1942, 1979, and 1992, separating four periods. After a stagnation up to World War II (a), with an average of 7 percent of the total, one can observe the steadily rising trend of the ratio up to 1979 (b), reaching 27 percent. The leap was accomplished during the 1980s (c), up to 46 percent, went on growing at a slower rate, and stagnated during the later decade (d), at a plateau of about 50 percent.

Source: Bureau of Economic Analysis (BEA), Fixed Assets Tables, Table 2.7: "Investment in Private Fixed Assets, Equipment, Structures, and Intellectual Property Products by Type."

We interpret the outstanding technico-organizational performances during T1 as an effect of the managerial revolution. As profit-rate maximizers and, more generally, as agents of increased efficiency, managers were the architects of the new techniques and organization, actually the agents of the general progress of management (besides what is shown in the figures, in trade, accounting, financing, the management of the labor force, etc.). A time span of about two decades was required before the effects of the new managerial relations reached their mature forms in the new complex of techniques and organization, but the outcome was spectacular. In the pure logic of profitability and production efficiency here considered, the outcome was highly beneficial. The features of this second phase were gradually generalized from industries with high rates of "throughput,"[5] as Alfred Chandler put it, to practically all sectors including mass distribution (in department stores).

During the following decades, information and communication technologies were at the root of a new wave of technical and managerial efficiency. (The first forms were the telegraph and telephone, early in the twentieth century.) As shown in Figure 13.3, new trends were established after World War II, when the ratio began to rise, with an exceptionally steep growth during the 1980s, introducing to the so-called boom of information and communication technologies during the 1990s (see the commentary below the figure). The key instruments increasingly became computers, software, and the internet. The impact was expressed within the workshop in new procedures of automation. Information and communication technologies are also crucial components of management and supported a revolution of management.

Robert Solow's 1987 quip "You can see the computer age everywhere but in the productivity statistics" is famous. The truth of the matter is that the gains resulting from the new wave of technical change were hidden by the erosion of the earlier wave. The ensuing combined trend was finally expressed in the ephemeral course of T_2.

It is still too early to formulate a reliable prognosis regarding the third trajectory à la Marx, M_3. (The link is obvious with the presently ongoing debates in the United States regarding the "secular stagnation."[6])

The technicalities inherent in the above analysis should not hide the importance of the conclusions regarding the historical dynamics of modes of production, specifically obvious during T_1: (i) The progress of the managerial component of relations of production in managerial capitalism was a major countertendency to the traditional pattern of technical and distributional change à la Marx; (ii) The fundamental trajectory was restored after a few decades.

Revolutionary and routine trajectories

The acknowledgement that all phases in the history of capitalism do not display features à la Marx may be shocking to Marxist economists. The discovery that the 2007–8 crisis was not caused by a declining profit rate was never fully accepted by a fraction of Marxist scholars, either by mistake or wishful thinking, and led to fanciful constructs.

The link is obviously tight between the no-way-out assessment of the historical dynamics of technology and distribution, the determination to safeguard the *Manifesto*'s view regarding capitalism's violent agony in a paroxysmal crisis, and the denial of the superseding of capitalist relations of production in a new mode of production.

Trajectories à la Marx are typical of what we denote as the "routine" course of capitalist relations of production as opposed to revolutionary phases.[7] In England, as well as in other countries, we believe, capitalist relations of production developed in agriculture and manufacture much before the Industrial Revolution, usually dated to 1770–1830 in England. The new relations of production originally progressed on the basis of the old techniques (as in the putting-out system), allowing for the formation of a capitalist class. The emerging capitalist relations paved the way to the forthcoming wave of technical change in the Industrial Revolution per se. When this wave occurred, the implementation of the new techniques in the context created by the factory system were the basis of outstanding profits for capitalist owners and had disastrous effects on small masters and workers still working along traditional lines. The dramatic gains for capitalists stimulated the trends of mechanization supporting the Industrial Revolution in a cumulative fashion. These benefits were, however, transient, as the new techniques were progressively generalized, domestically and internationally. This development marked the entrance into the trajectory à la Marx that, one can at least surmise, supported the formulation of Marx's thesis in the mid-nineteenth century. We do not know of reliable sources allowing for the empirical analysis of these early developments. One can also surmise that this period of astounding social violence was also a period of dramatic enrichment of capitalist classes.

To sum up, a "revolutionary trajectory" is the expression of the transition from a technico-organizational paradigm to the next, while a "routine trajectory" mirrors the intrinsic dynamic of a given paradigm. The industrial and managerial revolutions were the two main revolutionary trajectories. The first conferred on rising capitalist relations of production their form in mature capitalism (the channel of exploitation in the wage relation and the extraction of surplus-value, as analyzed in *Capital*), and the second, during T1, marked a major step forward in the progress of the new relations of production (with the ensuing features conferred on wage hierarchies), which made of the post-World-War-II decades the archetypical form of managerial capitalism.

Paving the way to the second social order and the turn to neoliberalism

A preliminary observation is that all the elements required by the interpretation of the Great Depression have been introduced.[8] The depression was the joint effect of the heterogeneous features of the production system and unbridled perilous financial innovation. The technico-organizational paradigm described earlier developed within the sector of the new corporations, while the traditional sector of smaller firms was lagging behind. (As contended in Chapter 10, the sector had been protected by the antitrust legislation, while the new sector of large corporations was in full expansion.) When the economy entered into recession in 1929, large segments of the old sector were eliminated, adding to the crisis but also confirming underlying tendencies (as shown in Figure 13.1, where one can observe the high degrees of capital productivity after the depression, surviving to the boom during the war).

After World War II, the exceptional course of technical and distributional changes, inherited from the first half of the century, the depression, and war, was a crucial determinant in the implementation of the postwar social compromise between managers and popular classes. In Chapter 10, the emphasis was on the conditions created by the occurrence of the Great Depression and the dynamics of the worker movement worldwide as circumstances supporting the implementation of the new social order, but no mention was made of the outstanding historical trends of technology and organization. During T1, the antagonism typical of income distribution within class societies had apparently been superseded. The rapid growth of the purchasing power of wage earners from the 1920s onward remained compatible with the rise of the profit rate to the mid-1960s.

It is, however, important to stress that the upward trend of the profit rate in the above definition (a broad measure of profits divided by the stock of fixed capital) did not benefit firms but was transferred to the government through taxation after World War II. The capability of the state to intervene in the economy was dramatically increased. Overall, these favorable trends resulted in two well-known features of the postwar compromise, namely the rise in the purchasing power of workers, as in Figure 12.3, and large government expenses, as in Figure 6.1.

These conditions were unsettled by the trend downward of the profit rate from the mid-1960s onward (reflecting the trend of the productivity of capital shown in Figure 13.1). Correspondingly, a stagnating trend was substituted for the earlier exceptionally fast rise in real wages with the entrance into the neoliberal decades (Figure 12.3). Profitability was only partially restored, and a new period of stagnation of the profit rate established. At the same time, the taxation of corporate profits was gradually alleviated, thus diminishing the effects of the underlying tendencies on firms' after-tax profit rates.[9]

Combining the analyses in the present and previous sections, the overall chain of causation can be summarized as follows:

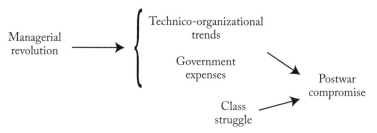

Determinism and political contingency

There is no denying the fact that the interaction between the various factors is in no way easy to decipher, and Marx's theory of history and political economy are here tightly intertwined. In our opinion, the pieces of the puzzle are, however, neatly assembled and quite adequately match Marx's general analytical framework:

1. The dynamics of productive forces and relations of production, as expressed in the rise of the managerial component of production relations within managerial capitalism;
2. The corresponding tendencies of technology and distribution and, more specifically, the crucial role played by profitability trends and the ensuing crises;
3. Other forms of structural crises, namely the Great Depression and the crisis of 2007–8 (with their apprentice-sorcerer aspects, as in the *Communist Manifesto*); and
4. Class struggle accounting for the political orientations of the sequence of social orders in the context created by structural crises: (i) the financial hegemony prior to the Great Depression; (ii) the new social order supported by a compromise to the left after the crisis; and (iii) the compromise to the right in neoliberalism after the crisis of the 1970s.

Returning to Marx's famous statement quoted in Chapter 3, regarding the capability of human beings to interfere with the course of history given ongoing "circumstances," the question must be raised of the respective degrees of historical determinism and contingency governing the course of historical dynamics.

The terminology itself ("making history" under given "circumstances") may be questioned. Nonetheless, even if the theoretical foundations underlying such distinctions remain fragile, there is a straightforward way out, namely the contention that margins of freedom are inherent in political developments, as opposed to degrees of determinism being inherent in the tendencies of economic variables. Or, to put the matter in an even stricter Marxian formulation, a degree of indeterminacy is expressed in "men's"—actually classes'—capability to impact the course of history in the conduct of class struggle, given the degree of indeterminacy surrounding possible outcomes of class conflicts.

Along such lines, the implementation of social orders can be understood as key historical breaking points—"bifurcations," as we will contend—potentially opening new political orientations. For example, it must be emphasized that there was nothing in the origin and nature of the crisis of the 1970s that required a transformation of the postwar compromise to the benefit of the alliance between upper classes in neoliberalism. The degree of contingency lay in the coincidental encounter between autonomous developments, such as the erosion of the political foundations of the postwar compromise (the expression of a broad institutional-political complex of factors) and the occurrence of the economic crisis grounded in the historical trends of technology and distribution. In Marx's terminology, circumstances were created, but the outcome, that is, the determination of one specific configuration of class alliance and domination, remained contingent and determined by political circumstances.

PART III

Past Attempts at the Inflection of Historical Dynamics

Despite the variegated violences and sometimes distinct outcomes of class struggle among countries or regions, a recurrent theme within the previous chapters was the stubborn character of the historical dynamics of productive forces, relations of production, and class struggle. This was a basic component of Marx's analysis of history, as discussed in Chapter 3, and one of the lessons learnt from the analysis of the great historical precedent, considered in Chapter 8. As of the early twenty-first century, what we know of the rise of managerial relations of production adds to this conviction.

In one way or another, a common feature of the failed attempts at the transformation of social relations from the Peasant wars of the early sixteenth century to the "pre-Marxian" struggles of the nineteenth century was their utopian character. The purpose of the present part is not, however, the criticism of historical endeavors for their lack of realism. One should not yield to the derogatory use of the term "utopia." How could human societies be transformed for the best without also "stubbornly" overstepping the borders of sheer realism?

Two symmetrical facets can be distinguished in the analysis of the implacable character of the dynamics of social relations: (i) All struggles aiming at the blocking of the advance of relations of production were discouraged; and (ii) the same was true of endeavors anticipating the course of history. Chapter 14 discusses the attempts by the most progressive segments of political forces (that is, going in the direction of "social progress") at the establishment of advanced forms of democratic political regimes in the context of societies dominated by the rise of capitalist relations of production during the French and English revolutions. In both instances, these endeavors were defeated by the continuing advance of capital accumulation, the concentration of capital beyond the limits of small ownership, and the reshuffling of social forces.

Chapter 15 is devoted to two bold categories of undertaking: On the one hand, utopian socialisms, which were the victims of the tension between communist idealism and the authority inherent in managerial organization; on the other, the anarchism of small ownership and communist anarchism, interpreted as two brands of outright rejections of authority. Finally, Chapter 16 attends to the construction of "scientific socialism" during the first half of the twentieth century as the most dramatic try at accelerating the course of history.

At a general level of analysis, the weight of existing production relations and class patterns is huge. There is, notably, little autonomy of political superstructures.

14

Utopian capitalism
in bourgeois revolutions

Important lessons regarding historical dynamics can be drawn from the analysis of bourgeois revolutions, notably the French Revolution, which played a crucial role in the formation of Marx's thinking. Several revolutions were actually "encased" within what is known as "the revolution." Beyond the bourgeois revolution, the second revolution was conducted by La Montagne [The Mountain] during the National Convention, under the banner of democracy; the third was the projected coup of Gracchus Babeuf and the Conspiracy of the Equals, in the name of communism. And the link must be established with the struggles of the Levellers and Diggers in England, almost 150 years earlier.

The bourgeois component was well attuned to the maturation of relations of production and class patterns and, not coincidentally, succeeded. The main thesis in the present chapter hinges around the respective climaxes reached in the struggles of the Jacobins (usually identified with the so-called La Montagne during the Convention) in France (in 1793) and the Levellers in England (in 1649). Both revolutions culminated in attempts to establish advanced forms of political democracy without basically questioning the private ownership of the means of production, though, at least implicitly, relying on a notion of limitation of private property in what we denote as "utopian capitalism." They failed.

These endeavors should not be contemptuously dismissed as the expressions of "petty-bourgeois" ideology. The point is rather that the unchecked continuation of capitalist accumulation entailed a reshuffling of class dominations and alliances (as in social orders, see Chapter 10), supported by the underlying transformation of relations of production. Behind these patterns of social confrontation loomed the features of the new epoch in the history of human societies known as the age of modernity. Common to all European countries and the United States, "capitalist modernity," more than a contradiction in terms, provides a compact expression of the final outcome of a chain of social struggles that indeed remained compatible with the march forward of capitalist social relations, but marked a crucial historical step in the history of human societies. There is no possible discussion of the capability of the forces of social struggle to inflex the course of history, as in the title of the present part, independently of these historical developments.

The French Revolution beyond the bourgeoisie

The original bourgeois nature of the French Revolution is still in debate. In these controversies, the "bourgeoisie" is not meant in its early sense of the inhabitants of cities in the Middle Ages, but as a class in full historical progress, even if the reference to the contradiction "bourgeoisie-proletariat" remained anachronistic (Chapter 8). (In the present context, we use "bourgeois class" and "capitalist class" as synonyms, without specific mention of landowners.) For example, François Furet— to whom reference was made in the appendix to Chapter 5 as the most sophisticated critic of Marx's and Marxist analyses of the French Revolution—had, in the last instance, to acknowledge the bourgeois foundation of the French Revolution despite his rejection of Marx's reliance on class mechanisms in the analysis of history (which Furet execrated).[1] As Furet convincingly contended, the difficult issue in the assessment of the continuing course of the revolution was that the bourgeois revolution had been accomplished during the first steps of what is traditionally called "the revolution":

> As early as 1789–1791, the bourgeois revolution is done and completed without any compromise with the old society. From 1790 onward, all the key components of the new bourgeois order that constitute our contemporary societies are there, namely the abolition of Orders [the nobility, the clergy, and the third estate] and "feudality," career paths opened to skills, the substitution of the social contract for the monarchy by divine right, the birth of the *homo democraticus* and the representative regime, free labor and free enterprise, are all established with no possible return.[2]

The reference to "contemporary societies" or "free enterprise" is specifically telling.

One can agree with Furet that, despite the often-dramatic violence inherent in the accomplishment of such historical transformations, a bourgeois parliamentary monarchy was in hand in France from the beginning of the revolution. In many places in Europe, even the storming of the Bastille on July 14, 1789 was hailed by broad fractions of upper classes, including royal courts. As could be expected, the more the *sans-culottes*, that is, activists from popular classes, engaged in the new course of social transformation (that is, marched in the streets), the more upper classes panicked. (*Sans-culotte* means "without breeches to the knees," that is, wearing pantaloons, in contrast to the nobility.) New dynamics were actually launched, culminating in the paroxystic stage during the National Convention (1792–5) and the proclamation of the French First Republic in September 1792. Was the bourgeois revolution pushed to its utmost conclusion? Or were the boundaries of a bourgeois revolution overstepped?

The question of private property, first of all land ownership, was a pivotal issue, but a more general one was the emerging capitalist features of society, of which land ownership was only one component. At the beginning of the Convention, the confiscation of properties already had a several-year-long history. The properties of the clergy had been seized at the end of 1789; the properties of the *émigrés* and the Crown were next in the list, fueling bourgeois land ownership. Even bourgeois property was potentially in question, due to the continuation and radicalization of social struggles.

Many among the philosophers of the enlightenment had already unambiguously condemned the private holding of large estates. One can quote here the well-known statement by Gabriel Bonnot de Mably:

As soon as I see the landed property established, I see unequal wealth. And how could this disproportionate wealth not arouse the vices of poverty, mental debilitation, the corruption of civil morals, and all the prejudices and passions that will eventually stifle the perceptions on which our philosophers, nonetheless, place their hopes? Open any history book and you will find that all peoples have been plagued by unequal wealth.[3]

Despite the popular origin of the Convention, the rightist fraction of the deputies, the Girondins, remained hegemonic for about nine months. Most of the roughly 150 Girondins were lawyers, medical doctors, and surgeons, as typical of the actors of the French Revolution (with a minority of nobles and merchants). It is important to stress, however, that 20 years later, the majority of the approximately 100 who had survived was composed of landowners, as they had inherited from their fathers, and this observation is telling of their social status. In addition, many had largely benefited from the purchase of confiscated lands.[4] The Girondins passed a decree stipulating that the mere reference to the *loi agraire*, that is, the distribution of large estates to small owners, was punishable by the death penalty.[5]

In June 1793, La Montagne took hold of power in a dramatic context of civil war and external warfare, ushering in the circumstances known as the Terror. The conduct of events changed radically. La Montagne, whose main figures were Maximilien de Robespierre and Louis Antoine Léon de Saint-Just, conducted policies of strong intervention in the economy, notably in order to ensure the supply of armaments and food to the armies, and the control of the price of corn (the Law of the Maximum). In addition, La Montagne repealed the martial law which allowed the army to shoot at demonstrators (a key component of the much-celebrated Loi Le Chapelier).[6] A second revolution was under way.

Robespierre himself thought that the culture of land in common was impracticable. Though the analysis of Robespierre's views regarding private property remains controversial, Robespierre was unquestionably hostile to large social inequalities.[7] A bold agrarian reform (the distribution of land to poor people) was enacted by the Ventôse decrees of February 1794 in the aim of establishing democracy on stronger social foundations.

Robespierre was known as "the incorruptible." His speeches were full of "virtue" and "democracy" in the rhetorical style of the period, and his main concern was with democracy. In Robespierre's views of social relations, there was, however, a clear antagonism between advanced forms of democracy, that is, democracy supporting the "popular cause," and the concentration of wealth, hence his fight against the rising bourgeois trends and the republic of upper classes (though Robespierre saved many Girondins[8]). We quote here Robespierre:

> Before the abolition of the nobility and the crown, the schemers, whose single concern was to establish their wealth on the ruins of the court, were fighting on the side of the friends of freedom and shared with them the title of "patriots." Hence the manifold meta-

morphoses of so many characters, whose civic virtue expired as soon as it began to contradict their ambitious speculations. Thus, the nation seemed divided into two parts, the royalists and the supporters of the popular cause. Today, as the common enemy has been eliminated [*the aristocracy*], you will see those mistakenly united under the name of patriots split into two classes. One part will be determined to continue the Republic for their own sake; the other part, for the people, in conformity with the motive that had so far excited their revolutionary diligence. The former will strive to alter the forms of the government in line with aristocratic principles and the interest of the rich [...]; the latter will strive to establish the Republic on the principles of equality and the general interest.[9]

There was no awareness of relations of production in the strict sense in Robespierre's mind, but an astoundlingly clear consciousness of the changing course of the revolution: Robespierre did not want what is nowadays called a bourgeois revolution (that is, actually to the benefit of the rising upper bourgeois class) but much more.

Among those who strove "to establish the Republic on the principles of equality and the general interest," one small component went very far, much further than Robespierre. A crucial new divide was, thus, established, pitting the supporters of limited private property against a radical minority to the left, which, independently of the exact terminology in use, acted in defense of emerging "communist" trends in Gracchus Babeuf's Conspiracy of the Equals (paving the way to neo-Babouvism during the first decades of the nineteenth century).[10] The program of the Conspiracy of the Equals was an ambitious communist program.[11] Babeuf thought he could convince rapidly, and had asked the Convention to allow him to conduct his experiment in a region to be determined (which he called a "republican Vendée"[12]). His demand was, obviously, dismissed. A third revolution was actually planned.

After the Thermidor reaction in July 1794, in which the Jacobins were defeated and La Montagne crushed, the Thermidorians continued the fight in favor of the unchecked rise of capitalist relations of production. Private property was finally guaranteed beyond any doubt, as declared by François-Antoine de Boissy d'Anglas in front of the Convention in June 1795—the unambiguous statement of what class democracy amounts to and the exact opposite of what Robespierre had been fighting for:

You must, at last, guarantee the property of the wealthy. [...] We must be governed by the best ones; the best ones are the most educated and having the strongest interests in the preservation of law. With very little exception, you will only find such men among those who, possessing a property, are attached to the country in which this property is contained as well as to the laws that protect this property, namely men who owe their education to property and the well-being this property ensures, that the education that made them able to debate wisely the benefits and drawbacks of the laws determining the fate of the homeland.[13]

The Conjuration was eliminated in 1797 and Babeuf executed.

The failures of the attempts by La Montagne and the Equals to interfere with the course of productive forces and relations of production—as promoted by the leading forces of the rising bourgeoisie—can be described as "symmetrical" developments:

1. Robespierre tried to "graft" advanced democratic forms on to the society of the late eighteenth century. Was the defense of the existing relations of production and class powers the force that hampered the progress of democracy beyond the "class democracy" compatible with the capitalist social dynamics on the rise during those years? The answer is unquestionably "Yes." And, in this respect, Robespierre was right but underestimated the degree to which the French society of the late eighteenth century had already been subjected to the advance of capitalist trends, as was dramatically confirmed during the ensuing years of the Directorate (1795–9). In this respect, Robespierre's attempt can be deemed utopian. No political exercise of violence in favor of virtuous democracy or small property was able to interrupt the concentration of the property of the means of production associated with the march forward of the new relations of production. In this respect, Furet was right, La Montagne did not fight with the aim of bringing the bourgeois revolution to its "natural" boundaries, that is, a revolution in the name of the bourgeoisie, which had been reached earlier, but acted in favor of a second revolution actually contradicting the bourgeois foundations of the new regime: Bourgeois democracy could not be what Robespierre was fighting for, that is, a utopian democratic capitalism based on the small ownership of the means of production.

2. In contrast, the relevance of the undertaking in the Conspiracy was later criticized as anticipating the course of history. "Pre-proletarian" popular classes were not suited to the task. One must obviously question such judgements assessing Babeuf's project in the light of the 1917 revolution in Russia. In retrospect, one can, however, contend that the success of the undertaking of the Equals was outright implausible, not simply because it came too early, but on the same grounds as utopian socialisms, to be discussed in Chapter 15, or the future of the proletarian revolution, in Chapter 16.

A brief comparison with seventeenth-century England

The comparison between the French Revolution and the social strife in England during the seventeenth century goes beyond the limits of the present study. Regarding England, even the reference to a "revolution" is controversial.

The dramatic events of the 1640s and 1650s—the Civil War(s) and the wars with "foreign" countries, the Commonwealth and the Protectorate, and the Restoration—were followed by the so-called Glorious Revolution of 1688 (also termed a Dutch invasion), ushering in the new regime of bourgeois constitutional monarchy. Fundamental issues should be raised—from which abstraction has been made regarding France, with the exception of Furet's questioning—first of all, the discussion of what should be called a revolution, more specificaly a "bourgeois revolution." Gerald Aylmer's book *Rebellion or Revolution: England from Civil War to Restoration*, is typical of such uncertain characterizations regarding England.[14] One can, however, contend that, considered from sufficient historical distance, the events of the seventeenth century in England unquestionably testified to the rise of the bourgeois class toward fullfledged political power, even if the reference to "a revolution" does not match the gradual features of the historical process.

Limiting the discussion to the period presently considered, at least three distinct uses are actually made of the term "revolution" regarding France and England:

1. A bourgeois revolution is a social transformation expressing the rise to power of the new bourgeois class in its *economic* and, first of all, *political* aspects. The seventeenth and eighteenth centuries in

England and France were periods of bourgeois revolution in this sense.

2. A bourgeois revolution is "only" a major step forward in the above longer and necessarily stepwise process of the rise to power of the bourgeois class. This is, for example, the sense given to the term by Furet in his analysis of the French Revolution as bourgeois revolution, stating that the revolution had been acomplished in 1789, as discussed earlier in this chapter.

3. The use of the term "revolution" may be restricted to the most radical episodes of struggles, such as 1649 in England or 1793–4 in France, while the return to standard bourgeois dynamics may be termed counter-revolutionary, that is, contrary to social trends assessed as progressive by left scholars, although the course of bourgeois revolution per se is continued. "Revolutionary" in this sense means "progressive" and counter-revolutionary "regressive," according to given criteria.

These uncertain definitional boundaries do not change the fact that the actions of the distinct social forces supported by, respectively, segments of the House of Commons, the Levellers, and the Diggers, can be interpreted as early anticipations on the three revolutions identified in the course of the French Revolution in the previous section, namely, the bourgeois component, the democratic revolution of the Jacobins, and the communist project of the Equals. And the correspondence is, obviously, not fortuitous but rooted in the common aspects of the ongoing transformations of relations of production.

Beginning with upper classes, the position of member of the House of Peers was hereditary, and the house was composed of members of the nobility, namely with the ranks of Duke, Marquess, Earl, Viscount, and Baron, and high members of the clergy. The members of the House of Commons were local landowners who did not hold peerages or, to a much lesser extent, merchants. The members of the two houses represented upper classes, with the split between royalists and the supporters of the new political trends to be expressed during the Civil Wars and the Commonweath.

Relevant to the present analysis are specifically the actions and views manifested by the Levellers, the representant of middle classes, during the Civil Wars, and the ephemeral popular experience of the Diggers. One can only recommend here Brian Manning's book *1649 The crisis of the English Revolution.*[15] As is well known, the role of the middle classes echoed by the Levellers was crucial in the New Model Army (fighting the king's cavaliers) during the Civil Wars. Oliver Cromwell allowed these forces to organize and lead the struggle to victory before suppressing them (sending remaining segments of the army to Ireland and shooting three leaders). In this latter respect, Cromwell was acting as leader of the classes represented in the House of Commons, once purged of the element that did not support the high hierarchy in the army. Conversely, the Levellers are usually described as a party of progressive petty bourgeoisie of yeomen and craftmen, with comparatively advanced political views, supported by a proportion of the population in London and regiments in the New Model Army. The most famous theorist was John Lilburne. Perez Zagorin referred to the Levellers as the "first left-wing party in England."[16]

To what extent did the views of the Levellers anticipate the progressive components of the French Revolution, namely, La Montagne of Robespierre? The comparison is obviously questionable (notably given the gap created by the transformation in the ideological background and the approach to religious issues at a distance of almost 150 years), but basic common traits must be stressed, defining what we in this chapter call "utopian capitalism":

1. There was no outright attack by the Levellers against private property (though the distribution of land to soldiers was contemplated);
2. both the king and nobility had to be dispensed with; and
3. the key point was the establishment of advanced forms of democracy, with the right to vote given to the poorest.[17]

The main thinker of the "utopian communism" of the Diggers was Gerrard Winstanley. Still following Zagorin:

> When at last he [*Winstanley*] took his pen in hand in 1648, he put forth an unpolitical book about religion. Yet within a few months after this, Winstanley was communist.[18]

The experiment of the Diggers aimed at creating a Christian communist utopia was almost immediately dispersed. In basic respects, this short episode was reminiscent of Christian communist attempts by Baptists in Munster and during the Peasant wars in the early sixteenth century, more than the Conspiracy of the Equals, whose main historical reference was the land reform of the Gracchus brothers.

Overall, three common points with the French Revolution must, thus, be emphasized:

1. Radical attempts at the transformation of social relations occurred during the seventeenth century in England as expressions of the rise of progressive social traits, overstepping the boundaries of the emerging power of the bourgeois class (also revolutionary in another sense) supported by the rise of capitalist relations of production.
2. Short windows of opportunity allowing for the expression of progressive trends were opened to the extent that the dynamics of capital accumulation were hampered by the actions of surviving upper classes from an earlier mode of production.
3. These attempts were irrepressibly brushed aside, in what has been earlier termed as "counter-revolutions." No stable historical grounds have ever been found for a society of small capitalist ownership and the corresponding political institutions.

The social foundations of the "counter-revolution"

Many distinct social traits were involved in the respective ideologies of the main social forces in France and England during the revolutions. The views of the radical components hinged around the notion of "democracy": quantitatively more or less advanced degrees of democracy and qualitatively distinct contents. They were supported by the participation of what the forces engaged in the English Revolution called "the middle sort of people" and the "poors": both in France and England, the values of modernity—small ownership, participation in production, and market relations between equal partners—matched the social status of middle and lower classes. The contrast was sharp between the ambitions of the most progressive or, equivalently, radical segments of the population in the two revolutions—namely the Jacobins and *sans-culottes*, and the Levellers—and the ambitions of the unvarnished bourgeois components and the final outcomes of social confrontation.

That fractions of the bourgeoisie and nobility were, at some point, fascinated by the philosophy of enlightenment in France and the philosophers of the English seventeenth century, say Locke's political philosophy,[19] in England, does not call into question the relevance of these social foundations. The same is true of the observation that large segments of the middle classes did not support radical trends.

In each instance, the main features of what has been denoted above as "outcomes" were the dominance of the upper segments of the bourgeois class in alliance with the descendants of the old ruling class undertaking new steps in their own process of metamorphosis, and the split within lower classes:

1. *The alliance at the top of social hierarchies under the leadership of the new class.* The notion of alliance at the top of class hierarchies is crucial here, though it must also be "blended" with the further notion of unequal social compromise, given the leadership of the new class, the bourgeoisie, inseparable from the gradual transformation of the old class (the remnants of the aristocracy or traditional gentry inherited from feudal social relations). As long as the tensions between the two components of uppper classes were maintained, the violence of historical dynamics was, somehow, contained; when the victory of the new component was established, there was no reservation.

2. *The split within lower classes.* At the same time, the relationship between middle and popular classes was gradually eroded by the development of capitalist relations, as contended in Chapter 8, with the upper segments of middle classes joining the ruling classes, at least regarding its political inclinations. The underlying social tension led, abruptly, to Thermidor in France and the elimination of the Levellers in England; in the longer run, the consequences of the political shift also cleared the way for the most violent forms of exploitation.

Although, regarding politics and social circumstances, the progress of the new mode of production was in no way hampered, but rather stimulated, one can speak of a "counter-revolution" as defined in the previous section.

Underlying the above dynamics of class structures, powers, and alliances, was the march forward of relations of production.

Epilogue

The conclusions of the episodes of class struggle in the previous sections are well known. The promises of utopian capitalism were rapidly frustrated.

The power of the upper segments of the bourgeois class was firmly established in the wake of the French Revolution. The republican "cladding" of the new political edifice during the Directory (1795–9), formally prolonging the Convention, paved the way to the personal power of Napoléon Bonaparte (with the famous coup of the Eighteenth Brumaire in November 1799) and the Empire, the return of the Bourbons during the Restoration, the July Monarchy, and the Second Empire after the short republican episode between 1848 and 1852.

The bourgeois foundations of the sequence of new regimes were not unsettled, despite the return of the old nobility and the emergence of the new nobility of the French Empires. The key point is that authoritarian regimes did not mark the end of the French Revolution as, in the last instance, *a bourgeois revolution*. Forms of social compromise were found between the new ruling class and the descendants of the earlier nobility (supported by the underlying hybridization process), but under the hegemony of the capitalist class. The same was true of the Third Republic in the wake of Paris Commune, when the capitalist class found what Marx considered the bourgeoisie's favorite form of government after decades of what may be called "republican activism" and the decisive impetus of the struggle of the productive classes of small masters and salaried workers in the three revolutions of 1830, 1848, and 1871.

Beginning with the elimination of the Levellers by Cromwell in 1649 and the dismantling of the most committed segments of the army, similar foundations of the new power structure were established in England, with the compromise at the top in the so-called Glorious Revolution of 1688 and the ensuing constitutional monarchy of Mary II and William III, and the Hanoverian dynasty since 1714.

"Capitalist modernity"

The notion of modernity is used by historians in reference to post-medieval Europe, culminating in the new political configurations associated with the philosophies of enlightenment during the eighteenth century. (After 1789, societies are said to enter into the "late modern period," in French *l'Époque contemporaine*.) Be it in England in the seventeenth century or in France in the eighteenth century, the relationship between the new era of modernity, on the one hand, and the rise of capitalist relations of production and the bourgeois revolutions, on the other, is blatant but fraught with major ambiguity.

The entrance into modernity is considered a major step forward in the history of humanity in the direction of social maturity regarding citizenry, the state as administrative body, nation-states, and the like. There is obviously a Rousseauian flavor in the notion, beginning with the famous statement regarding freedom and equality:

> Even if each man could alienate himself, he could not alienate his children: They are born men and free; their liberty belongs to them, and no one but they has the right to dispose of it.[20]

The third article of the Constitution of 1793 stated "All human beings are equal by nature and before the law." And the political philosophy of modernity cannot be separated from the new role conferred on sciences and the corresponding setback of religion and theology. Modernity was thus hailed as the new reign of reason.

As recalled, such themes had emerged during the seventeenth century in England. Christopher Hill quoted the Presbyterian Edwards pointing to the view that "by natural birth all men are equally and alike born to like property, liberty and freedom" as a "heresy" of the Sectarians.[21] Obviously, reference should also be made to similar trends in continental Europe, notably aspects of the Dutch golden age, roughly coinciding with the seventeenth century.

As is often the case, the issue is one of exact content and boundary. The action of the French La Montagne must be assessed in this perspective. Liberty and equality: Where should the border be set between such generous social values and the private ownership of the means of production? The second article of the Constitution of 1793 stipulated the following list of rights: "equality, liberty, security, property." Is "capitalist modernity" a contradiction in terms? Or, to the contrary, were capitalist relations of production the only social ground on which the values of modernity could be established?

Given the chronology of events, there is no questioning the link between, on the one hand, the transition between feudalism and capitalism and, on the other, the rise of modernity (in the multi-secular perspective of Chapter 8). This seemed all the more obvious regarding the early forms of capitalism in which, to a large extent, production was still performed in the context of family agriculture and the manufactories of small masters in the late eighteenth and early nineteenth centuries (and even more so during the seventeenth century); and these views were correspondingly supported by the middle classes during the two revolutions. These social structures could easily be mistaken for pre-capitalist small-commodity production, thus overseeing the grasp of capitalist merchants, rich farmers, and landowners, as well as the social forces underlying these dynamics: Hence the ideology of the market foundations of democracy that seemed to match so well the new economic trends. The opposite was actually demonstrated by the course of events during the later phase of the bourgeois revolutions, the bourgeois trends exported to the United States before independence and confirmed after, and the struggles in the early nineteenth century aiming at the consolidation of the rising power of capitalist classes.

Much more than a "link" between the rise of capitalist social relations and modernity is, however, involved. Returning to the dual theory of human societies in Chapter 5, the age of modernity is actually the name given to capitalism when considered from within the theory of sociality: respectively, "capitalism" from the viewpoint of the theory of class societies and "the age of modernity" from the viewpoint of the theory of sociality. There is a correspondence in terms. As could be expected, the emphasis in the theory of class societies is on relations of production; in the theory of sociality, on social values. The relationship is all the more striking when it becomes clear that, as we will contend in Chapter 18, it can be extended to the new mode of production, managerialism, which conveys its own set of meritocratic values, defining a "managerial modernity."

The simultaneous rise of capitalist relations of production and modernity should not reduce the reference to modernity to sheer capitalist ideology with the aim of the bolstering of the new relations of production. Within feudal social relations, men were actually born unequal, and many unfree. The establishment of capitalist relations of production paved the way to the possible emergence of a new set of social relations and values and, one can contend, gradually brought them closer to their necessary character.

The contradictory aspect of the new social relations was, however, immediately perceived by the best thinkers of the eighteenth century: The equality between "social conditions" that founded the values of modernity was deemed illusory, given the dramatic economic inequality inherent in capitalist relations of production (as shamelessly claimed in the quotation from Bonnot de Mably earlier in this chapter).[22] The hiatus was at the root of "modern" communist ideologies, that is, communism emancipated from the reign of god on earth (a slow and painful disconnection).

The three political currents in the French Revolution—respectively, supported by the bourgeois segment, the Jacobins, and the Equals—and the earlier trends during the seventeenth century in England or elsewhere in Europe must, thus, be assessed in the context of the above tensions inherent in capitalist modernity, given the degrees of correspondence and mismatch involved.

There is probably no better historical illustration of the relationship between infra- and superstructures than this relationship between the mode of production and the emerging "systems of thought," at least up to the contemporary stages of managerial capitalism, which provided a second dramatic illustration of such mechanisms, as we will contend. A dialectical articulation is implied in the second sense of the notion in Chapter 3, as the interaction between contradictory components. The link between the systems of thought and the corresponding relations of production was straightforward; likewise the so-called reciprocal action of systems of thought on relations of production as ideological buttress. But the tension between claims and facts was never superseded, and could not be superseded on the basis of the ongoing dynamics of relations of production.

The paradox is, however, that the era of modernity ushered in the appalling social features of the capitalist factory system and the Industrial Revolution.

Utopian socialism and anarchism

The combination of the dreadful situation of working classes during the late eighteenth and early nineteenth centuries—despite or "as a product" of the advance of productive forces and relations of production—on the one hand, and the ideas of the enlightenment and modernity on the other, led to the conduct of repeated experiments aiming at the outright implementation of dignified social conditions. This was performed independently of the continuing bourgeois power, in what is known as utopian socialism. These experiments were supported by the emigration to the paradise lands of the United States.

The constraints posed by the historical dynamics of relations of production were again manifested in the fact that all of these undertakings were unsettled by the tensions inherent in strong "managerial" features, despite communist ideologies. The tension between authority and democracy was one of the key factors, if not the key factor, accounting for the failures of these endeavors. Thus, the notion of the "stubborn character" of the dynamics of productive forces and relations of production in the context of the rise of capitalism, as in the previous chapter, was extended to the historical emergence of managerial traits.

As could be expected, the pivotal and excruciating debate around authority and emancipation (actually a debate around managerialism), undermining the march toward emancipation of human societies, was very clearly set out during the nineteenth century in the confrontation between what was known as Marx's state socialism and anarchist socialism (or anarchist communism). This defines the second object of the present chapter, after a brief evocation of Proudhonian anarchism. The link with Marx's and Engels' political views and action is thus established as a key step toward the analysis of self-proclaimed socialism in the next chapter, which concludes the present part.

Utopian socialism: The tension between democracy and authoritarianism

The project of building socialism in the nineteenth and early twentieth centuries was the outcome of a long chain of heroic initiatives with the

aim of the eradication of the social roots of individualism and dominations, from the early Christian communities of the first centuries,
through the millenarian undertakings inspired by the gospel in the
Middle Ages, and the Peasant wars in the early sixteenth century. We
will not do justice to these early endeavors, nor shall we consider the
products of sheer human imagination, such as Thomas More's famous
Utopia, which coined the term, or Francis Bacon's *New Atlantis*.

The discussion in the remainder of this section is confined to the
experiments initiated in Europe or the United States during the
nineteenth century. Four monumental figures must be mentioned,
namely Robert Owen (1771–1858), Charles Fourier (1772–1837),
Étienne Cabet (1788–1856), and Wilhem Weitling (1808–71) (to
which, at least, Hugues-Félicité Robert de Lamennais, 1782–1854,
or Fourier's disciple, Victor Considerant, 1808–93, should be added).
They were very different persons, acting within quite distinct contexts.
And these differences were reflected in their thinking and practices, as
documented in the appendix to the present chapter.[1]

Underlying these experiments lay the same conviction that society can
be changed from the inside, that is, without the preliminary revolution-
izing of general relations of production. There was a widespread belief
that the improvement of the condition of human societies would be so
spectacular that the entire population, including upper classes, would
be convinced and join. All utopian socialists conceived of their plans as
befitting more or less rapid generalization.

While the early Christian communities had been built in the expectation of the return of Christ on earth and in line with imaginary views
of what the first communities were (or even as a replica of the paradise
on earth of Adam and Eve), the socialist-communist communities must,
in our opinion, be understood in the context of the new organizational
trends in the nineteenth century. (We recall here the analysis of early
managerial trends in the second section of Chapter 5, "The socialization
of production: Capitalists and managers" which provides the historical
background.) All leaders were social architects, engineers, actually
managers: the leaders of "managerial utopias." And it is probably not
coincidental that the most successful endeavor was conducted by Owen,
a bright manager.

A first obvious issue was individualism. When the situation of workers
improved, they found it difficult to bear the discipline of communities.
Specifically relevant to the present study is, however, authority, obviously

tightly linked to discipline. The prerogatives inherent in these hierarchies were strongly manifested in the conduct of the experiments. Cabet and Weitling were utterly possessive in their control over all members of the communities. Facing the failure of his projects, at the end of his life, Weitling kept claiming that he held responsibility for his too-weak command. Had his system been applied, Fourier would have been even more controlling, as manifested in his maniacal pursuit of the preservation of the details of his system (to such a point that Considerant could hardly collaborate at the end of the master's life). Owen also remained at the helm, though he apparently did everything possible to transfer power to local democratic institutions.

Returning to the figure of Babeuf discussed in the previous chapter, the problem of authority had already been raised in two respects. On the one hand, the organization of production and the distribution of the product had to be placed in the hands of "magistrates"; on the other hand, the discussion went on among the Equals regarding the leadership of the Conspiracy: Had the power to be placed in the hands of a leader? A set of members of the Conspiracy were in favor of a strong leadership; others objected on behalf of the similarity with the monarchy.

A new obstacle on the road toward the emancipation of mankind was thus dramatically expressed. All men could be born equal; production could be organized collectively and distributed fairly. Now barring the way, implacably, was the concentration of authority within the hands of a minority, if not a single person, and the constraints inherent in strict organization. Private property had been superseded (with the exception of Fourier's phalanx) but the managerial concentration of power stood as the new obstruction.

This is precisely when Marx and Engels stepped onto the social scene under the banner of "scientific socialism." The utopian bias could apparently be superseded, at least this was Marx's and Engels' conviction, but it is no coincidence that the issue of authority came immediately center stage.

Doing without central authority: Anarchist communism

It is impossible to do justice here to the rich history of anarchism. We first establish the link with the rise of utopian ideas in the mid-nineteenth century, as in the previous section, then move to the context of the First International.

The term "anarchist" had already been used during the French Revolution in a derogatory sense to refer to people fighting authority in general. The modern sense, as a political doctrine, is attributed to Pierre-Joseph Proudhon in his book *What is Property?*[2]

The social circumstances that presided over the rise of anarchist views in their first form, which we attribute here to the person of Proudhon (1809–65), have been described in the second section of Chapter 8, devoted to the complex of hybrid class patterns during the late eighteenth and early nineteenth centuries. Besides the agriculture of small peasants, the early forms of industry were still to a large extent performed within the workshops of small masters, to which the raw material was supplied by capitalist merchants also buying the product; to these structures, one could add retail trade. Proudhon's system was conceived in a spirit of preservation of these social structures (contrary to that of utopian socialists). Two economic problems had to be solved. First, small producers, for their lack of capital, worked under the sway of the rising capitalist class. The remedy was mutual banking, a pillar of Proudhon's system. The second key component was fair trade, also among small producers, including small peasants, that is, what can be interpreted as the direct opposite of the unequal exchange between producers and capitalist merchants typical of the period.

Rising social trends were already at odds with Proudhon's view. First, a capitalist agriculture in which the manorial land was farmed, with rapidly increasing rents, had already developed prior to the French Revolution, even if land was less concentrated than in England.[3] Second, as recalled, during the first decades of the nineteenth century the factory system was progressing, paralleling earlier other forms of organization, as in mines. Proudhon had difficulty adapting his doctrine to the rise of large units, for which he envisioned "worker companies." This was done in a study published in 1851, but remained an uneasy facet of Proudhon's thinking.[4] One can also recall that Proudhon was very critical of the utopian experiments listed in the previous section, which he described as "systems" and charged with "dogmatism." To this, one can finally add that Proudhon was radically opposed to the ongoing struggles for national unity in Poland or Italy, due to his rejection of strong central governments.

Proudhon's views had a very broad echo within what he himself had called "myriad" small producers, to such a point that his conceptions dominated at the beginning of the First International during the 1860s (the International Workingmen's Association, IWA). Marx had to show patience and perseverance, as his views differed radically from Proudhon's.

As is well known, the main blow came, however, from Mikhail Bakunin, a flamboyant figure, originally an aristocrat and an outstanding actor in social struggles during the mid-nineteenth century, with a personality and approach hugely distant from Proudhon's narrow moral bonds, sexism, and economic views turned to the past. It would be difficult to find an equivalent to the social foundations of Proudhon's system in the doctrine of Bakunin; the common ground was the rejection of state institutions in a broad sense, as contended by Bakunin:

> If there is a State, there must be domination of one class by another and, as a result, slavery; the State without slavery is unthinkable—and this is why we are the enemies of the State.[5]

The division within the IWA led to the dismantling of the organization.[6] Bakunin referred to a "fight to the death" against the supporters of "state communism."[7] The prognosis regarding the authoritarian aspect of Marx's views regarding socialism and neoBabouvian communist ideology in general was actually widespread during the nineteenth century, and Bakunin's views had a very large impact.

We enter here the new field of the analysis of centralization and bureaucracy, at the center of the next chapter, devoted to self-proclaimed socialism. Bakunin, as early as 1872, with amazing farsightedness, foresaw the risks inherent in the construction of "state communism." Bakunin's above declaration went on:

> What does it mean that the proletariat will be elevated to a ruling class? Is it possible for the whole proletariat to stand at the head of the government? [...] The Marxist theory solves this dilemma very simply. By the people's rule, they mean the rule of a small number of representatives elected by the people. [...] This is a lie, behind which lurks the despotism of the ruling minority, a lie all the more dangerous in that it appears to express the so-called will of the people. [...] The Marxists say that this minority will consist of workers. Yes, possibly of former workers, who, as soon as they become the rulers of the representatives of the people, will cease to be workers and will look down at the plain working masses from the governing heights of the State; [...] They insist that only dictatorship (of course their own) can create

freedom for the people. We reply that all dictatorship has no objective other than self-perpetuation, and that slavery is all it can generate and instill in the people who suffer it. [...] They [*the new leaders*] will concentrate all administrative power in their own strong hands, because the ignorant people are in need of a strong guardianship; and they will create a central state bank, which will also control all the commerce, industry, agriculture, and even science. The mass of the people will be divided into two armies, the agricultural and the industrial, under the direct command of the state engineers, who will constitute the new privileged political-scientific class.[8]

Marx was himself an anarchist "in a second stage," unable to relax the tension between the managerial requirements of organization, on the one hand, and emancipation, on the other: The contradiction was superseded by the reference to the sequence *dictatorship of the proletariat—withering away of the state*, that is, postponing the creation of the conditions for emancipation. But this did not calm the quarrel.

It would be necessary to follow here the steps that governed the formation and rise of the Jura Federation of the International, not recognized by the General Council of the IWA, from the formation of the dissident federation in 1869 and its formal inauguration in 1871 at Sonvilier, condemning the London Council in Marx's home, to which we will return in the following chapter. It is the Congress of the dissident federations in St-Imier in 1872 that marked the creation of the Anti-authoritarian International.[9]

The early debates among anarchists hinged around the distinction between collectivism and communism, centralism, and the role of the state, at a considerable distance from Proudhon's views, with obviously a strong influence of the Paris Commune. All components of the movement rejected the state, and this rejection implied the renunciation to parliamentarianism. There was a general agreement regarding the socialization of the means of production (called wealth); in debate was the distribution of consumption goods as a function of individual contributions to production (in collectivism) or needs (in communism). The latter trend, communism, had the edge. In discussion was also the reference to "communes" in the traditional sense of the term (cities or villages) or purposely established geographical entities.

Peter Kropotkin became the dominant figure in the movement. Of aristocratic origin, and close to the tsar, Kropotkin fled from the Russian court to Siberia as an officer in the army, was placed under arrest because of his ideas and activism, and joined the anarchists in the Jura.[10] Kropotkin died in 1921 in the USSR. He refused the national funerals and his remains were followed by a crowd of people under very moving circumstances. The repression of anarchism was conducted in the wake of Kropotkin's death.

There is no need here to specifically describe Kropotkin's actions, but it is worth emphasizing that his ideas were the exact opposite of Marx's. One can mention the outright rejection of the view that capitalism would give birth to socialism (based, according to Kropotkin, on the observation that capitalism did not engender the concentration of capital as Marx expected), the refutation of the theory of value as naïve and the theory of surplus-value as misguided, etc. More interestingly and originally, Kropotkin elaborated on Darwin's theory of natural selection but inverted the proposition: The animal species that developed more efficiently were governed by principles of cooperation as opposed to internal rivalry. This statement matched Kropotkin's normative assessment of the social dynamics of human societies: Cooperation means efficiency but, obviously, under basic democratic arrangements.

The anarchist-communist prospect of outright emancipation by the implementation of highly decentralized procedures regarding the economy and politics fueled continuous struggles in the late nineteenth and early twentieth centuries and the so-called "propaganda by the deed." In this sense, communist anarchism was a major component of the worker movement.

At the root of the implacable character of historical dynamics

The lessons taught by the history of "pre-Marxian" social struggles, assessed at the light of Marx's theory of history, are severe.

The implacable character of the historical dynamics of productive forces/relations of production and class struggle was recurrently emphasized in the previous chapters. The conditions of popular classes in feudalism were appalling; there was, in the advance of productive forces associated with the Industrial Revolution, notably the progress of mechanization, a "potential" regarding the improvement of the conditions of life of the great mass of the population; the early developments of capitalist relations of production in the liberation of trade and the rise of the factory system were, however, at the root of new devastations hard to imagine today; after two further centuries of enhancement of productive forces and social struggle, dramatic conquests were realized by popular classes, but the social cost was huge. Nothing was obtained beyond what was compatible with the march forward of class societies, as demonstrated still by contemporary neoliberal trends.

The reasons are clear. Historical dynamics are not governed by popular or managerial projections of paradise on earth but by an evolutionary process of trials and errors, conflicts, and selections. New social structures are implemented that, quite independently of ensuing social damages, make the demonstration of their economic "efficiency" in the sense that they override earlier social arrangements. And the worst of all is that these configurations are supported by minorities, upper classes, drawing major advantages of the transformation in social relations.

Thus, the competition unfolds on two grounds. On the one hand, with outstanding rapidity, the increased efficiency resulting from the march forward of relations of production sweeps aside the earlier generation of social relations. This first competitive process unfolds *within relations of production and productive forces*, the better-performing social configurations ruling out the earlier. On the other hand, the concentration of income to the benefit of the actors of social transformation—in combination with their capability to organize centrally within efficient states—confers on upper classes dramatic powers regarding repression. And this defines the second facet of the social competitive process, as expressed *within class struggle*.

The sequence of attempts described in the previous sections and in Chapter 14 is directly illustrative of the violence inherent in historical dynamics. Without even mentioning the program of Babeuf and the Equals, the action of La Montagne during the French Revolution balked at the rising social forces of the new capitalist relations of production, much more advanced than is often thought, prolonging the path opened in England 150 years earlier. Many of the backward aspects of Proudhonian anarchism were abandoned by the definition of communist anarchism. But the project of doing without the state was an attempt at building a future for humankind independent of the march forward of socialization. As such, it was condemned from the outset, as Marx had well understood. In direct contrast to anarchist ideology, utopian socialism marked a first attempt at the immediate implementation of managerial organization. Bold experiments were conducted, and a first demonstration was made of the tension between tight organization and democracy.

Marx did not renounce his conviction. The resolution he proposed was the confrontation with the forces of domination on their own grounds, namely: (i) defeating upper classes politically in a single revolutionary blow, excluding potential restoration; (ii) temporarily placing an unprecedented power of repression in the hands of the proletarian class; and (iii) outperforming upper classes regarding the advance of productive forces within a highly centralized social framework. Along such lines, Marx and Engels channeled the forces of social emancipation into the dynamics of organization and mechanization under the banner of scientific organization. This is the subject of the following chapter.

APPENDIX TO CHAPTER 15: UTOPIAN SOCIALISTS

Beginning with Owen, born in 1771, Auguste Fabre's early study is adequately entitled *A Practical Socialist*.[11] Owen was originally a very successful businessman. His career was typical of the institutions of ownership and management in the middle of the nineteenth century, acting as manager and rapidly partner within partnerships. The success of his management in the industrial center of New Lanark in Scotland—in which more decent conditions of labor were provided to workers, notably children—was truly extraordinary. Owen devoted considerable amounts of money to the creation of nurseries and model schools; he demonstrated by doing that the amelioration of the conditions of workers and their families was fully compatible with the conduct of a profitable business. (The conditions of workers during the English Industrial Revolution were disastrous— and Owen proved they were counterproductive.) Owen was celebrated by top members of the upper classes, including the father of Queen Victoria, the Prime Minister Lord Liverpool and, later, Thomas Jefferson in the United States; but this was not enough. After a first trip to the United States, Owen established the ephemeral Community of New Harmony. The thorny issue was government. Owen was conscious that the people gathered in the establishment were not equal to self-government as he wished, and asked the participants to progress and be patient. A total of eight constitutions were enacted, but the community was dismantled. Up to the last days of his life (which he planned in the same way as he had organized businesses), Owen clung to his view that human beings had to be transformed by education, and this explained why he had placed so much emphasis on child education.

A thoroughly different character was Fourier, born one year after Owen, in 1772.[12] Not without foundation, Fourier was sometimes described as insane, with a rather strange life spent between his work as broker and an existence as "scholar" of the theory of almost everything, including astronomy, the history of mankind, and psychology. The charm of Fourier's writings lies in his vivid description of human behaviors and creeds. Interestingly, Fourier thought that earlier experiments in life in community had failed due to the requirement of the taming of human "passions" (which he carefully classified as "everything"). Adequate circumstances had to be created for the expression of passions, avoiding confrontations. Difficult. But Fourier considered himself an expert at everything.

In Fourier's analysis, the nineteenth century was described as the age of Civilization, a still-immature stage of social development, to be superseded by the new epoch of Harmony, on which Fourier's plans for social organization were based. Pairs of people, classified in 810 categories according to sophisticated patterns of passions, were supposed to live within each phalanx. Fourier was not a communist: The phalanxes were owned by rich participants, while the satisfaction of the basic needs of poor people was ensured, thus avoiding any form of envy. An attempt was made at the creation of a phalanx at the end of Fourier's life, but it failed. Fourier's main disciple, Considerant, was more successful, but his attempts, and several ensuing ones, did not survive. Fourier's system had, however, a huge impact.

With Cabet, born in 1788 (still 30 years before Marx), we enter a new epoch.[13] Communist ideas were developing in Paris, which Cabet joined after an early political career around the revolution of 1830. He published his famous *Voyage to Icaria* in 1840 (that is, three years before the arrival of Marx in Paris). The difficult issue became the relationship with the followers of Gracchus Babeuf, supported by the publication of Philippe Buonarroti's book on the Conspiracy of the Equals in 1828.[14] Cabet was an advocate of peaceful activism and alliance with the bourgeoisie. The clash was inevitable with other communists, notably Théodore Dézamy (1808–50). But during those years Cabet's ideas were by far the dominant within communist circles, and particularly strong within French cities like Toulouse and Lyon. Fleeing from "persecution," various groups of tightly selected disciples were sent by Cabet to the United States to found the colony of Icaria. The conditions they met were extremely severe. When the revolution broke up in Paris in 1848, Cabet decided to remain in the city, in the expectation of a new form of political action in alliance with a progressive fraction of the republicans. Thus, in April 1848, in between the upheavals of February and June, Icarian communists were chased through the city by the supporters of bourgeois families. Cabet, who maintained close contact with Owen, finally joined the communities in the United States. Cabet's direction was quickly questioned, and judged to be despotic and incompetent. The experiment ended in brutality hard to imagine within a community of which non-violence was a basic principle. In shock, Cabet died of "apoplexy" at the end of 1856. A few Icarian settlements survived to the end of the century.

Wilhelm Weitling was born in 1808 (that is, 10 years earlier than Marx).[15] He was the son of a maidservant in Magdeburg and a French soldier of Napoléon's occupying army. In Germany, as in other European countries, the 1830s and 1840s were the years of the rising capitalist relations described in the third section of Chapter 8, with the decline of the economy of small masters and skilled artisans, and the rise of the factory system and "big industry"; this was thus the period of the consolidation of the fundamental class antagonism between the bourgeoisie and the proletariat. New currents were developing with, for example, the publication of Friedrich Strauss's *Life of Jesus* in 1835,[16] one of the few books owned by Weitling, in which Hegelian philosophy was combined with Christianity.[17] This was also the period of Metternich's inquisition, and these rising trends were termed communistic. Weitling's communist-Christian views were formed in this social context, as later expressed in his main work, known under its German title *Garantien der Harmonie und Freiheit*, [*Guarantees of Harmony and Freedom*].[18] Weitling arrived in Paris in 1835, where he became the leading figure in the League of the Just. Despite important publications, Weitling, a tailor, was nothing of an intellectual. Although Marx hailed Weitling's work as early contribution to the formation of proletarian thinking in Germany, the relationship deteriorated rapidly. (Marx, known as "Jupiter Marx," was famous for his contemptuous attitude, and one can easily imagine the relationship with Weitling, who identified himself with the messiah or a prophet.[19]) Weitling went to the United States around the time of the 1848 revolution and created the community Communia in Iowa. The fate of Communia is directly evocative of the failures of other attempts; again, the key issue was the deliberate authoritarian direction of Weitling.

In each instance, the territories opened up in the United States appeared as a promised land, and the choice of the country by utopian socialists perpetuated a well-established trend, notably regarding Christian communities. A large population of German immigrants was already settled even prior to the 1848 revolution, then joined by the Forty-eighters. One can quote here the following list of the chronicles devoted to the colorful, often religious, colonies in the United States in Weitling's paper, *Die Republik der Arbeiter*, during the first half of the 1850s:

> *Die Republik der Arbeiter* carried interesting accounts of life at Oleana, the unsuccessful colony of Ole Bull, the noted Norvegian violonist; of Oneida, the community of the Shakers and Perfectionists; of Evenezer, a settlement of German Pietists near Buffalo; of the North American Phalanx at Red Bank, New Jersey, copied from Madam Anneke's *Frayebzeitung*; of the colony of Trappist monks in Iowa; of the New Buda of the Hungarian refugees in the same state; of Friedrich Rapp's Economy in Pennsylvania; and of Joseph Bäumler Zoar in Ohio.[20]

16
Self-proclaimed scientific socialism

The chain of experiments aiming at the superseding of capitalist relations of production as considered in the previous chapter culminated in the deliberate construction of socialism, with the victories of proletarian-peasant revolutions in various countries, notably Russia and China.

Seen from the early twenty-first century, the final outcome is all too familiar. These bold endeavors resulted in the implementation of what, in our conceptualization, should be termed managerial societies. Popular classes were not at the helm: A hegemonic class of officials wielded power in alliance with firms' managers; these societies were "bureaucratic managerialisms," with high degrees of centralization. But the epilogue is even more disappointing, since all of these experiments conducted in the name of scientific socialism failed, and the countries of self-proclaimed socialism joined the ranks of managerial capitalism.

The ambition of this chapter is not the specification of what "should have" happened in these countries but what was actually the course of events. In a similar manner, the purpose of the brief analysis of self-management below is not to determine whether these attempts could have succeeded but rather how they failed.

The alliance for revolution

Marx had high praise for the democratic character of the institutions of the Paris Commune: The majority of representatives were working men selected by universal suffrage with binding mandates and vulnerable to being recalled at any time.[1] The leaders received the same wages as other workers. The project was to extend the organization of Paris Commune to all cities or villages in France, with district assemblies sending delegates to a "National Delegation" in Paris. These observations did not change the fact that Marx and Engels saw in the highly democratic forms of organization a key root of the failure of the Commune, in particular regarding the conduct of military operations.[2]

In the wake of Paris Commune, and given the impossibility of organizing a new congress of the First International, a small conference was held in September 1871 at Marx's home in London, in which Marx's role was central. Resolutions were adopted. Resolution 8 unequivocally stated:

> In its struggle against the collective power of property-owning classes, the proletariat can only act as class by constituting itself into a distinct political party, opposed to all old parties of property-owning classes. This constitution of the proletariat into political party is indispensable in order to ensure the triumph of the social revolution and its supreme objective, the abolition of classes. The coalition of the forces of workers already obtained in the conduct of economic struggles must also be used as lever in the hands of the class in its struggle against the political power of its exploiters.[3]

Not only the conduct of economic warfare was implied but also the participation in elections. A major step forward toward the construction of an actual party in the full sense was accomplished.

The link between the new line and the failure of the Paris Commune was obvious. In January 1872, Engels also unequivocally stated:

> In my opinion, you [*Engels was writing to Carlo Terzaghi*] strongly overuse the words authority and centralization. I know of nothing more authoritarian than a revolution, and imposing one's will on others with bombs and guns is to exercise authority. It is the lack of centralization and authority that costed its life to the Paris Commune.[4]

It is probably worth recalling that Marx did not consider the Paris Commune to be a socialist movement. Much later, in a letter of February 22, 1881, Marx wrote to Domela Nieuwenhuis: "[...] apart from the fact that this was merely the rising of a town under exceptional conditions, the majority of the Commune was in no sense socialist, nor could it be."[5] The main currents were Blanquism and Proudhonism, that is, two inspirations that Marx and Engels held in contempt.[6] The genuine socialist movement was German and on the rise.[7]

This disenchanted assessment had a key impact on the definition of the strategies of the worker movement during the subsequent decades. The reliance on traditional political institutions, such as the creation of

an actual party or the participation in elections or, even more fundamentally, the role to be conferred on the state in the construction of
socialism, became the object of burning controversies. (As recalled in the
previous chapter, within the First International, Marx was already seen
as the emblematic leader of the party of authority, second to Auguste
Blanqui, however.)

The Social Democratic Party of Germany (SPD) was created in 1875,
that is, not much after the Paris Commune. After the banning of the
party by Otto von Bismarck in 1878, the party resumed its activity in
1891 (with the Erfurt Program in this same year).

It must be kept in mind that, following the strict reading of the
Communist Manifesto, the dominant view in the party during these early
years was the inescapable fall of capitalism in the near future. One can
read Karl Kautsky's *The Class Struggle*, published in 1888.[8] All pieces of
the puzzle were there, notably the disappearance of small production, the
falling profit rate, overproduction, and crises: Capitalism was doomed.
This is when the controversy with Eduard Bernstein erupted. Independently of the definition of any political strategy, Bernstein had a
much more realistic assessment of the future of capitalism. Bernstein
revisionism outraged Rosa Luxemburg, who wrote numerous articles
in rebuttal and publishing her *Social Reform or Revolution* in 1900.[9]
Luxemburg believed that if the prophecy in the *Manifesto* was wrong,
the struggle for revolution was in vain. But the controversy was much
broader. The epilogue is familiar: Kautsky would himself become a revi-
sionist, and Luxemburg died in the revolution!

The controversy around organization and leadership culminated in
Lenin's *The State and the Revolution*, published in 1917.[10] Lenin recalled
that a dramatic sequential "tipping point" was implied in Marx's view
of the conquest of power and the founding of a new society: a strong
leadership in the conduct of the struggle leading to the final abolition of
the state, both phases being separated by the dictatorship of the proletariat under the aegis of the implacable proletarian state with the aim of
the thorough elimination of capitalist relations.

Relevant to the present analysis is the observation that the alliance
between the members of the intelligentsia—transformed into active
political leaders—and popular classes led to the victory of revolutions
in two major countries, namely Russia and, later, China. (By "popular
classes," we mean here workers and fractions of the peasantry.)

There is no questioning the fact that only a very strong hierarchical organization could lead the struggle to victory. The proof is not only in the repression of revolutionary forces in Germany (the councils and the Spartakist league) in 1918 in the wake of the defeat of Germany and the betrayal of the SPD, but also the violence of repression everywhere (and in the mists of time). There is also no questioning the fact that Lenin's slogan in the pamphlet "All power to the soviets" did not survive the access of revolutionary forces to power.[11] The dreadful and bold character of the fight, notably the civil wars, do not alter the nature of the outcome. The chain of events marking the path towards Stalin's dictatorship is also well known. Assessing the political circumstances that led to the repression of the Kronstadt rebellion by Leon Trotsky[12] and the elimination of anarchists after Peter Kropotkin's death, both in 1921, lies beyond the limits of the present analysis.

Behind hierarchical organization loom the figures of leaders; and, when leaders coordinate their actions, a staff of officials is implied; when the commanding power of a staff of officials is institutionalized and reproduced, the ephemeral democratic features of the Commune are lost in the memory of heroic times.

Leaders and officials are segments of what this book broadly denotes as the managers of the government sector. But the economy must also be organized and controlled locally within firms. Thus was the twofold pattern of power established after the revolution in Russia (later in China) in the alliance between government officials and firms' managers (or the officials in charge of other decentralized institutions, such as schools, hospitals, or the like). The leadership was in the hands of the former; everywhere supported by the structures of the party.

Bureaucratic managerialism

There was nothing like a "state capitalism" in the USSR, that is, an alleged capitalist society without a flesh-and-bone ruling class.[13] The upper classes of the USSR and China (and other countries) were managers in the broad sense we give to the notion (including officials or Party cadres).[14] Interestingly, the notion of "state capitalists" was not associated with the reference to state capitalism to designate the members of the upper classes in these countries; the phrase "managerial capitalism" was not used, though this alleged capitalism was, indeed, very managerial.

In our terminology, "bureaucratic managerialism" is the most adequate charaterization of the USSR.

As a preliminary to this investigation, one can recall that the risks inherent in political centralization were repeatedly denounced prior to the October Revolution along lines evocative of Bakunin's much earlier assessment. Nikolai Bukharin was impressed by Robert Michels' "iron law" of oligarchy, formulated in 1910, stating that, for the mere sake of efficiency, any originally democratic complex organization would develop into an oligarchical organization. We quote here Bukharin, himself quoting Michels, and inserting his own comments marked as N.B. (for clarity, the quotation from Michels is indented):[15]

Professor Robert Michels, in his very interesting book, *Zur Sosiologie des Parteiwesens in der modernen Demokratie* (Leipzig 1910, p. 370), says:

"Doubts again arise on this point, however, whose consistent application would lead to an outright denial of the possibility of a classless state (the author should not have said 'state' but 'society'. N.B.). Their administration of boundless capital (i.e., means of production. N.B.) assigns at least as much power to the administrators as would possession of their own private property."

Viewed from this point of view, the entire evolution of society seems to be nothing more than a substitution of one group of leaders for another. [...] If this view is a correct one, Michels must also be correct in his conclusion, socialists may be victorious, but not socialism.[16]

In the subsequent sentences, however, Bukharin nonetheless expressed his final disagreement.

Besides the reference to Michels' theory of bureaucracy, Bukharin also discussed the analysis by Alexander Bogdanov, straightforwardly directed toward the USSR.[17] Bogdanov pointed to the lack of maturity of the proletarian class in the USSR, in the context of the well-known controversy regarding the required levels of development of productive forces on which the establishment of socialism could be premised.

Regarding the social nature of the USSR as it could be assessed after several decades of self-proclaimed socialism (and the dismantling of the USSR), the remainder of this chapter makes broad use of Moshe Lewin's work. Lewin was the most celebrated analyst of the USSR. His book *The Soviet Century*, published in 2005, offered a broad synthesis of the results of a lifetime of research.[18] After a penetrating analysis comes the concluding chapter (Chapter 27), under the promising title "What was the Soviet System?"[19] The USSR was "definitively not" a socialist system: "Socialism involves ownership of the means of production by society, not by a bureaucracy," and socialism means a "deepening—not a rejection—of political democracy."[20] On the same page, Lewin asserted "The USSR was not capitalist," and the sentence went on to explain that the "ownership of the economy and other national assets was in the hands of the state, which in practice meant the summit of its bureaucracy." Who was at this summit? The answer was again unambiguous: The bureaucracy "collectively acquired undivided and unchallenged power."[21] Do the collective owners of the means of production form a class? Lewin venerated Trotsky: A straightforward positive answer was unlikely. Lewin had already provided the answer, earlier in the book. At the top of social hierarchies, we find:

> [...] the members of the central ministerial core, who constituted the real ruling stratum. [...] To this hard core, composed of the heads of some eighty major government institutions, we must add the members of the Politburo, the heads of the party apparatus [...], and party secretaries in the regions and the capitals—a select group of some 1,000 people.[22]

Lewin went on:

> If the "ruling elite" is what we are interested in, then the first figure (1,000) is the relevant one, but if the "ruling class" is the subject of our study then the second (2,500,000) is appropriate.[23]

Lewin's analysis is telling of the uneasy character of the discussion. The word "class" is finally there, but almost inadvertently; it is not repeated in *The Soviet Century* and no discussion can be found there of the notion. When 2,500,000 people are the collective owners of the means of production and in power, Lewin could not avoid the reference to a class. His "bureaucratic absolutism" is an undemocratic managerialism with bureaucratic features. Interestingly, in Lewin's 1989–91 book *The Gorbachev Phenomenon*, the reference to a "ruling class" appears recurrently.[24]

Given the transformation of relations of production in the United States and Europe and the establishment of the second social order, the present discussion harks back to the analysis of the literature devoted to the rising managerial traits in Chapter 7, in the context of the theory of the convergence between systems. One can also mention Milovan Djilas' book *The New Class*, typical of another cluster of studies.[25]

The managerial organization of production

When the Bolsheviks were in power, the question was explicitly raised of the new relations of production to be implemented. Regarding the ownership of the means of production, there was no doubt: The answer was collective ownership by the state. Regarding organization and management, there was also no hesitation: The most advanced forms observed in the United States had to be imported. Lenin and Trotsky were on the same page. Beginning with Lenin in 1918:

> Socialism is inconceivable without large-scale capitalist engineering based on the latest discoveries of modern science. It is inconceivable without planned state organization, which keeps tens of millions of people to the strictest observance of a unified standard in production and distribution. We Marxists have always spoken of this, and it is not worthwhile wasting two seconds talking to people who do not understand even this (anarchists and a good half of the Left Socialist-Revolutionaries).[26]

Continuing with Trotsky in 1923:

> We did not invent planning. In its principle, it is the method used by Morgan and his staff (better than us) to manage his trust, namely, forecasting, coordination, direction. The difference (and it is large) lies in the fact that we must apply the methodology of planning to our trust of the trust, that is, the entire Russia.[27]

As could be expected on such grounds, the Mensheviks accused the Bolsheviks of guiding the country towards capitalism:

> The policy of Soviet power, from the very outset devoid of a genuinely proletarian character, has lately pursued more and more openly a course

of compromise with the bourgeoisie and has assumed an obviously anti-working-class character. On the pretext of nationalizing industry, they are pursuing a policy of establishing industrial trusts, and on the pretext of restoring the productive forces of the country, they are attempting to abolish the eight-hour day, to introduce piece-work and the Taylor system, black lists and victimization. This policy threatens to deprive the proletariat of its most important economic gains and to make it a victim of unrestricted exploitation by the bourgeoisie.[28]

But, as could be expected, the managerial aspect of the new relations of production was not perceived, or at least was denied. Interestingly, the Mensheviks identified the reliance on the managerial forms of organization with capitalism; the Bolsheviks, with socialism. Are managers capitalists or proletarians?

The difficulty with the adoption of managerial options was that, despite the progress of industry during the last years of the nineteenth century, there was certainly no numerous and advanced class of managers in Russia before the revolution.[29] Kendall E. Bailes' fascinating study *Technology and Society under Lenin and Stalin*, whose subtitle is "Origins of the Soviet Technical Intelligentsia, 1917–1941," is specifically telling. Bailes wrote: "The Soviet Union continued the prerevolutionary practice of wide technical borrowing from the West, and Western technology predominated in most areas of the economy."[30] The central theme was how "social conflicts involving the technical intelligentsia were handled in this period, and particularly the novel way in which Soviet society dealt with class conflict beginning in the mid-1930s."[31] The book tells the appalling story of the repression of managers, mostly engineers, during Stalin's dictatorship, the attempt to create a totally new generation of "politically correct" managers, and the eventual renewed conflict with Stalin revealing the profound nature of the antagonism. The problem of the relationship between firms' managers and the central bureaucracy in the conduct of the managerial new relations of production was actually never fully settled, though forms of compromise were found from Khrushchev's reforms onward.

Returning to the general historical process, what is truly astounding in the dynamics of self-proclaimed socialism was the crushing weight of "economic determinism." And this observation is obviously the expression of one among many fundamental principles governing the history of human societies. Was there no alternative to the reproduction of the social features of managerial capitalism regarding management or, more generally, organization? Had workers already been deprived of their organizational capabilities? Or had technology and organization become too complex?

Socialism in the USSR accomplished two dramatic steps forward in a sudden manner. There was no historical antecedent. On the one hand, regarding traditional government, the Bolsheviks solved the problem outright by the immediate dissolution of the power of the soviets and the transfer of political authority into the hands of the bureaucracy. A crucial feature of historical dynamics, evocative of the analysis Marx had given of the Second French Empire, was the necessary bureaucratic character of the strong state in a context of violent social strife. But do circumstances explain everything? During how many decades? On the other hand, regarding production, firms had to be placed under the control of managers. In this second respect, no leap forward to unexplored territories had to be realized: As clearly expressed in the above two quotations from Lenin and Trotsky, the organizational structures of production were imported from the most advanced configurations reached within managerial capitalism in the United States.

The failure of reforms

We cannot reproduce here Lewin's detailed account of the failure of reforms as of the early 1980s in the USSR in the context of the inefficient and corrupted administration of Leonid Brezhnev. Conversely, Lewin believed that Yuri Andropov and Mikhail Gorbachev had the capability to change the course of events:

> Paradoxically, to have stood a chance of success in 1982–3, the leader (or the leaders) would have had to recognize not only that the system was ailing (that had been clear to an Andropov or Kosygin for some time), but that several of its vital organs were already dead.[32]

Brezhnev was general secretary of the Communist Party up to his death in 1982, when the power was transferred to Andropov, who died prematurely in 1984, with extremely damaging consequences according to Lewin. (Among other measures, a program of economic reforms had been undertaken aiming at the complete self-financing of firms.) Under Andropov, new men were entering into the high spheres of the

Party, notably Gorbachev, to which Lewin devoted the complete book mentioned earlier (*The Gorbachev Phenomenon*). In the first version of this book, Lewin expressed the view that the perestroika had every chance to succeed (in the second draft, he had to acknowledge the harbingers of the incoming failure). Not only did Lewin think the transformation of the Soviet system was possible; he also passionately wished it would be accomplished. The USSR would become a genuinely socialist country, thus harking back to Lenin's project, or, at least, a hybrid social configuration. In Lewin's mind, the active social forces potentially apt to the task were unquestionably segments of what we denote as managers:

> Gorbachev has already opened new channels to educated professionals, the fastest growing group in Soviet society and the most politicized, or at least among the best informed. The entry of these professionals into the party has supplied the cadres for the Gorbachev line [...][33]

The failure of the new ruling class to implement "democratic" social structures—in the sense of "class democracy"—was, we believe, the crucial factor accounting for the inability of this class (the distinct components of the class) to reform the economy. The political and economic situations reached a dead end. The concentration of powers in the hands of what Lewin denoted as an "elite" did not allow for a broad social compromise between the two components of the upper class, namely state and party officials on the one hand, and firms' managers on the other. The extreme violence of Stalin's era had been superseded, but there was no space within state institutions for any creative expression and handling of internal contradictions. The concentration of wealth at the top was to be the main feature of the following transition in Russia, in perfect conformity with the earlier concentration of power and corruption within the topmost layers.

Self-management

Self-management appeared as an alternative to the centralized structures in Stalin's USSR. The difficulty in the analysis of these attempts at the construction of socialism "from below" is the very broad variety of experiments conducted under also quite distinct political and economic circumstances.

The concern of anarchists, as manifested within the structures of the First International, was primarily with the centralization of political power (the anti-state aspect), but this component of the worker movement cannot be separated from the cooperative movement during the nineteenth century in Europe and the United States. A study of self-management should begin with these early developments. To this it would be necessary to add the revolution in Spain during the second half of the 1930s, in which the anarchists were the leading force in the straightforward appropriation of the means of production.[34]

Considering contemporary developments, after the crisis of 2001 many businesses were recovered in Argentina or other countries of Latin America, with important successes. Even in the United States nowadays, one can find stores directly organized by rank-and-file members of cooperatives, and small firms of highly educated managers, like lawyers, surrounded by a few auxiliary employees.

In all experiments, a common difficulty is the necessary compromise between managers and basic workers within each configuration. Managing class hierarchies between production workers, clerical and commercial personnel, and managers, as within large corporations, is the challenging issue. The problem with these undertakings is often their ephemeral character and the lack of generalization. Basic ambiguities appear beyond the heroic stages of struggle when the new institutions must be stabilized, hence the interesting nature of the case of Yugoslavia, beginning after the 1941–5 revolutionary war and prolonged over several decades.

Was Tito's Yugoslavia a classless society? The issue is obviously controversial, but Darko Suvin's answer was unequivocal:

Did a ruling class exist in Yugoslavia? There was a group possessing a monopoly of power, control of the conditions of production, material privileges, and a collective consciousness; further, there was a class of manual workers: Since classes are relational entities, yes a ruling class existed. (Neither class was officially recognized, though Party ideologists rinsed their mouths with the working class from the 1960s on.)[35]

As acknowledged by Catherine Samary, however, the class division could not be referred to the traditional antagonism between proletarians and capitalists:

The reduction of contemporary domination/exploitation relations to the relationship between the bourgeois and the proletarian (or to capitalism, extending the notion beyond its specific aspect, that is, the logic of monetary accumulation and its appropriation by market dominant ownership relations) is an analytical impoverishment. It is a manifestation of blindness in front of an issue that Marx had not foreseen.[36]

In any instance, it is hard to think of any other ruling class than managers. The Fundamental Law of 1950 explicitly distinguished between workers' councils and management boards; only later did this distinction disappear in favor of allegedly undifferentiated "working people."

The social organization of production went through successive phases, reflecting the changing power configurations and hierarchies between the fractions of managerial classes:

1. Prior to the excommunication of Tito by Stalin in 1948, the power was concentrated in the hands of central managers as the economy was governed in the Soviet style.

2. Between 1953 and 1965, investment was decided centrally, but a larger autonomy was conferred on firms' managers regarding production. During these two first phases, the relationship remained rather tight between firms' managers and workers, as the main tension was expressed vis-à-vis central managers.

3. From 1965 onward, the mechanisms of both production and investment were decentralized, structures of "group ownership" were implemented, and the role of banks increased. The antagonism between firms' managers (whose powers where enhanced and wages increased) and workers reached new degrees. Inequalities were rising not only inside the firms but also among firms and republics. A first example was the unequal positions of individual firms in the economy. Some firms benefited from comparatively "comfortable" situations while others were subject to strong competition. Funding (derived from unequal self-financing) had to be reallocated among distinct firms and industries. This task was performed by banks, but the functioning of banks was itself transformed, with an increasing role of profit rates. A multiplication of strikes was observed.

4. After 1971, a march backward was initiated, with a return towards more centralized mechanisms. Large enterprises were divided in

order to counteract their growing powers. This was also a period of rising inflation rates.

No "balance" was ever found. Anyway, in the 1980s came the switch toward neoliberal managerial capitalism.

Brief remarks regarding China

The course of events in China was simultaneously similar and distinct from those of the USSR and Yugoslavia, with the Great Leap Forward in 1958, the Cultural Revolution in 1966, the program of reforms led by Deng Xiaoping in 1978, and the present march towards managerial capitalism under the leadership of the Communist Party.

The Cultural Revolution is specifically relevant to the analysis of managerial trends, or could at least be judged so. When the Cultural Revolution was engaged in China by Mao Zedong in 1966, the Sixteen Points targeted "those people in authority who are taking the capitalist road," notably within the bureaucracy.[37] The revolution could thus be interpreted as a last-ditch attempt at the reversal of the process of power concentration in the hands of a managerial elite. No mention was made, however, of a managerial class in the sense we give to the notion, though the elimination of the remains of capitalist classes in the strict sense was obviously not the key objective, as explicitly acknowledged. The reference to "people in authority" taking the wrong road was unequivocal: People in authority were managers (including party cadres). Liu Shaoqi could be considered as the leading figure in a trajectory strengthening the march of China toward a more efficient bureaucratic managerialism. (Liu was elected President of the People's Republic of China in 1959 in the wake of the disaster of the Great Leap Forward and died in prison in 1969.) Was a new road toward actual socialism beyond managerialism opened by the Cultural Revolution? The unfolding of the struggle and its outcome proved the opposite.

Alain Badiou can be considered a major exception regarding the interpretation of the course of the Cultural Revolution. The responsibility for the failure of the revolution was pinned on Mao himself by Badiou:

> But Mao is also a man of the party-state. He wants its renovation, even a violent one, but not its destruction. In the end he knows full well that by subjugating the last outpost of young rebellious "leftists",

he eliminates the last margin left to anything that is not in line (in 1968) with the recognized leadership of the Cultural Revolution: the line of party reconstruction.[38]

We do not, in any respect, believe Mao's abandonment of the party would have paved the way to actual "communism" in China beyond bureaucratic managerialism, be it reformed or continued in its earlier forms.[39]

The remainder of the drama is well known. The explosion of the Soviet Union appeared to Chinese leaders as a dreadful development, with a high probability that it would be reproduced in China unless a quite distinct course was followed. The institutions of political power were preserved, and the rush to capital accumulation and the concentration of wealth placed under the sway of the party apparatus (and under the shameless banner of "Socialism with Chinese characteristics").

Joining the ranks of managerial capitalist countries

Under quite distinct circumstances in the USSR, China, and Yugoslavia, a process of convergence toward the social configurations prevailing within the countries of managerial capitalism was finally undertaken during the 1980s. When this occurred, the United States and Europe had entered into the neoliberal phase of managerial capitalism with, notably, the dramatic trends towards the concentration of income at the top within Anglo-Saxon countries.

There is no mystery in the observation that upper classes in the countries of self-proclaimed socialism understood the benefits they could derive from this transition. As is obvious and described by Lewin in 1991 during the course of the events, the move was "launched 'from above' by the party leadership."[40] As usual, specific paths were followed within distinct countries, namely Russia, China (where the "national factor" as defined in Chapter 10 was the strongest), and Yugoslavia, but the fundamental nature of the transition was or will finally be the same.

The following points must be emphasized:

1. Prior to the final move, both the USSR and Yugoslavia undertook reforms aiming at the establishment of managerial societies, though Yugoslavia went much further.
2. In both instances, a first issue was the inability to establish a class democracy within the various fractions of the managerial classes.

3. In the two countries, the bridge between popular classes and managerial classes had been broken rather early and was never rebuilt. There were no grounds for an alliance between segments of the managerial classes and the popular classes. Given the above lack of class democracy, there was also no way toward a social compromise between, respectively, managerial and popular classes in the confrontation with the countries of managerial capitalism.

4. Managerial classes were devastated in China by the course of the Cultural Revolution. The cohesion of all managerial classes was ensured by the Communist Party in the course toward managerial capitalism, to date still distinct from neoliberal trends.

The reference in the present chapter to class patterns, class dominations, and class alliances is at the root of an important common aspect between the analyses of, respectively, the chain of social orders in the countries of managerial capitalism and the sequence of events in the countries of self-proclaimed socialism. In a social order like the postwar compromise, the two components of managerial classes (officials and firm managers) were able to gain significant autonomy from capitalist classes, entering into social alliance with popular classes; and, almost a century later, to jointly undertake the switch to neoliberalism, that is, moving from the alliance to the left to the alliance to the right. Within the countries of self-proclaimed socialism, the balance of power between the two components of managerial classes was more unequal and the nature of the relationship varied significantly as an effect of distinct institutional arrangements. The conduct of a sharp social transformation required, however, a collaboration. The convergence occurred, but the common ground was the rush toward managerial capitalism—in its neoliberal configuration, in Russia, or not, in China, at least up to now.

PART IV

Prospects for Human Emancipation Within and Beyond Managerialisms

The first statements in the Introduction to this book expressed our faith in the potential of popular struggle. This assessment was, however, immediately tempered in the next paragraph by the thesis regarding the contemporary transition from capitalism to a new antagonistic mode of production called managerialism. Given the stubborn reproduction of class dominations, as in Part III, what may remain of the prospects open to popular classes in their attempt at the inflection of historical dynamics in the direction of a dignified future?

First, "managerialism" refers to societies having acquired advanced levels of sociality regarding production and, more generally, social relations under the aegis of managers. This is the point now reached, or on the verge of being reached, within contemporary societies. In this respect, there is no alternative: No stroke of a "magic wand" will dissolve managerial hierarchies outright. Second, a broad variety of such social structures exist or existed decades ago, supported by distinct economic and political institutions. They may be located in distant positions on the democracy–authoritarianism spectrum. In this respect, any movement in one direction or the other is of utmost political importance regarding present conditions and future prospects. Chapter 17 analyzes these alternative trajectories denoted as "managerialisms"—and here the plural is the key point.

There is no determinism—notably, no economic determinism—in the selection of either one of the above trajectories. Chapter 18 discusses the power of popular classes to inflect the current path toward managerialism under neoliberalism in the direction of social progress.

The general interpretation can be summarized in a few key propositions: (i) Layers of gradual social progress accumulate along the sequence of modes of production—even "capitalist modernity" created such opportunities, and the same will be true of what we denote as "managerial modernity"; but (ii) the march forward is delayed by lasting phases of regression, as during the Industrial Revolution and neoliberalism; and (iii) the internal economic and political contradictions of these trajectories, in combination with the strength of popular struggle "bending" the course of history "to the left," are the social forces capable of destabilizing these dynamics for the best.

The link is, thus, established with the failures of earlier attempts at the inflection of the course of history as discussed in Part III. A utopia for the twenty-first century must, on the one hand, acknowledge the reproduction of relations of production and productive forces, notably their implications in terms of class struggle, but, on the other, impart a strong dynamic of social progress, overstepping the boundaries of the conquests of the postwar compromise, toward a future of emancipation beyond left-wing managerialism.

17

The economics and politics of managerialisms

The location of managerialism as the latest link in the historical chain of class societies—feudalism, capitalism, and managerialism—and as a new step forward in the course of socialization defines the main axis around which the entire demonstration in this book revolves. The outcome of the revolutionary leap forward under the banner of communism in the countries of self-proclaimed socialism was the establishment of bureaucratic managerialism; beyond the failure of these radical attempts at the acceleration of historical dynamics, the hybrid structures of relations of production in the countries of managerial capitalism testify to continuing managerial trends; and the contemporary structures of neoliberal managerial capitalism do not mark the end of history but prepare a new managerial configuration.

As suggested in the introduction to this fourth part, an important thesis is that, beyond the deterministic statement regarding the transition from capitalism to managerialism, large degrees of indeterminacy are preserved. No forms of managerialism are identical; far from it. Some among these trajectories can be mistaken for continuing sheer capitalism, as is presently the case in neoliberalism; others for preliminary steps toward socialism, as was the case within the social democracies during the interwar years and the early postwar social compromise in Europe. But these interpretations are misguided. Managerialism continues down its path.

For lasting periods of time, the concrete forms of managerialism will retain the imprint of their origins. (Chapter 6, "Managerialism and managerial capitalism," already pointed to the strength of historical hysteresis.) The first sections that follow recall the basic characters common to all trajectories toward managerialism, in particular the managerial class as upper class and the high degrees of socialization; but close attention is also paid to the differences. The end of the chapter

202 · MANAGERIAL CAPITALISM

attends to the political facet of managerialisms in the same spirit of comparison.

Trajectories and outcomes

Three specific historical routes toward managerialism were considered in the previous chapters. They point to distinct brands of the same basic structure:

1. *Bureaucratic managerialism in the USSR or China (from World Wars I or II onward, to the 1980s).* Radical breaks with capitalism occurred with the victory of the revolutions in Russia and China, leading to the implementation of bureaucratic managerialisms. Market mechanisms were ruled out; the ownership of the means of production was transferred to the state; a key role was conferred on central institutions, notably regarding investment. Yugoslavia stood out as an exception to the highly centralized procedures in USSR and China, but no stabilized arrangement was found. The experiences conducted in these countries are particularly relevant to the present discussion of historical perspectives—"counterfactually," one might say—regarding the social relations to which they could have led if the course of reforms had not been abandoned in favor of managerial capitalism. As suggested by the theories of the convergence between systems after World War II, there was the potential for the implementation of alternative structures.

   In these countries, the first and dominating configuration of managerialism was self-proclaimed socialism (bureaucratic managerialism); the second, the more decentralized configuration of self-management; and the third, any of the virtual configurations of what a reformed self-proclaimed socialism could have been.

2. *Managerial leadership in the countries of managerial capitalism (the post-depression/postwar decades).* In the wake of the managerial revolution at the transition between the nineteenth and twentieth centuries and what Chapter 6 denoted as the governmental revolution in the early twentieth century, an alternative gradual path toward managerialism was initiated within the main capitalist countries.

   The basic features of the new institutions and mechanisms were described in Chapter 10, devoted to the sequence of social orders. Private and government managers acquired a large autonomy vis-à-vis capitalist classes; conglomerates diversified their fields of activity rather independently of financial institutions; important horizontal networks of management of nonfinancial corporations were implemented in the system of interlocking directorships; the networks directly linking nonfinancial corporations dominated; the role of state or para-statal institutions was increased in the conduct of policies, notably regarding the macroeconomy and the struggle against inequalities; financial mechanisms were subjected to important regulation.

Even within the confines of the postwar compromise, variegated paths were followed in the United States and the various European countries, with sometimes quite significant differences.

3. *The managerialism of financial hegemony (from the 1970s onward)*. The alliance between managerial and capitalist classes defined the configuration of neoliberal managerial capitalism, also pointing to distinct forms of managerialism. The network of ownership and control and the interface ownership-control/management were established worldwide under the hegemony of the United States in what we called an economic governing core (Chapter 12, "The politics of social change"). In tight collaboration with or under the sway of this central power, governments performed the expected tasks regarding the liberalization of international trade and the free movement of capitals worldwide, within neoliberal globalization.

Again, significantly distinct trajectories were followed in the United States and the various countries of continental Europe. The first appendix to Chapter 10, devoted to the sequence of social orders within continental Europe, referred to forms of "financial orthodoxy" that might more adequately account for the situation within continental Europe, in particular in Germany, rather than outright neoliberalism. A significant degree of uncertainty still surrounds the new social trends in the United States. Three potential trajectories were considered: (i) the continuation of ongoing tendencies; (ii) "administered neoliberalism," that is the above supported by a strengthened action of central authorities; or (iii) a "neomanagerialism," that is, a new social order under the stricter guidance of private and government managers, but without the features of the postwar compromise reflecting the alliance between managerial and popular classes.

Degrees and forms of socialization

The accomplishment of a sudden step forward in the historical process of socialization was part of the deliberate program of self-proclaimed socialism in which the economy and broader social mechanisms were supposed to be monitored centrally. "Planning" was the key word, and high degrees of efficiency were expected from the abandonment of the chaotic course of market mechanisms. The unrestrained projection of the rule of central organization—actually, the expression of the ambition of the new class—paradoxically appeared as a fundamental weakness in the march toward sustainable forms of managerialism in these countries.

Though at a considerable distance from the above bold endeavor, advanced forms of sociality were reached within the countries of managerial capitalism. Considering the postwar compromise and neoliberalism jointly, there is no need to return here to the high degrees reached by the socialization of production in these countries and the establishment of multifaceted private networks, notably financial networks. As shown in Chapter 11 ("Class and imperial power structures"), under contemporary circumstances, the collective aspect of capital ownership, control, and management has reached tremendous degrees in the United States. The governmental aspect of socialization was no less spectacular. This is true even where it could be less expected, within the neoliberal United States, the dreamland of market mechanisms (see Chapter 6).

Combining the governmental and private aspects of socialization, U.S. neoliberal managerial capitalism is a "collective managerial-capitalism." (Obviously, the collective aspect does not contradict the very high degrees of inequality in the country.)

Less capitalism—More managerialism

Besides the continuing process of socialization, the trajectories toward mature managerialism in the countries of self-proclaimed socialism and during the postwar compromise manifested in important transformations of economic mechanisms, the expressions of the growing distance from the economics of capitalism.

Regarding market mechanisms, for example, a broad range of combinations was manifested. Earlier structures were either preserved, biased, or fully eliminated, depending on the role conferred on prices and the rules of their determination. The abandonment of market mechanisms was obviously a basic feature of the economies of self-proclaimed socialism, but important exceptions to market mechanisms were also observed in the economies of the postwar compromise, and with a tendency to be more so, notably with the development of nonprofit institutions.

The procedures guiding investment decisions are of crucial importance. Within the countries of self-proclaimed socialism and during the postwar compromise (notably in Europe), a central role was played by governments. Overall, the dynamics of the postwar compromise headed towards more balanced multiform procedures, in which firms, financial institutions, and governments interacted.

Regarding neoliberalism, a crucial aspect in the implementation of the new social order was the distance taken from self-proclaimed socialism or any hybrid form of socialism, as within the social-democracies of the first postwar decades in Europe (described by the promoters of neo-liberalism as the anteroom of totalitarianism[1]). The managerial ideology of economic organization, as in the guidance of exchanges by planning or mixed forms of government–private determination, was abandoned regarding exchanges between goods and services as well as investment. A deliberate emphasis was placed on market mechanisms (given the general difficulty of distinguishing between market and capitalist relations of production, in the left as well as the right), as expressed in the notion of neo-"liberalism." A frequently emphasized effect of neoliberalism was, thus, the "commodification" of earlier non-market relationships. Regarding investment, the criterion of sheer profitability was restored, as within the new institutions of ownership and control described in Chapter 11. The imposition of rates of return on own funds, sanctioned, notably, by the selling of the stock shares of the corporations not measuring up to the norms defined centrally, is evocative of capitalist dynamics (as in the analysis of competition in Volume III of *Capital*). The crucial transformation lay, in fact, in the high degrees of centralization reached within the network of neoliberal financial institutions (a tight web of reciprocally owned corporations) and the direct intervention of the managers of these institutions within the boards of directors as outsiders. Year after year, these mechanisms increasingly manifested in features akin to central "planning." Besides the arbitration between various industries, a prominent role is also played by the decisions made within the same institutions regarding the international movement of capitals.

In the new combination between market mechanisms governing exchanges and the simultaneous reliance on the allocation of resources in their "collective hands," managerial classes had finally found the winning combination along the path leading to their hegemony over popular classes, as well as, under distinct conditions, capitalist classes.

Subduing capitalist classes—Helping towards their reconversion

All managerial capitalisms in the past, as trajectories toward mature managerialisms, were the vectors of the elimination of capitalist classes, and it is still the case within neoliberalism. The single exception was the first financial hegemony under the aegis of large capitalists during the first decades of the twentieth century; the entrance into managerial capitalism in this first configuration actually defined a process of concentration, with the decline of small ownership and the formation of the new financial institutions; but the power of managers within boards of directors was on the rise. Along the three later trajectories considered in the previous sections, mechanisms tending to the eradication of capitalist classes were underway.

There is not much to be said regarding the countries of self-proclaimed socialism, since capitalist classes were eliminated outright, or after short episodes, such as under the New Economic Policy (NEP) in the USSR. Moving to the postwar compromise, rather than the sudden elimination of capitalist classes, we referred in Chapter 10 to a process of gradual "euthanasia" of capitalists *as capitalists*. One can recall the sharp decline in the income of the best-accommodated household sectors to which large capitalists belong, as in Figure 10.1; the dramatic rise of tax rates for upper incomes, as in Figure 10.2; the new trends of wealth inequality, as in Figure 9.3, etc. Even more specifically than income tax rates, one can recall the rise of inheritance taxes that affect the transmission of wealth, notably capital.

There was a capitalist reaction. The earlier unraveling of the privileges of capitalist classes came to an end as a result of the neoliberal (counter) revolution. Seen from the early twenty-first century, the neoliberal institutions of ownership and control, as notably supported by financial institutions, might be understood as the expression of a return towards earlier capitalist trends. The rules of the maximizing of shareholder value restored the rigors of the valorization of capital. Several figures in the previous chapters documented the sharp transformation in firms' management, for example, the distribution of dividends (Figure 10.3). Stock-market indices skyrocketed (Figure 10.4). Jointly considered, these tendencies support the unquestionable observation that neoliberalism was built on the new social alliance between managerial and capitalist classes, with significant benefits for capitalist owners and the use of capitalist mechanisms by managers to their own advantage. *And one should not forget the formation of a class of billionaires at the top.*

As already stated, these interpretations carry, however, a dangerous risk of a misreading of historical dynamics. The neoliberal alliance was placed under managerial leadership, and gradually more so. Pushing the new social structure to degrees of utmost managerial consistency, the power or the sheer existence of capitalist classes would be offset to the benefit of a fully managerial rule. This point has not yet been reached, but the institutions of neoliberal managerial capitalism testify to the advanced degree of the transition.

The truth of the matter is that for the earlier "euthanasia" of capitalists during the postwar compromise was substituted a programmed "metamorphosis" of capitalist classes, monitored from the summit. Within the alliance at the top, a chance was given to capitalist families to accomplish the transition between the two sets of production relations, capitalism and managerialism, under the most advantageous and secure conditions. The old and the new components of the upper classes walk hand in hand in this respect, but one component shows the way.

Hierarchies

The reference to managerial classes considered globally is a useful but major simplification. The class is divided in multiple respects.

A first commonsense criterion suggests a separation between multiple categories of skills in a straightforward manner. Within corporations, one can cite engineers still engaged in tasks of research and organization of production; managers active in accounting, the hiring and firing of the workforce, marketing, and the like; or, obviously, financial managers. To these fractions of the private managerial class, one must add senior government officials. Powers are distributed on these grounds, and incomes are unequal, depending on capacities and education.

Distinct managerialisms differ significantly in the following respects:

1. The spectrum of powers and incomes may be broader or narrower. Notably, the patterns of income inequality documented in Chapter 9 ("Varying trends of inequality") revealed larger degrees of inequality

among managers within neoliberalism than during the postwar compromise. And the trends also manifested in widening divergences.

2. The institutional structures of each configuration are also involved. For example, within the societies of self-proclaimed socialism, powers and income (independently of their practical forms) were concentrated in the hands of the high *Nomenklatura* within central institutions or the party. A more balanced pattern prevailed during the postwar decades in the countries of managerial capitalism. Neo-liberalism opened broad institutional breaches, as between financial and nonfinancial managers (see Chapters 11 and 12).

In all respects so far considered, ongoing trajectories point to variegated power and income configurations. Managerialisms could be classified by degrees of managerial hierarchies, as well as by trends toward widening divergences. In this game, neoliberalism would have the edge over the postwar compromise.

A managerialism bent to the left?

"Democracy," as political régime, is part of the basic concept of the theory of sociality, along with citizenship, nation-state, and similar notions. Again, the mighty figure of Jean-Jacques Rousseau looms here in the background, with the self-limitation of individual freedom in the social contract as the primary attribute of "Liberty."[2] From a Marxian viewpoint, there are, however, very strong limits to the exercise of democracy in a class society. Chapter 15 recalled the circumstances of the French and English revolutions and the struggles of radical segments in favor of so-called "virtuous" forms of democracy; the failure of the fight was pinned on the utopian character of advanced democracy within class societies. It is not possible to progress in this discussion without distinguishing between two facets of democracy, namely: (i) the relation-ships *within* given classes (notably, between fractions of classes), be they upper classes or popular classes, that is, intraclass democracy; and (ii) the relationship *between* upper classes and popular classes.

The notion of intraclass democracy played a pivotal role in Marx's analysis in *The Eighteenth Brumaire*, as recounted in Chapter 5 (notably in the appendix to that chapter). Marx judged the bourgeois republic as the favorite form of government of the bourgeoisie for allowing the assertion of the internal contradictions of the class, while the reliance on a strong authoritarian government was the response of upper classes to the rising degrees of social threat. The democracy inherent in the bourgeois republic to which Marx referred was obviously an intraclass democracy. One can also understand from Marx's analysis that intraclass democracy typically conveys degrees of freedom beyond the boundaries of upper classes, as in the freedom of expression, for example the liberty of the press, though often in an ephemeral fashion. (Not only the bourgeois press was involved in the mid-nineteenth century but also the press of popular classes, including communist papers).

A looser notion of democracy is, thus, required to account for the set of social practices allowing for significant degrees of expression of class contradictions than is implied in intraclass democracy. Popular classes may weigh, sometimes to significant degrees, on policies and reforms through the mechanisms of formal democracy such as free elections; they may express their demands by social struggles within rules defined by the law; the violence of repression will also differ strongly within distinct historical circumstances. In this sense, a political regime may be described as "more or less democratic."

The importance of intraclass democracy should not be underestimated. In Chapter 16, the failure of reforms (paralleling the lack of democracy in the general sense above) was pinned on the deficient degree of intraclass democracy in the countries of self-proclaimed socialism. But the discussion is no less relevant regarding the historical dynamics of managerial capitalism. The key observation is that there was a greater degree of "democracy" during the postwar compromise than within neoliberalism in the two respects, namely intraclass democracy or democracy in the broad sense above:

1. During the postwar compromise, a rather balanced pattern of powers was maintained between the various fractions of the managerial class—namely the private managers of nonfinancial corporations, the managers of financial corporations, and government managers—supporting advanced forms of intraclass democracy. The social order being based on an alliance between managers and popular classes, exceptional degrees of "democracy" were also reached. Notably, popular classes were represented within assemblies or governments by actual left parties, with significant bearings on policies. Agreements were negotiated between workers and employers, either locally within distinct firms or industries, or nationally under the

aegis of government institutions. Trade unions played a crucial role in these respects. The postwar compromise can be interpreted as a trajectory of managerialism "bent to the left," giving to "left" the sense defined at the end of Chapter 10. At least, the social order was pointing to such social relations.

2. Conversely, the alliance between upper classes during the two financial hegemonies was, by nature, associated with "less democratic democracies," one might say. Focusing on contemporary neoliberalism, stronger authoritarian hierarchies prevail within the ranks of managerial classes, as between financial and nonfinancial managers; independently of the divide at the top, the concentration of powers within the interface between ownership-control and management, as compared to the remainder of managers, is also acute. But, on the other hand, the previous degrees and forms of "democracy" during the postwar compromise were dramatically reduced.

Given the current deteriorating political trends observed within neoliberalism, it is useful to recall Marx's highly pertinent statement: When the threat of social confrontation becomes unmanageable, upper classes may relinquish the privilege inherent in the free expression of their internal divergences in a form of authoritarian government. The harbinger is the increasing toleration by upper classes vis-à-vis the rise of populism. The breaking point has not yet been reached within the main managerial-capitalist countries, but the remaining distance is diminishing and would shrink further in the event of growing popular struggles.

18
The potential of popular struggle

This concluding chapter raises the most difficult of all issues, namely the assessment of the capability of popular classes to inflect the course of history to their own benefit, under present circumstances and in the future (given the analysis of past experiences in Part III). The matter under consideration is not the organizational capability of popular classes, which will remain beyond the limits of the present study, but the historical circumstances conducive to this historical achievement.

We recall the three theses put forward in the introduction to this fourth part: (i) the accumulation of layers of social progress along the sequence of modes of production; (ii) lasting phases of social regression; and (iii) the power of popular struggle to override such episodes and consolidate the general advancement.

Under the common heading "The historical dynamics of emancipation and regression," the two first sections of this chapter hark back to the sequence of modes of production and the potential inherent in managerialism as a new step forward in the historical dynamics of relations of production: "managerial modernity" on the tracks of "capitalist modernity." As was the case in the emergence of capitalist relations within Anciens Régimes, the contemporary transition to managerialism is also the vector of "progressive" developments (still in the sense of going in the direction of social progress), but barred by the concentration of powers in the hands of the upper fractions of class hierarchies—actually a reaction to the emancipatory potential conveyed by the new relations of production. In the same spirit of historical comparison, the next section further elaborates on the class foundations of such sequences of "revolutions" and "counter-revolutions" (as defined in the analysis of the French and English revolutions in Chapter 14).

Building on these historical foundations, the subsequent section returns to the post-World-War-II sequence of social orders, discussed in Chapter 10, and the contemporary agenda of popular struggles: Neoliberalism must be understood as a new lasting regressive configuration—introduced by the counter-revolution of the 1970–1980s—in which the dynamics of class domination seem to irrepressibly have the edge and block the route of social progress. Once again, popular classes are confronted with the immense task of "shoving aside" historical obstacles: a "bifurcation" from the current trajectory. The remaining sections discuss the economic and political circumstances capable of supporting popular struggles under present circumstances. The 2007–8 crisis did not destabilize the neoliberal trajectory, but all underlying contradictions have not been offset and new crises will likely erupt during coming decades. In our opinion, the Achilles heel of neoliberalism lies, however, in its politics, as was the case with previous reactionary political endeavors in the past. And the economics and politics of neoliberalism might combine their effects.

The potential inherent in the recuperation of the capacity of popular classes to inflect the course of history beyond the dramatic course of present trajectories—the obvious difficulty of the task—must be considered in the light of earlier endeavors targeted towards human emancipation, discussed in Part III. There is no possible way out in the march toward human emancipation in the symmetrical attempts at stopping or boldly anticipating the course of history. The path of social struggle must be "tuned" according to the historical dynamics of relations of production and productive forces, though certainly not passively—"complying" always meant regressing—but in the footsteps of the twofold dynamics of sociality and class societies. This is what was meant by "bending managerialism to the left," that is, driving a dynamic of progress beyond managerialism itself, as in the title of the present part and the last section of Chapter 17. Two basic aspects must be distinguished in the historical challenge to which popular classes are confronted: (i) reversing the regressive trends of neoliberalism; and (ii) building a dignified future on the most progressive traits of managerial modernity, beyond the privileges of ownership and the monopoly of initiative and decision-making at the top of social hierarchies (within government institutions and firms).

The historical dynamics of emancipation and regression I: Capitalist modernity

The theory of class societies does not deny the accumulating progressive gains resulting from popular struggles. Freed from cataclysmic bias and combined with the dynamics of sociality, the theory accounts for the maintenance of class hierarchies along the two-sided historical march forward of human societies. Despite the stubborn reproduction of class dominations, popular struggles had a major impact on the course of history within the space remaining opened to social progress. Overall, nothing was given, but a lot was gained. The political difficulty in the march forward of class emancipation lies in the observation that the historical dynamics of progress are delayed by lasting episodes of aggressive strengthening of class dominations. Under such circumstances, the earlier forms of organization of popular classes are dismantled and the existing balance of social forces unsettled. There is a name for these trends: Reaction. This contradictory course of events, made of advancements and regressions, is typical of the ambivalent character of capitalist modernity.

As stated in Chapter 14, the declaration of capitalist modernity— proclaiming the realm of liberty and equality (and general happiness), associated with the break from the feudal ideology of "blue blood" and supported by the rise of capitalist relations of production—opened new territories to the demands of bourgeois classes within the confines of the earlier society. The values of modernity can be interpreted as a capitalist ideology deprived of its class-contradictory aspect or, equivalently, as contended in Chapter 14, the capitalist mode of production seen from the viewpoint of the theory of sociality: We are all born equal in a world of equality, freedom, and fraternity, a fascinating advancement—and an object of narcissistic investment on the part of upper classes. The political threat was obvious. A breach was opened in the seamless front of upper-class ideology. Decade after decade, popular classes made their way in.

The period of the industrial revolutions, in the wake of victorious bourgeois revolutions, can probably be considered as the most dramatic episode of social regression in the past. The bourgeois revolutions, which resulted from the development of capitalist relations of production prior to their industrial stage, were followed during the industrial revolutions (during the later decades of the eighteenth century and the first decades of the nineteenth century in England, and somewhat later in continental Europe) by periods of what can be called social "devastation." We recall that crucial factors were the course of mechanization and the confiscation of commons, which placed irrepressible tools in the hands of the rising capitalist class in alliance with the remnants of feudal relations. It is not necessary to restate here the terrible conditions created by the pressure placed on popular classes within the context of the early forms of exploitation associated with the rise of capitalist relations of production, ushering in the development of the factory system. It is enough to read Engels' *The Condition of the Working Class in England* or E. P. Thompson's *The Making of the English Working Class*,[1] but the conditions of labor and life have been described so many times (notably, children's and women's labor). The contrast with the promises of modernity was acute. It is no coincidence that this period stimulated the rise and marked the apex of the socialist-communist systems of thought and social confrontation in 1830, 1848, and 1871.

Our general assessment is that, considering history from a sufficient distance, the fight of popular classes consolidates important advancements and, century after century, layers accumulate. The march of capitalism under the banner of modernity during the centuries following the Industrial Revolution can certainly not be taken at face value, but the progress of sociality and productive forces opened new paths to the conquest of popular classes in the context created by, at least, facets of capitalist practices and ideologies.[2] Despite the social devastations caused by the industrial revolutions, popular struggles, overriding the forces of exploitation during the first half of the nineteenth century, finally imposed new conquests that can be retrospectively interpreted as among the promises of modernity. Obviously, only conquests that did not straightforwardly contradict the private ownership of the means of production or the political power of upper classes were on the agenda, for example, free basic education for all or universal suffrage. Education had long ago been considered by advanced segments of capitalist classes as favorable to the progress of capitalism (and a favorable factor in international competition); it was also clear that the risks inherent in universal suffrage could be superseded by the control of education and information. But each social conquest also conveyed progressive components whose accumulation threatened class dominations and supported the struggles of upper classes in the imposition of new reactionary trends during phases of regression. However, the accumulation of "progressive layers" was also a crucial factor in the transition to the new, managerial, mode of production.

The historical dynamics of emancipation and regression II:
Managerial modernity

There is no accepted term for managerialism from the viewpoint of the
theory of society, as "non-class-contradictory depiction of managerial
trajectories." For this reason, we coined the term "managerial modernity,"
based on the model of capitalist modernity. The correspondence is,
however, straightforward between: (i) capitalism as mode of production
and the epoch of democratic values of bourgeois revolutions; and (ii)
managerialism as new mode of production and, using the terminology
introduced in Chapter 6, the epoch of the "meritocratic" values of the
managerial revolution.

In their own way, the rising managerial trends within managerial
capitalism also forged new paths toward mature forms of organization
and conveyed new social values, as manifested during the first post-
World-War-II decades. The advance of managerial traits, associated
with the rise of the new relations of production, gradually dismantled the
foundations of capitalist practices as well as the ideologies of the private
ownership of the means of production, including its hereditary transmission, under the banner of meritocracy. And much more would have
been implied if popular classes had not been defeated at the transition
between the 1970s and 1980s.

Again, a lasting phase of reaction in neoliberalism barred the route
towards social progress. We do not mean that the violence of neoliberalism, at least within the most advanced countries, measures up to
the devastations of the Industrial Revolution, which would amount to
an outstanding performance. Distinct historical stages of development
have obviously been reached between the eighteenth and twenty-first
centuries along the general course of historical dynamics. But, *mutatis
mutandis*, neoliberalism supported and still presently supports such
regressive trends.

The potential of popular struggle is still there. Even assuming that the
"key foundations of managerialism" as mode of production-socialization
(the concentration of initiative, power, and income in the hands of a
minority) will not be questioned by social strife, much can be conquered
beyond neoliberalism. These conquests would prolong the dynamics of
some among the alternative managerial trajectories during the post-
World-War-II compromise, as described in previous chapters. They
would also be evocative of what reformed self-proclaimed socialism

could have been (if it had not been defeated), if oriented to the left as an effect of popular struggle.

The foundations of the continuing belief in a future of emancipation must be sought in the interaction between the historical dynamics of sociality and class societies in their present configuration, as Marx and Engels did in the nineteenth century; and the struggle of popular classes remains the single social force capable of opening the path, as Marx and Engels also believed. But the coincidence between the attainment of "social organization" and "social emancipation" cannot be taken for granted. No popular class will simultaneously perform the two tasks in one revolutionary blow, as Marx and Engels optimistically expected.

One can, however, "speculate" regarding the entrance into an even further stage opened up by the progressive trends inherent in managerial modernity. Given the enhancement of, notably, social interaction and education, the monopoly of social initiative on the part of minorities would become more and more difficult to sustain along the course of a managerialism sufficiently bent in a direction of social progress. A new trajectory would, correspondingly, be opened up towards class emancipation. The patient conquests of popular classes would, once again, stimulate the superseding of the current class foundations of relations of production.

This perspective harks back to the most ambitious plans of all architects of utopian or scientific socialisms, despite their de facto strong managerial inclinations. One can, notably, think of Marx's views regarding the superseding of the difference between manual and intellectual labor, and Lenin seeing in all workers the potential engineers of the future.

The class foundations of revolutions and counter-revolutions

There is more to be learnt from the parallel between the social conflicts that respectively marked the sequence of events underlying the rise of capitalist and managerial relations, specifically regarding class confrontations.

Returning to the analysis of bourgeois revolutions in Chapter 14, we recall the distinction made between two categories of social forces: (i) the strictly bourgeois component involved in the spiral of capital accumulation and concentration; and (ii) the radical progressive component rooted in small ownership and the "poors." The sequence revolution/

counter-revolution was discussed in this context, in relation to the interplay between these two components. The middle classes behind small ownership and the most popular social forces were the spearhead of social dynamics leading beyond the limits of bourgeois conquests in the strict sense. The victory of the bourgeoisie cleared the path to the rise of capitalist relations of production and the corresponding exploitation of popular classes during the Industrial Revolution.

A closer analysis reveals that two aspects of social dynamics combined their effects, accounting for the final bourgeois outcome of the revolution: (i) the alliance at the top of social hierarchies between the remnants of the old classes—now landowners or engaged in businesses—under the leadership of the upper fractions of the new bourgeois class; and (ii) the split within lower classes, separating between, on the one hand, prosperous segments of middle classes, rallying the alliance at the top, and, on the other, impoverished components.

A similar chain of events can be identified in the sequence of the postwar compromise and neoliberalism. The gradual rise of managerial trends during the first half of the twentieth century and the shocks of the Great Depression and World War II—given the strength of the worker movement worldwide—stimulated the radical change in the politics of social orders, paving the way to the establishment of the postwar compromise. The fact that the sudden social transformation was not described as a "revolution" was probably the expression of the contrast with the earlier—successful or failed—proclaimed socialist revolutions. But two social trends were underway, clearing the path to the neoliberal counter-revolution, directly evocative of the above reshuffling of class configurations and forces:

1. As in the case of the radical components of bourgeois revolutions, the ongoing social trends underlying the postwar compromise were more in line with the middle or lower segments of the managerial classes or fractions of these classes still related to production—the new brand of "middle classes" in the context of managerial relations of production—given that, in any case, top managers had not yet attained the summits reached in neoliberalism. The gradual consolidation and concentration of powers at the top of managerial hierarchies, notably within financial sectors, and the new alliance with capitalist classes created the conditions conducive to the

"neoliberal counter-revolution," the contemporary phase of social regression, with the alliance at the top of social hierarchies.

2. The trends of income inequality in Chapter 9 ("Varying trends of inequality"), with the stagnation of the average purchasing power of the great mass of wage earners in the United States and the dramatic improvement of the income of managerial classes (and gradually more so, when upper layers are considered in the managerial hierarchy, as in Figure 9.2) suggests a process of polarization (sometimes referred to as the "unraveling" or "end" of middle classes).

Both the transformations of class patterns and hierarchies of domination and alliance as typical of social orders were and still are key determinants. On such foundations, one can surmise that decades of popular struggle will be necessary to correct for the regressive effects of the neoliberal counter-revolution.

Bifurcating

The analysis of the economic and political circumstances that allowed for the correction of at least the most shocking aspects of the earlier phase of regression during the nineteenth century will remain beyond the limits of our investigation, notably, in France, the new currents of "republicanism" that paralleled and thrived in the wake of the failures of utopian socialisms and anarchisms, and deeply affected the politics of the Third Republic after the Paris Commune. Besides universal suffrage or free education, one should, at least, mention programs of social reforms (such as those undertaken by Bismark during the 1880s in the German Empire).

In Europe, both class struggle and the worker movement were obviously involved, but the course of historical dynamics was further impacted by the occurrence of the two world wars. One can only refer the reader to the first appendix to Chapter 10, "Managerial capitalism and social orders in Europe," which provides related information. And the social transformations in the United States would account for another facet of a similar story. In all instances, the early implacable dynamics of the Industrial Revolution were slowly attenuated as a result of obstinate popular struggle.

Regarding contemporary societies, the task on the agenda of popular classes is the reversion of neoliberal trends. The endeavor is directly evocative of the bifurcation from the first financial hegemony to the postwar compromise, heading toward potentially more progressive social configurations. During the interwar period—besides the historical dynamics of relations of production, the transformation of class patterns, and the occurrence of the Great Depression—the underlying factors that had made the bifurcation possible were the internal contradictions between capitalist and managerial classes underlying the transition from capitalism to managerialism, given the strength of the worker movement. (One can recall here Joseph Schumpeter's desperation vis-à-vis the future of capitalist relations of production in 1942, which Schumpeter pinned not on economic failures but on the transformation of "institutions," as discussed in Chapter 7.)[3]

At least four main sets of conditions had converged, paving the way to the postwar compromise: (i) Managerial classes considered globally were undergoing a dramatic episode in their historical ascension as a new upper class beside capitalist classes, seeking autonomy from capitalist classes, with very strong achievements to their credit; (ii) The Great Depression, notably its financial component, was blamed on capitalist owners, widening the distance between managerial and capitalist classes; (iii) The Depression and World War II pushed the governmental segment of managerial classes to a possibly even larger distance from capitalist interests than private managers; and (iv) The worker movement and the development of the countries of self-proclaimed socialism were still on the rise, and the strength of popular classes was becoming gradually more obvious. As contended, capitalist classes had to yield.

A balanced assessment of common points and differences must be made in the comparison between the interwar circumstances and World War II, which ushered in the postwar compromise, and contemporary trends. The most severe factor weighing on the contemporary dynamics of social change must be sought in political conditions, as expressed in the last statement in the above list, given the failure of the revolutionary trajectories of self-proclaimed socialisms and the dissolution of the postwar compromise.

Two important fields must thus be considered, namely the contemporary threat of an incoming new structural crisis and the stronger or weaker "cohesiveness" between the components of upper classes.

An incoming structural crisis?

The crisis of 2007–8 manifested the contradictions of neoliberalism, creating new expectations within the ranks of the radical left.[4] The crisis was, however, efficiently treated thanks to the dramatic intervention of governments and central banks; sufficient degrees of international cooperation were ensured. Nothing proves, however, that new threats do not accumulate.

Considering the four structural crises since the late nineteenth century, the crises of the 1890s and 1970s were profitability crises; the Great Depression and the crisis of 2007–8 crises of financial hegemony. Elaborating on this distinction, two scenarios can be contemplated for the forthcoming decades, though any combination is obviously possible.

Within an economy in which managerial traits have reached advanced degrees, the notion of profit rate must be considered cautiously. The main destination of the available "surplus," once taxes, financial incomes, and the wages of non-managerial employees have been paid, is the wages of private managers, notably at the top of hierarchies. As contended in our book *The Crisis of Neoliberalism*, during the 2007–8 crisis, dividends were cut while managers were still paying to themselves wages, bonuses, and supplements—a development testifying to the new balance of power at the top.[5] But sufficient amounts of the available surplus remain within corporations to finance new investments. The sum of the wages and bonuses/supplements of managers and retained profits is thus constrained by the "results" of corporations in this broad definition. The total amount is conditioned by the level of the wages of non-managerial workers and the profile of technical change, notably the trends of the productivities of labor and capital as analyzed in Chapter 13. That chapter pointed to the present establishment of an unfavorable pattern of technical change as expressed in the new trajectory à la Marx. If these circumstances were prolonged, it would become gradually more difficult to maintain the course of investment already on the wane.

The list of unsolved problems is long. One can recall the course of international trade and the rising exports of capitals within neoliberal globalization, the still-shy attempts at the taming of financial mechanisms, the continuing deficit of foreign trade, the stabilization of the debt of the government, and the rising debt of firms. The tendencies capable of leading to a new crisis of financial hegemony are still ongoing.

A key feature of the contemporary financial network is its strong anchorage in the hegemony of the United States, the expression of the financial domination of the country worldwide; and the dollar remains the international currency. The contrast is sharp with the decline in the comparative size of the U.S. economy, the low growth and investment rates (including the buybacks of their own shares by corporations, meaning a negative accumulation). We will only recall that, expressed in purchasing-power parity, between 1980 and 2016 the share of U.S. GDP in global GDP declined from 22 percent to 15 percent.

The future of what we call the economic governing core and its foundations in the power of the United States worldwide is fraught with significant growing weaknesses. New earth tremors are forthcoming.

Intraclass cohesiveness: A pending political crisis of neoliberalism?

In our opinion, the most threatening flaw in the continuing dynamics of neoliberal managerialism lies in current political conditions. We refer here to the alliance between the various layers of managerial and capitalist classes, with the leading role conferred on financial managers and the ongoing merger at the summit of social hierarchies between managerial and capitalist interests.

To date, these mechanisms allowed for the very strong leadership of the upper segments of managerial classes. The benefits of the managerial trajectory for managerial classes considered globally were spread upward, in a fan-like manner, but lower strata of the class (fractions distinct from the ownership-control/management interface) also benefited from the new trends, though to a lesser degree. This process was expressed in the spectacular rise of inequality documented in Chapter 9, in which the rise in the income and wealth of the most accommodated layers was paralleled by the less acute but still significant upward trends within the lower segments of upper classes (primarily regarding wages, as expected in an advanced managerial society). The same is specifically true of institutionally variegated fractions of managers, as expressed in the comparative rise of financial managers.

Two categories of development would destabilize the march forward of neoliberalism:

1. The growing internal contradictions between the components of upper classes; and

2. The simultaneous establishment of new relationships between segments of managerial classes and popular classes, as supported by the above tensions, thus allowing for forms of de facto cooperation, that is, weighing on historical dynamics in significantly converging directions or even "alliances" evocative of the postwar compromise.

Intraclass cohesion is supported by economic conditions: Unfavorable economic trends or the occurrence of a new structural crisis, as discussed in the previous section, would obviously unsettle the current status quo. But not only economic conditions are involved. As emphasized in the previous chapter, the strong internal hierarchical structure of the managerial class in neoliberalism and the dramatic deficiency of intraclass democracy add to the likelihood of growing divergences. A split could thus be expressed somewhere within the hierarchy separating the remnants of the class of large capitalists, top managers, and the lower fractions of managerial classes. This is what is meant by the potential "political crisis of neoliberalism" in the title of this section.

The transition from capitalism to managerialism within the countries of managerial capitalism is presently supported by a triumphant neoliberal ideology, feeding a significant restoration of capitalist mechanisms. The rise of managerial classes irredeemably conveys, however, new systems of thought. In numerous respects—ways of life, morals, social behaviors, etc.—a convergence is observed, or may be observed, depending on countries, between lower fractions of managerial classes and broader segments of the population, in particular regarding welfare, while the merger at the top feeds gradually more shocking exaggerations.

Within a managerial society, the limit of such convergences is obviously that the ideology and the corresponding practices of meritocracy are no more vulnerable to being superseded than the ideology of the private ownership of the means of production could be overcome within a capitalist society. In both instances, the limitation is the homology between ideologies and relations of production in the key relationship between infra- and superstructures. But how could the ideology of meritocracy remain unscathed in front of the concentration of powers and income at the top of social hierarchies in the new managerial-capitalist elite, in blatant contradiction of the alleged exclusive reliance on merit scales?

A lot can be achieved, thus destabilizing the neoliberal endeavor. Any forms of de facto cooperation between popular and at least fractions of managerial classes will, however, remain an interclass relationship: There will be no definite coincidence of interests between distinct classes. During a still-considerable period of time, there will be no paradise on earth, there will be managers within firms, and there will be a state and senior officials. But there is no alternative—as Margaret Thatcher said in support of the winning joint endeavor of capitalist and managers—to the striking of an alliance between popular and significant fractions of managerial classes. The present forces of reaction must be barred, as they have been stopped in the past, though much "more consistently."

A utopia for the twenty-first century?

The difficulty in the definition of a political program for a radical left lies in the intricate interaction between tasks obviously belonging to quite distinct timeframes. The timeframe of class emancipation is the course of history, along the sequence of modes of production and the progress of sociality; overcoming the forces of regression in neoliberalism, that is, superseding the rigors of the current social order, is only the beginning. But the enemy is strong.

All the pieces of the puzzle have been gradually introduced:

1. Capitalism is not "pregnant" of a classless society, to which "force" would give birth (paraphrasing Marx's statement related to the emergence of capitalist relations of production[6]). One can, at least, contend that it will not be directly so, since capitalism is actually giving birth to a new class society in managerialism. This is the pivotal thesis of this book.
2. There is no coincidence between the new era of organization and emancipation. Again, the force of class struggle will be required.
3. As contended in Part III, earlier attempts at stopping historical dynamics or anticipating future developments failed: (i) The endeavors of the radical components of the English and French revolutions (the Levellers and "poors," and the Jacobins and *sans-culottes*), blindly assuming the congelation of the historical dynamics of a capitalism of small ownership, could not resist the pressure of new, more efficient, capitalist developments, quite independently of the tremendous social cost; (ii) The projections onto the present realms of organization and emancipation, as in utopian socialisms and self-proclaimed socialisms, failed on the twofold account of the

ambitiousness of the task and the managerial class features that new forms of organization autonomously convey.

4. The potential inherent in the entrance into new modes of production may be blurred by the reaction of upper classes, as manifested during phases of regression, thus delaying the accomplishment of the new promises of sociality conveyed by "capitalist" or "managerial modernities." To date, the attenuation of the regressive social trends established in the wake of the bourgeois revolutions—in the extreme violence of capital accumulation during the first decades of industrial capitalism (at least in the first half of the nineteenth century)—is the single best example of such reversion. This achievement was the product of a several-decades-long phase of class struggle and the chaotic chain of events, notably in Europe, during the subsequent decades of the nineteenth century up to the first decades of the twentieth century. One can optimistically speculate that the current phase of regression in neoliberalism (now almost 40 years old) will be eroded in a similar fashion. More favorable conditions supporting the dynamics toward a left managerialism would thus be created.

There is, obviously, no way of jettisoning the designs of Marx and Engels—and of generations of utopian thinkers, revolutionaries, or reformists—to override class dominations in a dignified future for humanity. The political message in this book is that there will be no alternative to a managerialism sufficiently and consistently "bent to the left" under the pressure of obstinate class struggle.

The ultimate criterion in the identification of such a left-wing managerialism would be its capability to impose social dynamics, in the last instance, conducive to the gradual attenuation of what earlier in this chapter has been denoted as "the monopoly of social initiative" in the evocation of the prospects opened to a future of emancipation. Despite the overuse and distortion of the term, one may decide to call such a favorable trajectory "socialism," as the mark of a reclaimed affiliation with earlier endeavors.

Notes

Chapter 2

1. A. Silva and V. Yakovenko. "Temporal evolution of the 'thermal' and 'superthermal' income classes in the USA during 1983–2001." *Europhys. Lett.*, 69 (2): 304–10, 2005.
2. We use the Internal Revenue Service (IRS) definition of households, as tax units, as done by Yakovenko et al., as well as Thomas Piketty and Emmanuel Saez. In the U.S. Census Bureau, a household is a group of people living in the same home. In 2010, the total numbers of households in the United States for the IRS and the Census were respectively 155 and 117 millions.
3. A. Banerjee and V. Yakovenko. "Universal patterns of inequality." *New Journal of Physics*, 12: 1–25, 2010; and Y. Tao, X. Wu, T. Zhou, W. Yan, Y. Huang, H. Yu, B. Mondal, and V. Yakovenko. "Universal exponential structure of income inequality: Evidence from 60 countries," 2016 (https://arxiv.org/abs/1612.01624).

Chapter 3

1. For example, in *For Marx* (1966), Louis Althusser contrasted the "science of history" and Marx's "philosophy." L. Althusser, *For Marx*. Verso, London, New York, 2005, pages 59, 119.
2. K. Marx. "Theses on Feuerbach. Appendix to Ludwig Feuerbach and the end of classical German philosophy" (1845). In *Selected Works of Marx and Engels, Volume One*, pages 13–15. Progress Publishers, Moscow, 1969 (www.marxists.org/archive/marx/works/1845/theses/theses.htm).
3. K. Marx and F. Engels. *A Critique of the German Ideology* (1845). Progress Publishers, Moscow, 1968.
4. Ibid., "History: Fundamental Conditions."
5 Ibid., "The Essence of the Materialist Conception of History. Social Being and Social Consciousness."
6. K. Marx. *The Eighteenth Brumaire of Louis Bonaparte* (1851). International Publishers, New York City, 1963, Chapter I (www.marxists.org/archive/marx/works/1852/18th-brumaire/).
7. K. Marx and F. Engels. "Manifesto of the Communist Party" (1848). In *Selected Works of Marx and Engels*, pages 98–137. Progress Publishers, Moscow, 1973.
8. Marx was 41 years old and, ten years earlier, had read Engels' *The Condition of the Working Class in England*, published in 1845, written *A Critique of the*

German Ideology in 1845, and published *The Communist Manifesto* in 1848, both with Engels.

9. See J. Ritter. *Hegel and the French Revolution*. MIT Press, Boston, 1982, Chapter 6, §7 and 8.

10. G. Duménil. "Entre 'théorie de l'histoire' et 'économie politique du capitalisme': Y a-t-il chez Marx une théorie générale de l'exploitation?", 2014 (www.cepremap.fr/membres/dlevy/dge2014a.pdf).

11. K. Marx. Preface, *A Contribution to the Critique of Political Economy* (1858). Lawrence and Wishart, London, 1970. (Quoted from www.marxists.org/archive/marx/works/1859/critique-pol-economy/preface.htm.)

12. K. Marx. *The Grundrisse* (1857). Penguin Books, London, New York, 1993, pages 471–9.

13. G. Duménil. *Le Concept de Loi Économique dans "Le Capital,"* Avant-propos de L. Althusser. Maspero, Paris, 1978.

14. Marx. Preface, *Critique of Political Economy*.

15. Ibid.

16. Duménil. *Le Concept de Loi Économique*.

17. A useful reference is Bernard Bourgeois' Présentation to G. Hegel, *Encyclopédie des Sciences de la Logique. I – La Science de la Logique* (1817–30). Librairie Philosophique J. Vrin, Paris, 1970, pages 7–112.

18. The distinction between these two aspects of Marx's dialectics is explicit in Emmanuel Renault's study regarding Marx's dialectics. Renault established the link between Marx's dialectics and Kant's theory of "negative values." A link must be established between Marx's approach and "the Kantian theory of negative values, since this theory contends that the contradictions of knowledge and the real oppositions [*conflicts*] define two categories of heterogeneous oppositions [...]," E. Renault. *Marx et la Philosophie*. Presses Universitaires de France, Paris, 2013, pages 43–4 (translated by the authors).

19. K. Polanyi. "The economistic fallacy." *Review (Fernand Braudel Center)*, 1 (1): 9–18, 1977.

20. K. Polanyi. *The Great Transformation*. Rhinehart, New York, 1944, page 150.

21. É. Balibar. "The basic concepts of historical materialism." In L. Althusser and É. Balibar (eds), *Reading Capital (Part 3)*, pages 199–325. New Left Books, London, 1970, page 207.

22. K. Marx. *Capital, Volume I* (1867). First Vintage Book Edition, New York, 1977, page 914.

23. Marx and Engels. Preface, "Manifesto of the Communist Party." In *Selected Works*.

24. L. Althusser. *On the Reproduction of Capitalism. Ideology and Ideological State Apparatuses*. Verso, London, New York, 2014, page 163 (https://libcom.org/library/reproduction-capitalism-louis-althusser).

25. K. Marx. *Capital, Volume III* (1894). First Vintage Book Edition, New York, 1981, page 1025 (www.marxists.org/archive/marx/works/download/pdf/Capital-Volume-III.pdf).

26. V. Lenin. "The State and Revolution: The Marxist theory of the state and the tasks of the proletariat in the revolution" (1918). In *Collected Works, Volume 25*, pages 381–496. Progress Publishers, Moscow, 1974.
27. K. Marx. *The Poverty of Philosophy* (1847). Progress Publishers, Moscow, 1973 (www.marxists.org/archive/marx/works/1847/poverty-philosophy/), Chapter 2, Part 5. See E. Andrew. "Class in itself and class against capital: Karl Marx and his classifiers." *Canadian Journal of Political Science*, 16 (3): 577–84, 1983.
28. E. P. Thompson. *The Making of the English Working Class*. Penguin Books, London, New York, 2013.
29. Quoted in D. McNally. "E. P. Thompson: Class struggle and historical materialism." *International Socialism*, 61, 1993 (www.marxists.org/history/etol/newspape/isj2/1993/isj2-061/mcnally.htm). On these issues, see Thompson's pamphlet *The Poverty of Theory: or an Orrery of Errors* (1978). Merlin Press, London, 1995.
30. Thompson. *English Working Class*, page 9.
31. Marx. *Capital, Volume I*, pages 254–5.
32. Blatant conflicts between distinct approaches to the same course of events were detected here. D. F. Noble (ed.). *Progress without People: New technology, unemployment and the message of resistance*. Between The Lines, Toronto, 1995, Appendix: Karl Marx against the Luddites, page 146; V. Bourdeau, F. Jarrige, and J. Vincent. "Le passé d'une désillusion: Les Luddites et la critique de la machine." *Actuel Marx*, 39: 145–72, 2006.
33. E. P. Thompson, V. Bertrand, C. Bouton, F. Gauthier, D. Hunt, and G. Ikni. *La Guerre du Blé au XVIII⁰ Siècle*. Les Éditions de la Passion, Montreuil, 1988.
34. E. P. Thompson. "The moral economy of the English crowd in the eighteenth century." *Past & Present*, 50: 76–136, 1971.
35. F. Gauthier. "Une révolution paysanne", 2011 (https://revolution-francaise.net/2011/09/11/448-une-revolution-paysanne).

Chapter 4

1. K. Marx. *Capital, Volume III* (1894). First Vintage Book Edition, New York, 1981, page 516 (www.marxists.org/archive/marx/works/download/pdf/Capital-Volume-III.pdf).
2. As in the quotation regarding the definition of classes at the end of the previous chapter: the penultimate sentence of Volume III of *Capital*: "From this point of view, however, doctors and government officials would also form two classes, as they belong to two distinct social groups…"
3. Marx. *Capital, Volume III*, page 503.
4. K. Marx. *Capital, Volume I* (1867). First Vintage Book Edition, New York, 1977, page 482.
5. Marx. *Capital, Volume III*, Chapter 9.
6. Ibid., page 511.
7. Ibid., page 512.

8. G. Duménil and D. Lévy. "Production and management: Marx's dual theory of labor." In R. Westra and A. Zuege (eds), *Value and the World Economy Today: Production, Finance and Globalization*, pages 137–57. Palgrave, London, Basingstoke, 2004.
9. K. Marx. *Capital, Volume II* (1885). First Vintage Book Edition, New York, 1978, page 210.
10. Marx. *Capital, Volume III*, page 569.
11. Ibid., page 568.
12. K. Marx. *The Eighteenth Brumaire of Louis Bonaparte* (1851). International Publishers, New York City, 1963 (www.marxists.org/archive/marx/works/1852/18th-brumaire/, page 64).

Chapter 5

1. K. Marx. *Capital, Volume III* (1894). First Vintage Book Edition, New York, 1981, page 507. (Quoted from: www.marxists.org/archive/marx/works/download/pdf/Capital-Volume-III.pdf, page 260.)
2. Ibid. (First Vintage edn.), page 928.
3. F. Engels. *Socialism: Utopian and Scientific* (1880). International Publishers, New York, 1972 (www.marxists.org/archive/marx/works/1880/soc-utop/ch03.htm).
4. For example, mines at the beginning of the sixteenth century in Europe could be jointly owned by noble and commoner proprietors in the system of *comparsonnage*, placed under the conduct of early forms of management. G. Bischoff. *La Guerre des Paysans*. La Nuée Bleue, Strasbourg, 2010, pages 78–81.
5. S. Pollard. *The Genesis of Modern Management: A Study of the Industrial Revolution in Great Britain*. Edward Arnold, London, 1965.
6. Ibid., page 55.
7. Ibid., Chapter II, Section III. See also page 222.
8. J. Foster. *Class Struggle and the Industrial Revolution: Early industrial capitalism in three English towns* (Foreword by Professor Eric Hobsbawm). Weidenfeld & Nicolson, London, 1974.
9. Ibid., page 224.
10. Marx. *Capital, Volume III*, page 508. (Quoted from the URL, page 260.)
11. Engels. *Socialism: Utopian and Scientific*.
12. J. Bidet and G. Duménil. *Altermarxisme: Un autre marxisme pour un autre monde*. Presses Universitaires de France, Quadrige. Essais, débats, Paris, 2007, Chapter 4, "L'union manquée de l'organisation et de l'émancipation," pages 85–92.
13. E. P. Thompson. *Whigs and Hunters: The origins of the Black Act* (1975). Penguin Books, Harmondsworth (UK), 1990, page 261.
14. Ibid.
15. Ibid., page 262.
16. K. Marx. *The Eighteenth Brumaire of Louis Bonaparte* (1852). International Publishers, New York City, 1963 (www.marxists.org/archive/marx/works/1852/18th-brumaire/).

17. F. Furet. *Marx et la Révolution Française*. Flammarion, Paris, 1986.
18. Marx. *The Eighteenth Brumaire*, Chapter VII.
19. http://gallica.bnf.fr/ark:/12148/bpt6k9628969d.
20. Marx. *The Eighteenth Brumaire*, Chapter VII.
21. A. de Tocqueville. *The Ancien Régime and the Revolution* (1856). Cambridge University Press, Cambridge (UK), 2011, page 39.
22. Ibid., page 41.

Chapter 6

1. P. Payne. *British Entrepreneurship in the Nineteenth Century*. Macmillan, London, 1974, pages 14–15. Payne refers to "Extremely elaborate partnership systems," page 18. Within "common-law partnership," liability remained unlimited. Limited liability was introduced in 1856 and 1862 by the Joint Stock Companies Acts.
2. T. Veblen. *Absentee Ownership and Business Enterprise in Recent Times*. George Allen & Unwin, London, 1924; A. Berle and G. Means. *The Modern Corporation and Private Property*. Macmillan, London, 1932; A. Berle. *The Twentieth-Century Capitalist Revolution*. Macmillan, London, 1955; A. Berle. *Power without Property*. Harcourt Brace, New York, 1960; R. Dahrendorf. *Class and Class Conflict in Industrial Society*. Routledge and Kegan Paul, London, 1959; R. Marris. *The Economic Theory of Managerial Capitalism*. Macmillan, London, 1964; T. Nichols. *Ownership, Control and Ideology*. George Allen & Unwin, London, 1969; O. Williamson. *The Economics of Discretionary Behavior*. Prentice-Hall, Englewood Cliffs, NJ, 1964; T. Nichols. *Ownership, Control and Ideology*. George Allen & Unwin, London, 1969.
3. A. Chandler. *The Visible Hand: The managerial revolution in American business*. Harvard University Press, Cambridge MA, London, 1977.
4. G. Duménil and D. Lévy. *Capital Resurgent: Roots of the neoliberal revolution*. Harvard University Press, Cambridge MA, 2004a, Chapter 16: "Historical precedent: The crisis at the end of the nineteenth century."
5. H. Thorelli. *The Federal Antitrust Policy: Organization of an American tradition*. Johns Hopkins Press, Baltimore, 1955; G. Bittlingmayer. "Did antitrust policy cause the great merger wave?". *Journal of Law and Economics*, 28: 77–118, 1985.
6. W. Roy. *Socializing Capital: The rise of the large industrial corporation in America*. Princeton University Press, Princeton, 1996.
7. O. Sprague. *History of Crises under the National Banking System*. National Monetary Commission, Government Printing Office, Washington, 1910.

Chapter 7

1. See, for example, Y. Moulier-Boutang. *Le Capital Cognitif: La nouvelle grande transformation*. Éditions Amsterdam, Paris, 2007.

2. M. Hardt and A. Negri. *Empire*. Harvard University Press, Cambridge MA, 2000.

3. N. Poulantzas. *Classes in Contemporary Capitalism*. New Left Review Press, London, 1975, page 181.

4. C. Baudelot, R. Establet, and J. Malemort. *La Petite Bourgeoisie en France*. Maspero, Paris, 1974.

5. A. Bihr. *Entre Bourgeoisie et Prolétariat: L'encadrement capitaliste*. L'Harmattan, Paris, 1989.

6. Ibid., page 8 (translation by the authors).

7. Ibid., page 408.

8. E. Olin Wright. *Class, Crisis and the State*. New Left Books, London, 1978.

9. Ibid., pages 61–2.

10. Olin Wright was actually heading toward a Marxist sociology of capitalism, extending the ensuing categories to students, pensioners, unemployed, and the like. Ibid., pages 92–3.

11. E. Olin Wright. *Classes*. Verso. New Left Books, London, New York, 1985, page 43. One can also consult the section "The theory of history," pages 114–18.

12. L. Boltanski. *The Making of a Class: Cadres in French society*. Cambridge University Press, Cambridge (UK), New York, 1987.

13. S. Mohun. "Class structure and the US personal income distribution." *Metroeconomica*, 67 (2): 334–63, 2016.

14. G. Duménil. *La Position de Classe des Cadres et Employés: La fonction capitaliste parcellaire*. Presses Universitaires de Grenoble, Grenoble, 1975, page 102 (translated by the authors).

15. J. Burnham. *The Managerial Revolution: What is happening in the world*. John Day Co., New York, 1941.

16. A. Hughes. "Managerial capitalism." In J. Eatwell, M. Milgate, and P. Newman (eds), *The New Palgrave: A Dictionary of Economics*, pages 293–5. Palgrave Macmillan, London, Basingstoke, 1987, page 295.

17. Notably, C. Kerr. *Industrialism and Industrial Man: The problems of labor and management in economic growth*. Harvard University Press, Berkeley, 1960; and R. Aron. *The Industrial Society*. Weidenfeld & Nicholson, London, 1967.

18. J. Schumpeter. *Capitalism, Socialism, and Democracy*. Harper and Brothers, New York, 1942, page 61.

19. Ibid., pages 423–4.

20. Burnham. *The Managerial Revolution*. It might be the case that Burnham's thesis actually reproduced Bruno Rizzi's analysis published in 1939 in Paris: B. Rizzi. *L'URSS: collectivisme bureaucratique. La bureaucratisation du monde* (1939). Champ Libre, Paris, 1976.

21. J. Galbraith. *The New Industrial State*. Princeton University Press, Princeton, 1967, pages 86-87.

22. C. Mills. *The Power Elite*. Oxford University Press, New York, 1956; G. Domhoff. *The Power Elite and the State: How policy is made in America*.

Aldine de Gruyter, New York, 1990; and G. Domhoff. *Who Rules America?: Power, politics, and social change.* McGraw-Hill, New York, 2006.

23. M. Zeitlin and R. Ratcliff. *Landlords and Capitalists: The dominant class of Chile.* Princeton University Press, Princeton, 1988; and M. Zeitlin. *The Large Corporation and Contemporary Classes.* Rutgers University Press, New Brunswick, 1989.

24. P. Bourdieu. *State Nobility: Elite schools in the field of power.* Stanford University Press, Stanford, 1996.

25. P. Bourdieu. "Sur le pouvoir symbolique." *Annales*, 32 (3): 201–211, 1977, page 207.

26. For example, P. Bourdieu. "Esprits d'État. Genèse et structure du champ bureaucratique." *Actes de la Recherche en Sciences Sociales*, 96 (1): 49–62, 1993.

27. T. Le Texier. "La rationalité managériale, de l'administration domestique à la gouvernance" (thèse de doctorat). Université de Nice Sophia-Antipolis, 2011.

28. Bourdieu. *State Nobility.*

29. M. Foucault. *The Birth of Biopolitics.* Palgrave Macmillan, New York, 2008.

30. J. Bidet. *Foucault with Marx.* Zed Books, London, 2016; and J. Bidet. *Marx et la Loi Travail: Le corps biopolitique du Capital.* Éditions Sociales, Paris, 2016.

Chapter 8

1. K. Marx. Preface, *A Contribution to the Critique of Political Economy* (1858). Lawrence and Wishart, London, 1970. (Quoted from: www.marxists.org/archive/marx/works/1859/critique-pol-economy/preface.htm.)

2. A useful review of the controversies surrounding the origins of the early Industrial Revolution in England and the international leadership of the country during the nineteenth century can be found in H. Heller. *The Birth of Capitalism: A twenty-first century perspective.* Pluto Press and Fernwood Publishing, London, Halifax and Winnipeg, 2011. One can, for example, cite Robert Brenner's work (R. Brenner. "Agrarian class structure and economic development in pre-industrial Europe." *Past and Present*, 70: 30–75, 1970; R. Brenner. "Symposium. Agrarian class structure and economic development in pre-industrial Europe." *Past and Present*, 97: 16–113, 1982). Brenner is debating with a set of scholars, notably the French historian Emmanuel Le Roy Ladurie, regarding the so-called crisis of feudalism during the thirteenth to fourteenth centuries and the emergence of capitalist relations of production in Europe. Brenner challenged Le Roy Ladurie's Malthusian (that is, hinging around demography) interpretation of the transition between feudalism and capitalism as defining a form of "orthodoxy." Le Roy Ladurie's overall interpretation confers a crucial role on a "demographic cycle" (from the late Middle Ages to the eighteenth century): "A broad agrarian cycle, observed in its entirety and stretching from the end of the fifteenth century to the beginning of the nineteenth century, such is the central character in my book." (E. Le Roy Ladurie. *Les*

Paysans de Languedoc. Flammarion, Paris, 1969, page 345, translation by the authors). In his refutation, Brenner emphasized the diversity of geographical developments, and this is where class patterns and powers come to the fore as a substitute for demography per se.

3. J. R. Farr. *Artisans in Europe 1300–1914*. Cambridge University Press, Cambridge (UK), New York, Melbourne, 2000.

4. See, notably, C. Hill. *The English Revolution 1640*. Lawrence and Wishart, London, 1940, Section "Industry and Trade" (www.marxists.org/archive/hill-christopher/english-revolution/).

5. Reference is generally made to the study by François-Louis Ganshof, first published in 1944: F.-L. Ganshof. *Feudalism*. University of Toronto Press, New York, London, 1964. A broader definition can be used, in which the clergy is incorporated (M. Bloch. *Feudal Society*. University of Chicago Press, Chicago, 1961).

6. K. F. Werner. *Naissance de la Noblesse*. Librairie Arthèmes Fayard, Paris, 1998.

7. Ganshof (*Feudalism*) brings up interesting information regarding the first steps in the establishment of feudal relationships during the Merovingians and Carolingians. But the focus is, as often, on the link between the lords and the vassals, not the extraction of surplus labor.

8. For example, Louis XVI abolished slavery and serfdom on royal land in 1776.

9. "[...] les nobles possédant fiefs percevaient sur les paysans les droits féodaux (on pouvait d'ailleurs être nobles sans posséder de fief, et être roturier et posséder un fief noble: toute connexion avait disparu entre noblesse et système féodal." A. Soboul. *La Révolution Française*. Messidor / Éditions Sociales, Paris, 1982, page 59.

10. F. Gauthier. "Une révolution paysanne" (https://revolution-francaise.net/2011/09/11/448-une-revolution-paysanne, 2011).

11. E.-J. Sieyès. "What is the Third Estate?" (1789) (http://pages.uoregon.edu/dluebke/301ModernEurope/Sieyes3dEstate.pdf).

12. Hill. *The English Revolution*, Section 2: "Economic Background of the English Revolution", (b) Industry and Trade. See also C. Hill. *The Century of Revolution 1603–1714*. Van Nostrand Reinhold (International) Co. Ltd, London, 1961.

13. Hill. *The English Revolution*, Preface.

14. Hill. *The English Revolution*, Section 3: "Political Background of the English Revolution," (a) The Tudor Monarchy.

15. A.-R. Turgot. *Reflections on the Formation and the Distribution of Riches* (1770). Macmillan Publishers, New York, 1898; A. Smith. *An Inquiry into the Nature and Causes of the Wealth of Nations* (1776). Dent and Son, London, 1964.

16. A.-C. Hoyng. *Turgot and Adam Smith: Une étrange proximité*. Honoré Champion, Paris, 2015.

17. B. Manning. *1649: The Crisis of the English Revolution*. Bookmarks, London, Chicago, Melbourne, 1992, pages 32–4.

18. M. Dobb. *Studies in the Development of Capitalism*. Routledge, London, 1950, page 17.
19. W. R. Rubinstein. *Men of Property: The very wealthy in Britain since the Industrial Revolution*. Social Affairs Unit, London, 2006, page 51.
20. Ibid., page 53.
21. F. Furet. *Penser la Révolution Française*. Gallimard, Paris, 1978, page 168.
22. S. Hupfel and G. Sheridan. "A la recherche d'une démocratie d'ateliers. *L'Écho de la fabrique* des canuts." In T. Bouchet, V. Bourdeau, E. Castleton, L. Frobert, and F. Jarrige, (eds), *Quand les Socialistes Inventaient l'Avenir, 1825–1860*, pages 113–26. La Découverte, Paris, 2015.
23. M. Gribaudi. *Paris Ville Ouvrière: Une histoire occultée 1789–1848*. La Découverte, Paris, 2014, Chapter 4.
24. M. Chase. *Chartism: A new history*. Manchester University Press, Manchester (UK), 2007.
25. E. Evans. *Britain before the Reform Act*. Routledge, Abingdon, New York, 2014, page 94.
26. J. Foster. *Class Struggle and the Industrial Revolution: Early industrial capitalism in three English towns* (Foreword by Professor Eric Hobsbawm). Weidenfeld & Nicolson, London, 1974, Chapter 7: "Liberalization."
27. Evans. *Britain before the Reform Act*.
28. Foster. *Class Struggle*, Chapter 3: "Labour and state power."
29. H. de Saint-Simon. "L'organisateur" (1819). In *Œuvres complètes III*, pages 2099–237. Presses Universitaires de France, Quadrige, Paris, 2012; H. de Saint-Simon. "Du système industriel" (1820). In *Œuvres complètes III*, pages 2342–632. Presses Universitaires de France, Quadrige, Paris, 2012.
30. H. de Saint-Simon. "Nouveau christianisme: Dialogues entre un conservateur et un novateur" (1825). In *Œuvres complètes IV*, pages 3184–226. Presses Universitaires de France, Quadrige, Paris, 2012.
31. P. Enfantin et al. *Doctrine de Saint-Simon: Exposition, première année, 1828-1829*. L'organisateur, Paris, 1830 (http://gallica.bnf.fr/ark:/12148/bpt6k85469w).
32. The communist periodicals were: *Le Moniteur Républicain*; *L'Homme Libre*; *L'Intelligence*; *L'Égalitaire*, *Journal de l'Organisation Sociale*; *La Fraternité*; and *Le Travail, Organe de la Rénovation Sociale* (A. Maillard. "Egalité et communauté, la presse communiste." In T. Bouchet et al. (eds), *Quand les Socialistes Inventaient l'Avenir, 1825–1860*, pages 168–80).
33. J. Reynaud. *De la Nécessité d'une Représentation Spéciale pour les Prolétaires* (1832). Chapitre.com, Paris, 2013, pages 12–13 (translation by the authors). See: A. Aramini and V. Bourdeau. "Synthèse et association. la *Revue encyclopédique* de Leroux, Reynaud et Carnot." In T. Bouchet et al. (eds), *Quand les Socialistes Inventaient l'Avenir, 1825–1860*, pages 84–96.
34. Ibid., page 13.
35. The League of the Just was created in Paris in 1836 by German emigrants, notably Wilhelm Weitling, to which we will return in Chapter 15. C. Wittke. *The Utopian Communist: A biography of Wilhelm Weitling, nineteenth-century reformer*. Lousiana State University Press, Baton Rouge, 1950.

36. M. Léonard. *L'Émancipation des Travailleurs: Une histoire de la Première Internationale.* La Fabrique, Paris, 2011, Chapter II: "Ces ânes de proudhoniens" Une mise en marche laborieuse (1864–1866) ["These Prudonian asses." A difficult start (1864–1868)].

Chapter 10

1. H. Thorelli. *The Federal Antitrust Policy: Organization of an American tradition.* Johns Hopkins Press, Baltimore, 1955; G. Duménil, M. Glick, and D. Lévy. "The history of competition policy as economic history." *The Antitrust Bulletin,* XLII (2): 373–416, 1997.
2. H. Zinn. *A People's History of the United States.* Harper Perennial, New York, 1980.
3. In his 1968 book The *Corporate Ideal in the Liberal State,* James Weinstein defended the thesis that "big businessmen," contrary to "smaller manufacturers and commercial men," headed a movement of progressive social reform evocative of the programs of the 1960s in the aim of taming social strife (J. Weinstein. *The Corporate Ideal in the Liberal State, 1900-1918.* Beacon Press, Boston, 1968, page 92).
4. G. Duménil and D. Lévy. "Pre-Keynesian themes at Brookings." In L. Pasinetti and B. Schefold (eds), *The Impact of Keynes on Economics in the 20th Century,* pages 182–201. Edward Elgar, Aldershot, England, 1999.
5. G. Duménil and D. Lévy. "Costs and benefits of neoliberalism. A class analysis." *Review of International Political Economy,* 8 (4): 578–607, 2001.
6. This section heavily draws from G. Duménil and D. Lévy. *The Crisis of Neoliberalism.* Harvard University Press, Cambridge MA, 2011.
7. U.S. incarceration rates 1925 onwards: https://commons.wikimedia.org/wiki/File: U.S._incarceration_rates_1925_onwards.png.
8. Duménil and Lévy, *The Crisis of Neoliberalism,* Figure 4.2.
9. Ibid., Figure 8.2.
10. Duménil and Lévy. *The Crisis of Neoliberalism.*
11. An extensive discussion of profit-rate maximizing can be found in Galbraith's *Industrial State* (J. Galbraith. *The New Industrial State.* Princeton University Press, Princeton, 1967).
12. A. Chandler. *The Visible Hand: The managerial revolution in American business.* Harvard University Press, Cambridge MA, London, 1977, page 10.
13. The package was part of the Hiring Incentives to Restore Employment Act.
14. J. Schumpeter. "State imperialism and capitalism," 1919 (www.panarchy.org/schumpeter/imperialism.html): "Whoever seeks to understand Europe must not overlook that even today its life, its ideology, its politics are greatly under the influence of the feudal 'substance,' that while the bourgeoisie can asserts its interests everywhere, it 'rules' only in exceptional circumstances, and then only briefly."
15. A. Mayer. *The Persistence of the Old Regime: Europe to the Great War.* Verso, London, New York, 1981.

16. K. Polanyi. *The Great Transformation*. Rhinehart, New York, 1944, pages 3–4.
17. Ibid., page 10.
18. Ibid., page 13.
19. "Matériaux pour l'histoire de notre temps." *Vol. 17, Socialisme et classes moyennes en France et en Allemagne dans l'entre-deux-guerres. Dossier préparé par René Girault*, 1989.
20. G. Duménil and D. Lévy. *La Grande Bifurcation: En finir avec le néolibéralisme*. La Découverte, Coll. L'horizon des Possibles, Paris, 2014, Chapter 8.
21. M. Foucault. *The Birth of Biopolitics*. Palgrave Macmillan, New York, 2008.
22. Ibid., page 4.
23. Ibid., page 2.
24. Ibid., page 4.
25. Ibid., Lecture of January 10, 1979.
26. E. P. Thompson, V. Bertrand, C. Bouton, F. Gauthier, D. Hunt, and G. Ikni. *La Guerre du Blé au XVIIIe Siècle*. Les Éditions de la Passion, Montreuil, 1988.
27. Among many possible locations, pages 565 and 586 of E. P. Thompson's *The Making of the English Working Class*. Penguin Books, London, New York, 2013.
28. The *Annuaire du Collège de France*, 78e année. Histoire des systèmes de pensée, année 1977–1978, pages 445–9, 1978.
29. Foucault. *Biopolitics*.
30. Giscard d'Estaing was president of the French Republic between 1974 and 1981. Barre became Prime Minister in 1976 and resigned when Mitterrand was elected president in 1981.
31. G. Becker. *Human Capital: A theoretical and empirical analysis, with special reference to education* (1964). University of Chicago Press, Chicago, 1993; and, first published after Foucault's lectures, G. Becker. *A Treatise on the Family* (1981). Harvard University Press, Cambridge MA, 1991.
32. Ibid., page 42.
33. P. Dardot and C. Laval. *The New Way of the World: On neoliberal society*. Verso, London, New York, 2014.

Chapter 11

1. S. Vitali, J. Glattfelder, and S. Battiston. "The network of global corporate control." *PLOS ONE*, 6 (10): 1–6, 2011 (https://doi.org/10.1371/journal.pone.0025995); and S. Vitali, J. Glattfelder, and S. Battiston. "Supporting information: The network of global corporate control." *PLOS ONE*, 6 (10): 1–19, 2011 (https://doi.org/10.1371/journal.pone.0025995.s001). The first presentation we gave of this work was in G. Duménil and D. Lévy, *La Grande Bifurcation: En finir avec le néolibéralisme*. La Découverte, Coll. L'Horizon des Possibles, Paris, 2014, Chapter VII.
2. Vitali et al., "The network of global corporate control," page 3.
3. 2016 Annual Report of BlackRock.

4. Vitali et al., "The network of global corporate control," page 4.
5. Ibid., page 19.
6. The sources are:
    1. Wealth of the top 100 billionaires: www.forbes.com/billionaires/list/;
    2. Wealth of the poorest half of the world population: Credit Suisse Research Institute. "Global Wealth Report 2016." (www.credit-suisse.com/corporate/en/research/research-institute/global-wealth-report.html);
    3. Stock-market capitalization worldwide: www.world-exchanges.org/home/ index.php/files/52/Annual-Statistics-Guide/453/WFE-Annual-Statistics-Guide-2016.xlsx.
7. Vitali et al., "Supporting information: The network of global corporate control," Table S1.
8. S. Vitali and S. Battiston. "The community structure of the global corporate network." *PLOS ONE*, 9 (8), 2014 (http://dx.doi.org/10.1371/journal.pone.0104655). Regarding Europe, one can also cite S. Vitali and S. Battiston. "Geography versus topology in the European ownership network." *New Journal of Physics*, 13: 1–18, 2011.
9. A. Lenger, C. Schneickert, and F. Schumacher. "National elites." *Transcience Journal*, 1 (2): 85–100, 2010. See also M. Hartmann. "Internationalisation et spécificités nationales des élites économiques." *Actes de la Recherche en Sciences Sociales*, 5 (190): 10–23, 2011; and V. Burris and C. Staples. "In search of a transnational capitalist class: Alternative methods for comparing director interlocks within and between nations and regions." *International Journal of Comparative Sociology*, 53 (4): 323–42, 2012, with similar conclusions.
10. W. Carroll. "Transnationalists and national networkers in the global corporate elite." *Global Networks*, 9 (3): 289–314, 2009.
11. Ibid., page 289.
12. Ibid., pages 294–5.
13. Ibid., page 294.
14. Notably, L. Panitch and S. Gindin (eds). *The Making of Global Capitalism: The political economy of American Empire*. Verso, London, New York, 2012; and W. Robinson. "The fetishism of Empire: A critical review of Panitch and Gindin's *The making of global capitalism*." *Studies in Political Economy*, 93: 147–65, 2014. See also the special issue: *Actuel Marx*, 60, "Une classe dominante mondiale?" Dossier préparé par Gérard Duménil. Presses Universitaires de France, Paris, 2016.
15. A. Stephanson. *Manifest Destiny: American expansion and the empire of right*. Hill and Wang, New York, 1995.
16. A. Chandler. *Scale and Scope: The dynamics of industrial capitalism*. Harvard University Press, Cambridge, MA, London, 1990.

Chapter 12

1. G. Duménil and D. Lévy. *La Grande Bifurcation: En finir avec le néolibéralisme*. La Découverte, Coll. L'Horizon des Possibles, Paris, 2014, page 40.

2. H. Stein. *The Fiscal Revolution in America*. University of Chicago Press, Chicago, London, 1969.

3. New York Times, April 27, 1994 (www.nytimes.com/1994/04/27/business/market-place-wall-street-is-closed-to-honor-a-bear-market-president.html).

4. G. Duménil and D. Lévy. *The Crisis of Neoliberalism*. Harvard University Press, Cambridge MA, 2011.

5. H. Vatter. *The U.S. Economy in the 1950's: An economic history*. University of Chicago Press, Chicago, 1963.

6. "Financial Services Industry," The Industrial College of the Armed Forces, National Defense University, Spring 2010, page 2.

7. Ibid., page 3.

8. M. Useem. *The Inner Circle: Large corporations and the rise of business political activity in the U.S. and U.K.* Oxford University Press, Oxford, 1984.

9. Ibid., page 3.

10. Ibid., page 4.

11. Ibid., page 150.

12. C-SPAN, November 13, 1994 (www.c-span.org/video/?60409-1/journey-economic-time).

13. P. Mirowski and D. Plehwe (eds). *The Road from Mont Pèlerin*. Harvard University Press, Cambridge MA, London, 2009.

14. R. Ptak. "Neoliberalism in Germany. Revisiting the ordoliberal foundations of the social market economy." In P. Mirowski and D. Plehwe (eds), *The Road from Mont Pèlerin: The making of the neoliberal thought collective*, pages 98–138. Harvard University Press, Cambridge MA, London, 2009, page 125.

15. Ibid., page 112.

16. A. Giddens. *The Third Way: The renewal of social democracy*. Polity Press, Cambridge (UK), 1998.

Chapter 13

1. A useful synthetic description of the historical profiles of variables can be found in G. Duménil and D. Lévy. "The historical trends of technology and distribution in the U.S. economy since 1869. Data and figures" (www.cepremap.fr/membres/dlevy/dle2016e.pdf, 2016).

2. K. Marx. *Capital, Volume I* (1867). First Vintage Book Edition, New York, 1977, Chapter 25.

3. This account of mechanisms rephrases, for the best, Marx's analysis in *Capital*, in which the basic concepts are the rate of surplus-value, the organic composition of capital, and the like. Among the many studies we devoted to these mechanisms, see G. Duménil and D. Lévy. *The Economics of the Profit Rate: Competition, crises, and historical tendencies in capitalism*. Edward Elgar, Aldershot, England, 1993; and G. Duménil and D. Lévy. "The classical Marxian evolutionary model of technical change." In M. Setterfield (ed.), *Handbook of Alternative Theories of Economic Growth*, pages 243–74. Edward Elgar, London, 2011.

4. G. Duménil and D. Lévy. "The acceleration and slowdown of technical progress in the US since the Civil War: The transition between two paradigms." *Revue Internationale de Systémique*, 10 (3): 303–21, 1996.

5. A. Chandler. *The Visible Hand: The managerial revolution in American business*. Harvard University Press, Cambridge MA, London, 1977, Chapter 8.

6. D. Byrne, S. Oliner, and D. Sichel. "Is the information technology revolution over?" (www.federalreserve.gov/pubs/feds/2013/201336/201336pap. pdf, March 2013); C. Teuling and R. Baldwin (eds). *Secular Stagnation: Facts, causes, and cures*. CEPR Press, London, 2014 (www.voxeu.org/sites/default/files/Vox_secular_stagnation.pdf); and R. Gordon. "Secular stagnation: A supply-side view." *American Economic Review: Papers and Proceedings*, 105 (5): 54–9, 2015.

7. G. Duménil and D. Lévy. "Technology and distribution in managerial capitalism: The chain of historical trajectories à la Marx and counter-tendential traverses." *Science and Society*, 80, Special Issue: Crises and Transformation of Capitalism: Marx's Investigations and Contemporary Analysis: 530–49, 2016.

8. G. Duménil and D. Lévy. *Capital Resurgent: Roots of the neoliberal revolution*. Harvard University Press, Cambridge MA, 2004, Chapter 19.

9. G. Duménil and D. Lévy. "The crisis of the early 21st century: Marxian perspectives." In R. Bellofiore and G. Vertova (eds), *The Great Recession and the Contradictions of Contemporary Capitalism*, pages 26–49. Edward Elgar, Aldershot, 2014, Figure 3.

Chapter 14

1. F. Furet. *Penser la Révolution Française*. Gallimard, Paris, 1978, page 40.

2. Ibid., page 201 (translated by the authors).

3. G. Bonnot de Mably. *Doutes Proposés aux Philosophes Économistes sur l'Ordre Naturel et Essentiel des Sociétés Politiques*. À la Haye, Paris, 1768 (translated by the authors) (https://archive.org/details/bub_gb_UJoSAAAAIAAJ, page 12).

4. J. Chaumié. "Les Girondins et les Cent Jours: Essai d'explication de leur comportement par leurs origines géographiques et sociales et leur passé politique (1793–1815)."*Annales Historiques de la Révolution Française*, 43 (205): 329–65, 1971.

5. J. Grandjonc. *Communisme/Kommunismus/Communism: Origine et développement international de la terminologie communautaire prémarxiste des utopistes et des néo-babouvistes 1785–1842*. Éditions des Malassis, Paris, 2013, page 68, note 156. See also: J.-M. Schiappa. *Gracchus Babeuf avec les Égaux*. Les Éditions Ouvrières, Paris, 1991, page 153.

6. F. Gauthier. "Une révolution paysanne" (https://revolution-francaise.net/2011/09/11/448-une-revolution-paysanne, 2011).

7. M. de Robespierre. *Sur la Propriété. Projet de déclaration des droits de l'homme et du citoyen* (1793). F. Cournol, 1867 (https://fr.wikisource.org/wiki/). See also: H. Leuwers. *Robespierre*. Fayard, Paris, 2014.

8. Chaumié. "Les Girondins et les Cent Jours."

9. M. de Robespierre. *Œuvres, Tome 6, Discours, première partie (1789–1790)*. Presses Universitaires de France, Paris, 1950, page 17 (translated by the authors), as cited in T. Van der Hallen. "Corruption et régénération du politique chez Robespierre." *Anabases*, 6: 67–82, 2007.

10. The origins of the use of the term "communism" in Europe since 1785 have been traced by Jacques Grandjonc in his towering philological study *Communisme/Kommunismus/Communism*. It was only in the wake of the elimination of La Montagne after Thermidor that Babeuf, in an attempt at rallying the disappointed segment of the deputies, changed his view regarding Robespierre, then dead.

11. Regarding Babeuf and the Conspiracy of the Equals, one can consult Schiappa's book, *Gracchus Babeuf avec les Égaux*.

12. Schiappa. *Gracchus Babeuf*, page 206.

13. Boissy d'Anglas, Projet de constitution pour la République française, et discours préliminaire prononcé par Boissy d'Anglas, au nom de la Commission des onze, dans la séance du 5 Messidor an III-June 23, 1795. Quotation from Schiappa, *Gracchus Babeuf*, page 94 (translated by the authors).

14. G. Aylmer. *Rebellion or Revolution? England from Civil War to Restoration*. Oxford University Press, Oxford, New York, 1986.

15. B. Manning. *1649: Crisis of the English Revolution*. Bookmarks, London, Chicago, Melbourne, 1992.

16. P. Zagorin. *A History of Political Thought in the English Revolution*. Routledge, Abingdon, New York, 1954, page 6.

17. Ibid., page 13.

18. Ibid., page 43.

19. J. Tully. *An Approach to Political Philosophy*. Cambridge University Press, Cambridge (UK), New York, 1993.

20. J.-J. Rousseau. *The Social Contract or Principles of Political Right* (1762). (www.constitution.org/jjr/socon.htm, Section "Slavery".)

21. C. Hill. *The English Revolution, 1640*. Lawrence and Wishart, London, 1940. (www.marxists.org/archive/hill-christopher/english-revolution/, 4: "The revolution.")

22. Thus, Jacques Bidet quite convincingly refers to the "declaration of modernity"—all men are born free and equal—emphasizing by the term that, within capitalism, this declaration is a "claim," since men, though being born equal, are not equal. J. Bidet. *L'État-monde: Libéralisme, socialisme et communisme à l'échelle globale*. Presses Universitaires de France, Paris, 2011; G. Duménil. "Modernity and capitalism: Notes on the analytical framework of Jacques Bidet" (www.cepremap.fr/membres/dlevy/dge2013a.pdf, 2013).

Chapter 15

1. W. Sombart. *Le Socialisme et le Mouvement Social au XIXe Siècle*. V. Giard & E. Brière, Paris, 1898.

2. P. J. Proudhon. *Qu'est-ce que la Propriété?* A. Lacroix et Cie Éditeurs, Paris, 1873 (http://gallica.bnf.fr/ark:/12148/bpt6k111212d).

3. A key argument in Robert Brenner's analysis of the roots of agrarian capitalism (R. Brenner. "Agrarian class structure and economic development in pre-industrial Europe." *Past and Present*, 70: 30–75, 1970).

4. P. J. Proudhon. *Idée Générale de la Révolution au XIXᵉ Siècle.* Garnier Frères, Paris, 1851. (http://gallica.bnf.fr/ark:/12148/bpt6k6115074k/f6.image. See the summary, page 254.)

5. M. Bakunin. "Statism and anarchy," 1873 (https://theanarchistlibrary.org/library/michail-bakunin-statism-and-anarchy).

6. M. Léonard. *L'émancipation des Travailleurs: Une histoire de la Première Internationale.* La Fabrique, Paris, 2011.

7. Ibid., page 173.

8. Bakunin. "Statism and anarchy."

9. C. Cahm. *Kropotkin and the Rise of Revolutionary Anarchism, 1872–1886.* Cambridge University Press, Cambridge (UK), New York, 1989, page 29.

10. Ibid.

11. A. Fabre. *Robert Owen: Un socialiste pratique.* Bureaux de l'Émancipation, Nîmes, 1896.

12. J. Beecher. *Charles Fourier: The visionary and his world.* The Regents of the University of California, Berkeley, 1986.

13. F. Fourn. *Étienne Cabet ou le Temps de l'Utopie.* Vendémiaire, Paris, 2014.

14. P. Buonarroti. *Gracchus Babeuf et la Conjuration des Égaux.* BnF Gallica, Paris, 1828 (http://gallica.bnf.fr/ark:/12148/bpt6k835717).

15. C. Wittke. *The Utopian Communist: A biography of Wilhelm Weitling, nineteenth-century reformer.* Lousiana State University Press, Baton Rouge, 1950.

16. D. F. Strauss. *The Life of Jesus: Critically Examined* (1835). Cosimo Classics, New York, 2010. (https://archive.org/details/lifeofjesuscritioostraiala.) One can also mention the important influence of Lamennais.

17. Ibid., page 13.

18. W. Weitling. *Guarantees of Harmony and Freedom* [*Garantien der Harmonie und Freiheit*] (1842) (http://reader.digitale-sammlungen.de/de/fs1/object/display/bsb10862497_00005.html).

19. Wittke. *The Utopian Communist*, page 38.

20. Ibid., page 156.

Chapter 16

1. K. Marx. *The Civil War in France: The third address* (May, 1871). English edition, 1871. (www.marxists.org/archive/marx/works/1871/civil-war-france/, Section "Paris Commune.")

2. It is worth reading the narration of the disaster by Gustave Lefrançais, one of the leading participants; an outstanding mix of humor and emotion: G. Lefrançais. *Souvenirs d'un Révolutionnaire: De Juin 1848 à la Commune.* La Fabrique, Paris, 2013.

3. Translation by the authors of Marx's quotation in French of the resolution in K. Marx and F. Engels. "Marx to Hermann Jung (July 1872)." In *Marx and Engels: Collected Works, Letters 1870–1873, Volume 44*, pages 413–14. Lawrence and Wishart, electronic book, 2010.

4. K. Marx and F. Engels. *La Commune de 1871. Lettres et déclarations pour la plupart inédites (1866–1894)*. Union Générale d'Éditions, Paris, 1971, page 158 (translation by the authors).

5. www.marxists.org/archive/marx/works/1881/letters/81_02_22.htm.

6. F. Engels. "Introduction" (1895). In *K. Marx: Les luttes de classes en France (1848–1850)*, pages 11–36. Éditions Sociales, Paris, 1963.

7. Jean Longuet quoted Marx's astounding letter: J. Longuet. *La Politique Internationale du Marxisme, Karl Marx et la France*. Félix Alcan, Paris, 1918, page 199.

8. K. Kautsky. *The Class Struggle* (1888). Charles H. Kerr & Co, Chicago, 1910.

9. R. Luxemburg. *Social Reform or Revolution* (1900–08). Militant Publications, London, 1986 (www.marxists.org/archive/luxemburg/1900/reform-revolution/); H. Harmer. *Rosa Luxemburg*. Haus Publishing, London, 2008.

10. V. Lenin. "The State and the Revolution: The Marxist theory of the state and the tasks of the proletariat in the revolution" (1918). In *Collected Works, Volume 25*, pages 381–496. Progress Publishers, Moscow, 1974.

11. V. Lenin. "All Power to the Soviets!" (Pravda, July 18, 1917). In *Collected Works, Volume 25*, pages 155–6. Progress Publishers, Moscow, 1974.

12. L. Trotsky. "Hue and cry over Kronstadt." *The New International*, 4 (4): 103–06, April 2000.

13. R. Lew. *L'Intellectuel, l'État et la Révolution: Essais sur le communisme chinois et le socialisme réel*. L'Harmattan, Paris, 1997.

14. G. Duménil and D. Lévy. *Au-delà du Capitalisme?* Presses Universitaires de France, Paris, 1998.

15. R. Michels. *Political Parties* (1915). Transaction Publishers, Piscataway NJ, 2009.

16. N. Bukharin. *Historical Materialism—A system of Sociology* (1921). International Publishers Co., Inc., New York, 1925, pages 309–10. As could be expected given the explicit controversy during the First International, similar ideas were very widespread. One can mention here Jan Machajski, also from Poland and about the same age as Luxemburg, a careful student of Marxist work, of whom Luxemburg commented: "Machajski concluded that 'scientific socialism' was the theory of a new class of intellectuals that had appeared with industrial capitalism" (as stated by Harmer, *Rosa Luxemburg*, page 50).

17. Duménil and Lévy. *Au-delà du Capitalisme?*, page 65.

18. M. Lewin. *The Soviet Century*. Verso, London, New York, 2005.

19. The following analysis draws from: G. Duménil. "L'absolutisme bureaucratique selon Moshe Lewin." *Actuel Marx*, 39: 167–72, 2006.

20. Lewin. *The Soviet Century*, page 379.

21. Ibid., page 380.

22. Ibid., pages 345–6.

23. Ibid., page 346.

24. M. Lewin. *The Gorbachev Phenomenon: A historical interpretation.* University of California Press, Berkeley, 1992.

25. M. Djilas. *The New Class: Analysis of the Communist system.* Frederick A. Praeger Publishers, New York, 1957.

26. V. Lenin. "'Left-wing' childishness and the petty-bourgeois mentality" (1918). In *Collected Works, Volume 27*, pages 323–334. Progress Publishers, Moscow, 1972.

27. The English text is "incomplete." The quotation has been translated from the French by the authors from L. Trotsky. "Rapport au 12ème congrès du PCbR" (1923). In *La Lutte Antibureaucratique en URSS, Tome I*, pages 25–77. Union Générale d'Édition, Paris, 1975 (www.marxists.org/archive/trotsky/1923/04/industry.htm).

28. Lenin. "'Left-wing' childishness and the petty-bourgeois mentality." Lenin was quoting the Menshevik paper *Vperyod* of April 25, 1918.

29. V. Lenin. "The development of capitalism in Russia" (1899). In *Collected Works, Volume 3*, pages 21–608. Progress Publishers, Moscow, 1964 (www.marxists.org/archive/lenin/works/1899/devel/).

30. K. Bailes. *Technology and Society under Lenin and Stalin: Origins of the Soviet technical intelligentsia, 1917–1941.* Princeton University Press, Princeton, 1978, page 408.

31. Ibid., page 409.

32. Lewin. *The Soviet Century*, page 260.

33. Lewin. *The Gorbachev Phenomenon*, page 131.

34. B. Bolloten. *The Spanish Civil War: Revolution and counterrevolution.* University of North Carolina Press, Chapel Hill, London, 1991.

35. D. Suvin. "On class relationships in Yugoslavia 1945–1974, with a hypothesis about the ruling class." *Journal of Contemporary Central and Eastern Europe*, 20 (1): 37–71, 2012 (www.tandfonline.com/doi/abs/10.1080/0965156X.2012.747473).

36. Association Autogestion. *Autogestion. L'Encyclopédie internationale.* Édition Syllepse, Paris, 2015, page 1154 (translation by the authors).

37. Chinese Communist Party. "Decision of the Central Committee of the Chinese Communist Party concerning the Great Proletarian Cultural Revolution." *Peking Review*, 9 (33): 6–11, 1966.

38. A. Badiou. *The Communist Hypothesis.* Verso, London, New York, 2010, page 148.

39. A devastating account can be found in R. MacFarquhar and M. Schoenhals. *Mao's Last Revolution.* The Belknap Press of Harvard University Press, Cambridge MA, 2006.

40. Lewin. *The Gorbachev Phenomenon*, page 158. See also: D. Kotz and F. Weir. *Revolution From Above: The demise of the Soviet system.* Routledge, Abingdon, 1997; G. Duménil and D. Lévy. *Au-delà du Capitalisme?* Presses Universitaires de France, Paris, 1998; J. Bidet and G. Duménil. *Altermarxisme:*

Un autre marxisme pour un autre monde. Presses Universitaires de France, Quadrige. Essais, débats, Paris, 2007.

Chapter 17

1. F. Hayek. *The Road to Serfdom* (1944). The University of Chicago Press, Chicago, 1980.
2. J.-J. Rousseau. *The Social Contract or Principles of Political Right* (1762) (www.constitution.org/jjr/socon.htm).

Chapter 18

1. F. Engels. *The Condition of the Working Class in England* (1845). Oxford University Press, Oxford, 2009; and E. P. Thompson. *The Making of the English Working Class*. Penguin Books, London, New York, 2013.
2. One can parenthetically emphasize that communist values were to bureaucratic managerialism what the ideology of modernity was to capitalism. These values were apt to open new paths after the dreadful decades of Stalinism, thus manifesting a similar potential of progress.
3. J. Schumpeter. *Capitalism, Socialism, and Democracy*. Harper and Brothers, New York, 1942.
4. G. Duménil and D. Lévy. *The Crisis of Neoliberalism*. Harvard University Press, Cambridge MA, 2011.
5. Ibid., Box 9.2, pages 128–9.
6. K. Marx. *Capital, Volume I* (1867). First Vintage Book Edition, New York, 1977, page 916.

Index

Page numbers in **bold** refer to entire chapters or sections and in *italic*, to figures.

Investment, 54, 115, 134, 194, 202, 205, 213, 221
  Government in the financing of investment, 127, 205
  Investment in information technologies, *149*
IRS (Internal Revenue Service), 9
IS-LM model, 141
IWA (International Workingmen's Association), 175–7

Jarrige, 32n32
Jefferson, 180
Johnson, 134
July monarchy, 168

Kautsky, 67, 185, 185n8
Kennedy, 134
Kerr, 67n17
Keynes, 138
  See also Economic theory, Keynesianism; Keynesian revolution
Keynesian revolution, 61, 99, 145
  Separation between private management and the management of the macroeconomy, 134, 140
  See also Governmental revolution
Kosygin, 191
Kotz, 196n41
Kropotkin, 177, 178, 186

Ladurie, 71n2
Lamennais, 173, 240
Landowners
  In the transition between feudalism and capitalism, 74, 75, 77, 159
  – in Marx's class analysis, 28
Large industry, 44, 79
Late modern period, 168
Laval, 117, 117n33
Lawyers, 159, 193
LCC (Largest connected component), *119*, 120, *120*, 121, 123
Le Roy Ladurie, 231
Leadership (within class alliances), *See* Alliance between classes
Leadership within class alliances, *See* Alliance between classes
League of the Just, 182, 233
  See also Weitling

Lefrançais, 183n2, 240
Left or right, *See* Right or left
Lehman Brothers, 121
Lenger, 127n8
Lenin, 30, 30n26, 185n10, 186, 186n11, 189, 189n26, 190n29, 191, 192, 216, 242
Léonard, 84n36, 176n6
Leuwers, 160n7
Lew, 186n13
Lewin, 187, 188, 188n18, 188n24, 191, 192, 196
Liberal turn, 82, 233
  See also Foster; Evans
Lilburne, 165
Liu Shaoqi, 195
Liverpool, 180
Locke, 166
Longuet, 184n7, 241
Lord and vassals, 23, 24, 72, 74, 180, 232
Louis XIV and Louis XV, 75, 76
Louis XVI, 75, 232
Louis XVIII, 83
Ludlow massacre, 98
Luxemburg, 67, 185, 185n9, 241

Maastricht, *See* Europe, Masstricht Treaty
Mably, 159, 159n3, 170
MacFarquhar, 196n40
Machinery, 31, 32, 51, 79, 151, 180, 213
Macroeconomy (Management of the –), 46, 54, 61, 99, 109, 133, 134, 137, 141, 145
Madrid European Council, 114
Maillard, 83n32
Malemort, 63, 63n4
Managed classes, *See* Managerialism
Managerial capitalism, **57**
  Class structure of managerial capitalism, 57
  Collective managerial capitalism, 204
  Managerial-capitalist countries, 47, 210
  See also Hybrid relations of production
Managerial capitalism in Europe, **111–15**